# DEATH SQUADS OR SELF-DEFENSE FORCES?

# DEATH SQUADS

## HOW PARAMILITARY GROUPS

# OR SELF-DEFENSE

## EMERGE AND CHALLENGE DEMOCRACY

# FORCES?

## IN LATIN AMERICA

Julie Mazzei

The University of North Carolina Press

CHAPEL HILL

© 2009
THE UNIVERSITY
OF NORTH CAROLINA
PRESS
All rights reserved

Designed by
Kimberly Bryant
Set in Arnhem and
The Sans by
Rebecca Evans
Manufactured in
the United States
of America

The paper in this book meets the guidelines for permanence and durability of the Committee on Production Guidelines for Book Longevity of the Council on Library Resources.

*The University of North Carolina Press has been a member of the Green Press Initiative since 2003.*

Library of Congress Cataloging-in-Publication Data
Mazzei, Julie.
Death squads or self-defense forces?: how paramilitary groups emerge and threaten democracy in Latin America / Julie Mazzei. — 1st ed.
p. cm.
Includes bibliographical references and index.
ISBN 978-0-8078-3306-3 (cloth: alk. paper) —
ISBN 978-0-8078-5969-8 (pbk: alk. paper)
1. Terrorism — Latin America.
2. Paramilitary forces — Latin America.
I. Title.
HV6433.L3M39 2009
363.32 — dc22                2009009382

cloth     13  12  11  10  09   5  4  3  2  1
paper     13  12  11  10  09   5  4  3  2  1

*To my mom,* SUSAN,

      *who gave me my intolerance of injustice,*

   *and to* ZACHARY

# CONTENTS

# FIGURES & MAP

## Figures

## Map

## ACKNOWLEDGMENTS

In the years during which this project took shape, I have become indebted to a host of people — colleagues, peers, family, and friends — who have supported me and this research. To all of those who have offered advice and direction over the years, my gratitude. Special thanks is owed to my mentor and advisor, Dr. Bill LeoGrande, who has provided insights and counsel throughout the evolution of this project. Additional thanks go to Dr. Cathy Schneider and Dr. Joe Soss for their guidance and inspiration. To those at the UNC Press who have supported this project, particularly Elaine Maisner, Ron Maner, Tema Larter, and Julie Schroeder, thank you for your diligence and direction. Finally, thank you to my family — my mother and sisters for their endless encouragement, my stepsons for their patience with this project, and most of all my husband for sacrificing so I could complete this project, and for simultaneously bringing so much more to my life.

# INTRODUCTION

In October 1987, Juan Bautista was driving through Puerto Araujo, Colombia, transporting merchandise from the border with Venezuela. He was traveling with sixteen of his coworkers along a route dotted by military checkpoints. At the checkpoint in Puerto Araujo, a lieutenant made note of the fact that the men were carrying a "considerable quantity of contraband merchandise" but allowed them to pass. Shortly thereafter, Juan and the sixteen others were stopped by a group known as the Asociación Campesina de Ganaderos y Agricultores del Magdelena Media (the Association of Rural Ranchers and Farmers of Magdalena Medio, ACDEGAM), a group of citizens who had organized to protect their communities against the Colombian guerrillas. The self-declared "self-defense patrol" had been watching Bautista and his friends for some time; the men had refused to pay the ACDEGAM "protection taxes" and were suspected of supplying guerrillas with some of the goods they transported. When they were detained by the ACDEGAM on 6 October, the seventeen men were taken to the ranch of the ACDEGAM's leader, Henry Perez. There they were murdered and dismembered, and their remains disposed of in the Ermitaño stream (IACHR 2004:43).

Similar self-defense patrols were organized in several communities at the time of the massacre. The Colombian government disavowed any connection to the groups, referring to the *autodefensas* as "death squadrons" and as "organization[s] of hired murderers" (IACHR 2004:40, 43n). Despite these admonitions, the ACDEGAM and similar organizations continued to declare their legitimacy as defenders of public security. A sign posted by the self-defense groups outside one Colombian city proudly read: "Welcome to Puerto Boyocá, land of peace and progress, antisubversive capital of Colombia" ("Historia de la Autodefensa" 2003:3, translation mine; Chernick 1998:30; IACHR 1993: introduction).

Paramilitary groups (PMGs) like the ACDEGAM are not unique to Colombia—nor is the debate over whether they are defensive groups or criminal death squads. In September 1995, the Serbian onslaught against non-Serbs in Bosnia was well under way. But outside the city of Sanski Most, Bosnian forces were beginning to make progress in pushing back Serb forces. As the Bosnian forces made their way to the city, the Serbs called upon the private forces of Zeljko Raznjatovic to protect them and the city. Also known as Arkan, Raznjatovic led his "Serbian Volunteer Guard" (better known as the "Tigers") into the city and began taking control. On 20 September, Arkan and his men rounded up twelve non-Serbs, took them in a bus just beyond the city limits, and shot them each. Eleven were murdered; one survived. The next day, the group again forced several non-Serb men into their bus, then collected another group of about thirty-one non-Serbs whom they had been holding for some days. They raped their one female detainee before traveling on to a third location, where yet another group of non-Serbian men were forced onto the bus. The busload of civilians was driven to a location outside Sanski Most, and all were shot. Two survived; sixty-five were murdered (ICTY 1997:3).

Like the PMGs in Colombia, Arkan and his "Tigers" saw themselves as defending a civilian population under attack. In a 1999 interview, Arkan claimed that he and his men were "not against Moslems . . . [nor] Albanians. We are only against the terrorists who are calling themselves a liberation army" ("We'll Never" 2007). Outside of his nationalist Serb supporters, however, Arkan was known as the "butcher of Bosnia" (Bell 1999) and a "warlord" ("Kosovo; Citizen Arkan" 1993). While he declared his determination to fight "in defense of Kosovo," he was indicted by the International Criminal Tribunal for the Former Yugoslavia for crimes against humanity, including participation in the "ethnic cleansing" campaign against Croatians, Bosnians, and Kosovars (Allison 1999).

Arkan's Tigers and the ACDEGAM have joined the ranks of a particular type of violent political actor — a type of actor as yet underinvestigated by the academic community but increasingly important in a number of violent conflicts. Political science has long studied the use of violence by the State, generally as a tactic of repression or popular demobilization, and the ways in which revolutionary groups use violence to alter or overthrow the State. But paramilitary groups operate outside of these two recognized "sides" in political conflict. The ACDEGAM was among 140 PMGs operating in Colombia, none of which was a recognized part of the state security forces. Nonetheless, all of these groups claimed to be fighting against the revolutionary guerrilla groups alongside the State,* and they enjoyed some

---

*"State" will be capitalized throughout the book to refer to the institutions, individuals, and structures that make up the governance of what is commonly known as the nation-state at the federal level. When not capitalized, "state" refers to the regional divisions or subunits of a country.

unofficial support from elements within the political system. As a collective they wreaked havoc on the civilian population, causing millions of civilians to be displaced from their homes and killing thousands of those not fortunate enough to have escaped. Arkan's Tigers were among several PMGs participating in the "ethnic cleansing" in the former Yugoslavia and were responsible for many of the mass killings (HRW 2000c; 2001d). The groups operated outside the official bounds of the State, though as in Colombia they had connections with members of the State; they targeted non-Serbs, particularly Muslims and those assumed to be separatists.

Officials within the U.S.-supported "unity government" in Iraq had similarly "unofficial" ties to the "death squads" that began operating in Baghdad around 2006. As the murder rate escalated in the capital city to dozens per day, evidence of the connections between the perpetrators and their organizations and officials within the government were uncovered by journalists. Indeed, members of the Iraqi police forces were found to "overlap" with the individuals who collectively made up the paramilitary groups who were carrying out so many of the gruesome attacks and leaving a trail of corpses behind them (Hess 2006; "Slaughter" 2006).

As with these cases, the Janjaweed in Sudan do not have the official support of the state security apparatus, yet there is ample evidence of State complicity in their attacks against rebel groups and noncombatant civilians. Since their emergence in 2003, millions of Sudanese have been forced from their homes, and nearly 200,000 have been murdered (HRW 2005). The Janjaweed have been strongly criticized by the international community for their part for the genocide and displacement that is ongoing in the Darfur region. Paramilitary groups have operated in parallel fashion, causing instability and committing gross human rights violations in Northern Ireland, El Salvador, Guatemala, Indonesia, and Uganda among other countries (see Sluka 2000; and Campbell and Brenner 2000).

Despite the fact that paramilitary violence is an increasingly frequent and global phenomenon, we have very little analytic understanding of the circumstances under and process by which PMGs emerge. This study focuses on these exact questions, examining the conditions in which PMGs organize and the structural alignments that give paramilitaries the opportunity to mobilize. The importance of understanding PMG emergence cannot be understated neither for the academic world nor the thousands of victims who fall prey to PMGs every year. Thus this study contributes to both the academic and policy realms in important ways by offering an empirical look at the nature and emergence of paramilitary groups, filling a void in scholarship regarding this type of political violence, and speaking to vital policy questions of national and international security in regard to the prevention of paramilitary violence.

Of course the first step in understanding paramilitary emergence is distinguishing a PMG from the range of other politically violent actors. In the course of my fieldwork, I interviewed more than one individual who, rather than acknowledge the presence of paramilitaries in his country, would shrug his shoulders and ask, "Well, what is a paramilitary? A group of armed men? Sure, we have armed men. So does every country." And while the interviewees' objective might have been evasion, their point remains a legitimate one. Every country does have armed men. What distinguishes a paramilitary from a guerrilla group? From a mob family? From a covert military operation? The term "paramilitary" has been used to describe elite, well-trained portions of a country's military, rogue units, and death squads.[1] The fact is that the term "paramilitary" has been used colloquially as a sort of "catch-all" rather than with any sort of precision or analytic conceptualization. This lack of any definitive meaning is an obvious obstacle to both theory building and policy making.

PMGs often identify themselves as "self-defense" groups while their critics call them "warlords" or "death squads," but such terms get us no closer to understanding the groups themselves. They are helpful in understanding the "view of self" held by the organization, and the "view of other" held by opponents, but they are as analytically useful as terms like "freedom fighter" and "insurgent." In truth, "self-defense group" and "death squad" are rhetorical devices used by the organizations to insinuate virtuosity and legitimacy, and by opponents to indicate malevolence and illegitimacy. Such terms provide insight into the perceptions of the actors themselves, but they are only subjective reflections of two opposing perspectives. In order to conduct an objective inquiry that is analytically accurate and useful, we need to avoid rhetorical devices that insinuate that they are "bad guys" or "good guys."

Paramilitary groups are political, armed organizations that are by definition extramilitary, extra-State, noninstitutional entities, but which mobilize and operate with the assistance of important allies, including factions within the State. Thus while officially illegal, PMGs enjoy some of the resources, access, and status generally exclusive to the State but which is funneled off by political and military allies. This paradox is central to the nature of the paramilitary group. Paramilitaries are offensive, not defensive in nature; their very purpose is to eliminate those who are perceived as threatening the socioeconomic basis of the political hierarchy. Thus paramilitary groups do share some characteristics with Payne's (2000) "uncivil movements," for instance the use of violence to exclude.[2] The non-governmental organization (NGO) Global Exchange has pointed out that "paramilitaries do not exist to defend the interests of society as a whole, but rather the interests of a dominant privileged sector" (Arronte, Castro Soto, and Lewis 2000:112–13). Thus PMGs may be thought of as combatants in what Mary Kaldor calls "new wars," in which principal combatants "borrow from counter-insurgency techniques of destabilization aimed at sowing 'fear and hatred'" (2001:8). Like Kaldor's "new war" aggressors (among which she counts PMGs), paramilitaries use "expulsion through various means such as mass killing [and] forcible resettlements" (2001:8) to control or eliminate those they oppose.[3]

Paramilitary groups are not random gangsters nor vigilantes sponsoring their own adjudication of criminal offenses. They are not "mobsters" or organized crime families using violence for capitalistic or monetary gains. Nor are they "private armies" that carry out the personal agenda of a wealthy employer. They are not militias or elite military factions, organized or operating with the official blessing of the State. PMGs are political organizations, but they are not left-wing radicals fighting for reform or revolution. They are organized not to overthrow the State, nor to devise coups against it. Indeed, one might visualize PMGs as opposite a revolutionary movement along a continuum of collective action and noninstitutional political participation. If social movement organizations (SMOs) are a form of contentious politics that pursue reform through extrainstitutional means, and revolutionary movements are a form of contentious politics that may use violence to overthrow the State, and countermovements are organizations that use noninstitutional means to combat the movement's reform objectives (see Meyer and Staggenborg 1996), then PMGs may be conceptualized as a type of contentious politics that uses violence to protect the established order rather than overthrow it.[4] Thinking in terms of their position along this continuum allows us to understand the defining characteristics of PMGs: their opposition to reform and their relationship to factions within the State. It is the relationship between the PMG and significant factions within the State itself that both distinguishes PMGs from other violent actors and highlights one of the analytical weak spots in the literature on political violence.

While paramilitary groups are political in nature and — as the examples above clearly illustrate — violent, they are noninstitutional and thus retain neither the full range of resources nor the legitimacy of the State. None of the groups noted above was or is operating within the structures of the State itself. Nor, as has previously been noted, do PMGS have the desire to revolutionize the political system. Literature on political violence evolved relying on the "State/anti-State" categorization of actor, and it offered little in the way of classifying and thus understanding paramilitary groups. Previous works focusing on State-sponsored violence speak to why a regime may undertake violence against its own people, and work on revolutionaries speaks to why people might take up arms against the State. But paramilitaries fit neither of these characterizations.

Indeed, the paramilitary phenomenon problematizes scholarly treatment of civil society and the State as two distinct areas, or levels, of analysis. There are members of paramilitary groups who are civilians and who may or may not be acting at the behest of military personnel, though the military personnel may be off duty and are engaging in illegal activity outside the parameters of their official capacity. In other cases paramilitary members are members of the armed forces and may or may not be following illegal orders of their official superiors acting in an unofficial capacity. "[T]he creation of paramilitaries abolishes the dividing line between what is civilian and what is military. It utilizes civilians to carry out activities that contribute to the 'reestablishment of order,' civilians who are conditioned to clandestine mechanisms that hide their identities and guarantee their impunity." This conflation of what is "State" and what is "civil society," of what is "military" and what is "civilian" requires political scientists to seriously reconsider the typologies we have relied upon in the past to categorize actors, interests, and incentives (Arronte, Castro Soto and Lewis 2000:112-13).

The tactics and victims of paramilitary groups are reminiscent of the old counterinsurgency wars sponsored by some Latin American States during the late 1970s and 1980s, a fact which may encourage the faulty categorization of PMGS as "State-sponsored violence" and thereby lead to flawed theoretical and policy conclusions. State-sponsored violence and paramilitary violence are two very different phenomena: With PMGS, we see the usurpation or delegation of part of the State's monopoly over the legitimate use of violence to an extra-State actor. The "monopoly over the legitimate use of violence" is a defining characteristic of the State, which would seem to imply that a State that has lost or is sharing this monopoly would be weak. Yet in countries with paramilitaries, there is also a strong and active military. Thus not only is it erroneous to treat paramilitaries as synonymous with or a substitute for State-sponsored violence, but also this misconceptualization allows us to ignore the obvious and important question raised by paramilitary emergence: Why and through what process has the State allowed its monopoly over the legitimate use of force to be broken? And why has this not weakened the State, as one might have expected?

Bureaucratic authoritarianism (BA) is perhaps the premier theoretical model of extreme State-sponsored violence, designed to explain the economic modernization, authoritarianism, and political instability that was characteristic of much of Latin America during the 1970s and 1980s. O'Donnell (1979, 1988) argues that the violent repression characteristic of bureaucratic authoritarian States was the product of two dynamics: (1) the "normalization" economic model aggravated preexisting socioeconomic inequalities, intensifying the need to exclude certain already-disadvantaged groups, and (2) the attempt to "depoliticize the handling of social issues" and disconnect the State from civil society, closing any channels of access that previously connected the two. In order to achieve this economic and political exclusion of the popular sector, the BA State institutionalized "specialists in coercion" in the professionalized military and used them to "deactivate" mobilized groups and suspected subversives (O'Donnell 1988:31–33).

The strong-State foundation of bureaucratic authoritarianism leaves unanswered the question of why a state might defer or concede its monopoly over violence to an extra-State actor. If the State is capable of and willing to use violence, why is it allowing or even facilitating paramilitary violence? Scholars conceptualizing paramilitary groups as the State's means of privatizing violence view PMGs as a strategic tool used by governments trying to meet a myriad of demands. Bruce Campbell and Arthur Brenner argue that "subcontracting" became a "habit" of the modern State as industrialization and modernization put increasing demands on the governance infrastructure while "the means at the disposal of States [was] not always kept up." Death squads, Campbell and Brenner argue, may be conceptualized as a "more malevolent form" of the State's need to subcontract out certain responsibilities, in this case repression (Campbell and Brenner 2000:16–17).

Indeed, "privatization" theorists take this one step further and argue that the human rights and democratization demands of international actors have added new obligations and constraints to those faced by developing countries in an increasingly global political economy. According to this body of literature, States allow private, non-State organizations to perpetuate violence against State enemies in order to appear "clean" to international sources of development and military aid money (Vargas Meza 1998:25; Huggins 1991:11, 13). The objectives of State violence are seen here much as they are in the bureaucratic authoritarian model: The regime views repression and violence as a means of social control necessary for economic gain and demobilization of opposing social forces. But this literature adds two elements to the BA model: (1) recognition of the role of international actors and their demands on the State, and (2) a reconceptualization of the State, so that it may be willing to designate an extra-State actor to share in its monopoly over violence. As international aid and trade agreements become increasingly important to developing nations, so their "image" becomes increasingly important to the sources of aid. "International public opinion frequently condemns violent, overt State repression, making it necessary for elements in such states to relinquish some direct control over civil society to informal . . . death squads" (Huggins 1991:13).[5]

However, the privatization hypothesis lacks empirical evidence that definitively links PMG organization and mobilization with foreign military aid. Indeed, in the case of Colombia, early paramilitaries organized years prior to a 1994 cut in U.S. aid. Thus there is an empirical gap between the occurrence of the alleged explanatory variable and paramilitary emergence, rather than the evidentiary chain necessary for theoretical rigor (George and Bennett 2005:19, 207; Mahoney and Rueschemeyer 2003:323). Even a cursory examination into this "gap" exposes a significant theoretical oversight. The privatized violence model does not account for the simultaneous and at least equally important role played by domestic actors in State decisions. While it is true that developing countries often rely on international aid packages for economic stability, they also rely on internal allies for political stability.

Political decision makers often face domestic demands and internal conflicts, and the sometimes contrary demands of international actors. Thus, in order to sustain their economic interests, national leaders must placate international demands, but in order to maintain the stability of their regime and their own political power, they must also address the demands of various domestic actors. The quandary is particularly acute for leaders of developing states, who are often faced with aid packages that have strings attached, and who must then "sell" the aid package—and its strings—to their domestic constituencies. The "privatized violence" model fails to offer conceptual or analytic tools that incorporate the ways in which the domestic realm interacts with the international realm, or ways in which the regime's approach to handling the multiple demands becomes relevant to paramilitary emergence.

The simultaneous negotiations on the domestic and international stage are more accurately modeled in Putnam's two-level game model. Putnam argues that when states are engaged in international negotiations, whether it be trade agreements, aid packages, or other bilateral or international issues, leaders must simultaneously negotiate the "terms of the deal" with their domestic constituency (Putnam 1988; Evans, Jacobson, and Putnam 1993; LeoGrande 1998a). This model recognizes that international negotiations do not occur in a vacuum, but rather within the constraints posed by a domestic political environment that will only permit the leader to negotiate certain "win-sets," or terms that are agreeable to domestic actors at the international table. Thus, Putnam argues, rather than separating the two levels of analysis, models must be able to replicate the interaction and interdependence between international negotiations and domestic politics. The two-level game model allows us to conceptualize the privatization of violence as a "win-set" (Putnam 1988:435) for the regime — it can meet both external demands for cessation of State involvement in human rights violations and internal demands for continued repression.

This model seems to work, explaining why a seemingly irrational decision — delegating some of the State's monopoly over the use of violence — may indeed be quite rational, depending on the interests of and demands faced by policy makers. Yet the model does not account for the grassroots-level of activity required in the mobilization of paramilitary groups. It does not incorporate the interests, objectives, and incentives driving grassroots actors who become members of or involved with the PMGs. Without the interaction and willingness of political actors at this level, there would be no paramilitary emergence. Indeed, a more careful examination of the Colombia case reveals that PMG grassroots organization significantly preceded Plan Colombia. None of the State-centered models account for this aspect of the phenomena.

Studies looking at the strength or weakness of a State and its institutional and structural capacity for fulfilling the basic functions of a State have conceptualized the most extreme form of a weak State as "collapsed." Scholars who study the process of collapse define it as a "situation where the structure, authority, law and political order have fallen apart and must be reconstituted. . . . It is not necessarily anarchy. . . . [But], for a period, the State itself, as a legitimate, functioning order, is gone." The collapse of a State creates a power vacuum, where power is literally "up for grabs" and grassroots-level actors may vie or organize to reconstruct the State, or alternatively take advantage of the vacuum for their own goals and ambitions without actually building a new institutionalized State (Zartman 1995:1–10; 267–68). In a study of "protracted [internal] conflict," Crighton and MacIver (1991) argue that paramilitaries often emerge in such situations perpetuating an especially violent situation where the State has all but lost control over its theoretically assumed monopoly over power and violence. This is sometimes referred to as "Balkanization," referring to the process of Yugoslavia's dissolution.

The applicability of the collapsed State models to paramilitary violence is definitively undermined by the fact that paramilitary group emergence and sustainability is in part dependent upon the complicity of factions within the State. In the case of Arkan's Tigers in the Balkans and the Janjaweed in Sudan, as with the PMGs in Colombia and in other countries, the evidence linking paramilitary groups to members of the military, political elite, and economic elite is clear and overwhelming. If the collapsed State explanation fit, we would expect to find a severely weakened State that has lost its monopoly over power and violence. Instead, we find a State that, while factionalized, maintains control over its resources and is delegating some of those to extra-State organizations. While the Colombian State could not, under most definitions, be considered a *strong* State, neither Colombia nor Sudan is a State on the brink of implosion. Rather, they are most likely to, in the future, keep company with States such as Guatemala and El Salvador that experienced extensive PMG violence and yet survived as States. The relationship between the military and paramilitary makes it difficult to argue that the State has collapsed.

Thus the question of elite allies is raised. The importance of domestic elite alignments in the emergence of extra-State actors has been well documented by social movement literature. The division among political elites is a critical "signal" in the "opportunity structure" that "encourages . . . [political or social actors] to use their internal resources to form social movements" (Tarrow 1996:54). That is, elite disunity provides an opportunity for new or nontraditional political actors to enter the political arena. McAdam, McCarthy, and Zald argue that the most radical types of social movements, including revolutions, are facilitated not by "the routine" realignment of elites, but by "those momentous, if rare, cleavages in previously stable governing alliances" (1996:11), an observation demonstrated by this research to apply to paramilitary emergence as well.

More recent social movement literature uses a "political process model," which evolved out of the political opportunity structure concept. According to this model, a divided elite has the potential to offer a movement more than just the political opening created by a stalemate or internal conflict that leaves traditional actors impotent to act against new actors. A divided elite may additionally provide a new political actor with an ally among the political elite and therefore within the State (McAdam and Snow 1997; McAdam 1996). In other words, when the elite or factions within the State are divided, some splinter group may begin to look outside its traditional allies for support and become an ally to a grassroots-level actor. Elite allies give new or unconventional political actors a newfound access to resources and a voice within the formal, traditional political structure.

Regardless of the degree to which non-State organizations can access the political system or attract political allies, there must be an organization ready to emerge in the first place. Social movement literature suggests that among the key elements of nontraditional political organization is a sense of collective identity. Specifically, case studies of a variety of movements have found that a sense of shared grievance, or a collective identity grounded in a commonly experienced injustice, often lays the foundation for organization and mobilization (see Mueller 1994). Descriptive accounts of PMGs indicated that the concept of a collective identity, or "shared sense of grievance" would be a useful template for a group-level analysis of paramilitary formation. For instance, Salazar (1991) argues that the very poor self-defense patrols organized in Medellín, Colombia, were originally organized by individuals who shared a common fear and grievance against violent youth *sicarios*, mostly teenage boys or young men who found being a paid assassin one of the most viable "occupations" in the area.

Yet the critical differences between PMGs and social movement organizations in terms of objective and required resources suggest that the mechanisms facilitating their emergence must also differ. While revolutionary social movements aim to demand reform via the overthrow of the State, paramilitaries aim to prevent reform and protect the State. Social movements therefore often rely on broad-based popular support and demand access to an established political system, typically with the objective of pursuing the implementation of reform via that system. Revolutionary movements seek support again from the population, and create a broad network of resources that are extrainstitutional. Paramilitaries require a much smaller nexus of support from individuals who are often within the established institutions who can offer resources from those very same institutions — for instance, military personnel for weapons and training. And unlike social movement organizations (revolutionary or not), PMGS need the State to "overlook" them, or provide impunity.

I utilized these various discourses in the literature as blueprints for pursuing these questions of how and why paramilitary groups emerge when and where they do. The project was an inductive one with explanatory objectives, and thus it called for a comparative case study analysis. As has already been noted here, the range of cases where PMGS have emerged is broad; however, methodological requirements (and researcher skills) called for careful selection. As a Latin Americanist, my area of expertise and language skills focused my attention on Latin America. Methodologically, I needed to choose cases on the dependent variable (paramilitary emergence) with limited variation in order to search for a pattern of similarity.[6] That having been said, I was also interested in exploring cases with some temporal or variance in stages of paramilitary violence. To that end, I selected three cases of paramilitary emergence for in-depth study: Chiapas, Mexico, where PMGS emerged in the mid-to-late 1990s and continue to operate on a small scale; Colombia, where PMGS emerged during the 1980s and enjoyed widespread influence; and El Salvador, where paramilitaries operated during the civil war of the 1980s, but where they have ceased operation since the 1992 peace accord.

These three are cases of politically developing states with a history of political violence and periods of military activity unchecked by civilian authority. The cases are roughly similar in terms of region, geopolitical relationships, and cultural and religious diversity, and they share similar histories in terms of colonialism, ethnic diversity and conflict, coup d'état, and dictatorship. Each of the three has a history of feudal stratification binding peasant and wealthy landowner (*el hacendado*), with an emergent working class and entrepreneurial business class in more developed areas. Perhaps as a result, they also have in common a historic struggle between the rural, landless peasantry and the oligarchy over land reform and resource distribution. Of course these are rough similarities; there are differences and distinctions across cases. Nonetheless, in pursuit of the methodological value in having limited variation, these three cases fit the requirements.

Other cases within Latin America were considered for study. Guatemala was initially included as a case where PMGS had been active but had since dissolved, but events in the country during the course of the research suggested a possible reemergence of PMG-type activity, making its categorical placement questionable. In addition, Argentina was initially included as a case without PMG violence. Evidence was later uncovered regarding small PMG operations during the 1970s, which disqualified it. Similarly, the state of Guerrero in Mexico was considered as a replacement for the Argentina case, but it was also excluded due to reports of paramilitary activity. Given the goal of conducting a multicase comparative study, the methodological concerns, and my own professional interests and expertise, the cases of Chiapas, Colombia, and El Salvador emerged as the focal points of this study.

The objective was not to generalize to a broader population (as in statistical analysis), nor to discover a "covering law." The research was designed rather to establish, with decisive clarity, high validity, and detailed analysis, the causal variables necessary for paramilitary emergence, the ways in which those variables are conjunctural (if at all), and the causal mechanisms responsible for "activating" the chain of causation (George and Bennett 2005; Mahoney and Rueschemeyer 2003; Ragin 2000). The important policy potential inherent in these findings required a research design that could offer policy-makers a basis upon which to build realistic strategies for dealing with paramilitaries. In order for such potential to be realized, the research needed to provide rigorous analysis of the actual mechanistic relationship between conjunctural variables and the outcome of interest (Munck 2004:112; George and Bennett 2005:8; Ragin 2000:12–13, 33, 72).

Given these objectives, this research used what Mahoney and Rueschemeyer refer to as a "causal narrative," a method of tracing the process leading to the outcome of interest via within-case analysis as well as across cases "by comparing cases of highly disaggregated sequences of processes and events that lead to outcomes" (Mahoney and Rueschemeyer 2003:361). Building a causal narrative requires that a researcher identify not only what variables effect an outcome, but also how (or why) each variable comes to effect that outcome. In political science, this frequently involves the not-always-easy task of identifying which individuals or groups are making particular decisions, and why they are doing so. As Peter Hall writes, understanding causal processes requires that one understand the

> chains of choices that the actors make in response to each other through iterated rounds of interaction. At each point in time, the choices of actors may be influenced by the presence of specific types of institutions. . . .

The outcome usually depends on a further set of conditions — social, economic or cultural — that can be complex or evanescent. . . . It is usually difficult to reduce the chains of causation envisioned by such theories to a simple set of independent variables. (Hall 2003:384)

In his work on conducting rigorous case studies, Yin argues that a researcher may begin with "several cases known to have had a certain type of outcome," and legitimately conduct research as to "how and why this outcome occurred in each case" (1994:108). Yin suggests that this be conducted using a method he refers to as "pattern matching," where the researcher uses "rival explanations as patterns" and compares each of the selected cases against the rival explanations. This process of pattern matching increases a study's internal validity, testing what would be expected if the proposition (or hypothesis) of alternative explanations were correct, against what is found empirically.

This research project took pattern matching one step further and conducted what Yin refers to as "explanation-building" research, that is, case studies conducted with the intention of uncovering phenomenological explanations that "reflect some theoretically significant propositions" (Yin 1994:111). Such projects often begin with an incomplete or uncertain set of propositions. To that end, this research took cues from two-level game theory, looking at the various interests of and demands on decision makers, and how those might contribute to paramilitary emergence, as well as from social movement literature, researching grassroots-level actors and their interests, motivations, allies, and opportunities. Using these, I then designed the data-collection stage to include both top-down and bottom-up components[7] in order to facilitate a process-oriented, comprehensive model of paramilitary emergence.

Data was collected using a triangulation of methods for each individual case, allowing "converging lines of inquiry" and therefore more rigorous findings with stronger construct validity (Yin 1994:92). I began each case by conducting in-depth historical research. The primary benefit gained from this element of the research was the ability to understand the environment out of which paramilitaries emerged, and to dig for data that might contribute to understanding the root of paramilitary groups and activities. The historical component had three main objectives: (1) to provide sound historical meaning for the political structures, coalitions, and environment which existed as PMGs emerged, (2) to collect data that might contribute to an understanding of the process of PMG emergence, and (3) to collect event data on paramilitary violence in the cases where applicable. This research allowed the project to take a dynamic approach to looking at the way in which the process of variables interacting over time affected the emergence and role of PMGs in each case. While the vast majority of this research was conducted in the United States, it was complemented and substantiated by interviews and fieldwork.

The second stage of research had two main components. The first was documentary and archival research, which was used to document paramilitary historical and contemporary activity, to identify the objectives of paramilitary activity, to collect data on those involved in paramilitary activity, and to look for the presence or absence of relationships between political actors. Archives and documents were also used to search for evidence of State interest in, collusion with, or opposition to paramilitaries, and evidence that spoke to whether the paramilitary groups were self-initiated on a grassroots level or whether the process was initiated from above. Because documentation of events tends to downplay heavy-handed violence connected to the State (particularly where the press cannot operate freely) and generally does not report covert State actions (Stanley 1996:17), a great deal of this evidence was collected from reliable human rights and international legal organizations.

The second component involved fieldwork conducted in each of the countries studied, with the exception of Colombia, where travel was unsafe during the data-collection phase of this research. Particularly given that organizations such as the IACHR (Inter-American Commission on Human Rights) could provide reliable, serious, detailed data and other information on Colombia, travel there was not worth the risk to my personal safety. However, that is not to say that using interviews with other fieldworkers and documentary evidence can adequately substitute for the knowledge, experience, and information I might have gathered in the field. I know from experience working in other field settings that nothing can replace the firsthand encounters with the subject of a study. Nonetheless, the situation in Colombia became dangerous enough to make interviews in-country too risky.

While doing fieldwork, I conducted interviews with a wide range of individuals, including civil society organization leaders, human rights watch organizations, church leaders, military and former military personnel or spokespersons, government officials, former guerrillas and guerrilla supporters, and regular civilians whose "collective memory" of paramilitary violence, perceptions of the State, and perceptions of political violence in general added a great deal to my understanding not only of the situation, but also of how they understood the situation (see Jorgensen 1989:12–13, 69). For instance, observer accounts may distinguish between paramilitary and State violence, but do the average citizens make such a distinction? And if they do not, how does this affect the citizens' perceptions and understandings of their political environment — and thus their local support or opposition to paramilitaries, the State military, or guerrilla organizations?

The interviews and general experience of being in the field provided me with some degree of tacit knowledge, helping me to understand the community-level significance of historical events, figures, and issues. Many of the interviews also provided me with key information regarding the paramilitary groups, including characteristics and identity traits, how they were organized, what their objectives were, and where they fit in the broader political environment, particularly relevant to other political actors. In addition, the culmination of interviews with State-level officials made me privy to the extent of the division within the State. Through interviews, I gained insight into the reasoning (or excuses) used by many to deny or minimize paramilitary activity, as well as into the efforts (and frustrations) of some trying to expose the PMGs for what they were. This data therefore contributed significantly to reconstruction of the causal narrative.

### Theory of Paramilitary Emergence: The Triad

Paramilitary emergence results from a culmination of dynamics whose intersection provides the opportunity, resources, organizational structure, and motives for their organization. If, as suggested earlier, we think about PMGs as a violent form of countermovement organization (just as a revolutionary group is a violent form of SMO), then we might expect that the factors relevant here — and the ways in which they relate to one another — are similar to those relevant for movement emergence. And indeed that is the case. Understanding PMG emergence requires study of structural shifts, the perceptions of actors at various levels of political life, and organizational networks. While shifts in the distribution of power provide the resourced allies necessary to provide for PMGs, the perceptions of actors are critical in the motivation underlying the formation of paramilitary groups, and preexisting organizations provide a critical building block for the mobilization of the groups themselves.

*1. Structural Shifts.* Paramilitarization should first be understood as a strategy used to counter reform efforts. The setting for paramilitary emergence is a political environment traditionally ruled by an oligarchy whose monopoly over the country's resources and wealth has depended on an exclusive right of political participation. Typically this has been protected by a military or official security force whose job it has been to repress the masses, a job that has been regionally carried out by State-sponsored or condoned armed groups of civilians. Consequently, the political and military elements of the State have evolved around the purpose of protecting the economic elite and furthering their interests. The political elite are those who pursue the interests of the economic elite (and the two may overlap significantly), and the military thrives off of the financial support of the State and the wealthy, who need the military to put down periodic uprisings. This symbiotic relationship works well until there is significant internal and/or external pressure for an opening in the political system.

Perhaps due to conditions put on foreign aid, or to international press attention, or to a significant domestic political rival, the dominant power holders find themselves facing an opposition party or organization of considerable strength, one that is demanding reform of the symbiotic system. The group may be demanding a more democratic system of government, or a redistribution of wealth (via land reform or workers' rights, for instance), any of which would undermine and potentially end elite exclusivity. This threat becomes an impetus for interaction between actors at the State and grassroots levels. National power brokers and local decision makers see the opposition group and the reforms as a menace to their position and status.

Historically, such opposition was eliminated with relative ease, as that was the job of the military, sometimes delegated to legalized regional bands of armed civilians. But international pressure has been increasingly brought to bear on countries committing gross human rights violations, making it progressively more difficult for developing countries to secure the loans and investment they need when they are simultaneously eliminating unarmed civilians. Thus the overt repression so relied upon in the past is a less viable option for the State. Yet the political elite continue to need the support of the economic elite, whose interests are also served by repressive security forces and their supplemental regionalized armed civilian "forces." The political elite are caught: protecting the economic elite by using the security forces to put down the opposition will secure domestic support, while it simultaneously drives away needed international support. This creates a distinctive shift within the political, economic, and military circles. Decision makers divide, with hard-liners arguing that the opposition has to be repressed and moderates arguing for minor reforms that will placate the opposition without driving away foreign lenders and investors. When the moderates win in the policy arena, the military is reined-in, and the armed civilian groups disbanded or made illegal despite hard-liners' opposition. The consequence of this division is a shift in the distribution of institutional power such that the moderates dominate, sending hard-liners in search of extrainstitutional means of achieving their preferred ends.[8]

Critical to this theory is the conceptualization of the "State" as an arena where various actors with potentially differing interests and motivations are at play. Borrowing from literature that "deconstructed" the State (Mitchell 1991; Nordlinger 1981), Stanley found that "States are seldom unitary actors; rather, they include many components that follow different imperatives and frequently contradict one another" (Stanley 1996:12). Consequently, the "State" is not viewed as monolithic but rather as a collection of actors who may be playing on the same team or who may find themselves competing with one another, depending upon whether those interests are shared. The political elite, who had previously united around the objective of repressing the masses and pursuing the economic elite's interests, may have presented the illusion of a unified "State." But faced with potentially new incentives and objectives (for instance, winning international approval and financial assistance), the illusion disintegrates as some of the political elite are drawn to the new incentives and others remain loyal to the traditional system. This division is one of the critical elements contributing to the opportunity for paramilitary emergence, in that it creates potential allies with important resources for the PMG.

In each of the cases studied here, the faction of hard-liners was significant and maintained positions of power, legitimacy, and leadership within the State, as well as important allies in military and wealthy circles. Thus they were not an easy group to marginalize. Indeed, in these cases, while the moderates won in the policy arena, reform measures were taken largely to meet the demands of "appearance" on the international stage. It is not clear in any of the cases studied here that the moderates won because their vision of reform was actually the more popular among policy makers and political leaders. In addition, the political hard-liners maintained the symbiotic relationships so entrenched in the political system and thus had at their disposal the resources of hard-liner compatriots in the military and among the wealthy. The hard-liners were not marginalized politically by their policy loss; instead, they exercised their political strength outside the institutional and legal boundaries of the State.[9]

2. *Perceptions and Frames.* In addition to these changes in the political structure, the willingness of moderates to heed calls for reforms created a perception among hard-liners within political, elite, and military circles that the reform advocates were undermining a legitimate political system. Thus the moderates created not only a division among power holders and an opportunity structure for PMGs, but also a "frame" for action among those institutionally marginalized. "Frames" are the collection of perceptions and cognitive understandings of a situation that actors bring to the table. Understanding actors' subjective understanding of their reality is critical to explaining their actions. Indeed, social movement scholars argue that frames "mediate between opportunity, organization and action. . . . At a minimum, people need to feel both aggrieved about some aspect of their lives and optimistic that, acting collectively, they can redress the problem" (McAdam, McCarthy, and Zald 1996:5) in order to undertake collective action.

The hard-liners in each of the countries studied here viewed reform advocates as illegitimate and undermining an established system that defined not only rules of governance, but also distribution of wealth and power. The reforms, they believed, threatened the basis of wealth, the exclusivity of the political system, and the purpose of the military, which had (as noted above) always been to secure and protect the system itself. Thus the moderates, via the reform measures, created a deeply shared grievance among these factions. For hard-liners within each of these sectors, advocates of reform were dangerous to the system — insurgent sympathizers at best. Using paramilitary violence to repress a reformist (insurgent) threat was essentially a continuation of what had always been done to protect the system, except that it had to be carried out in an "unofficial," extra-State manner. This was viewed by the political hard-liners as (1) legitimate, because they were fighting the opposition, and (2) necessary, because the State itself would not or could not act. Hard-liners within the military viewed the paramilitaries as organizations capable of carrying out the military's duty while their hands were tied by an unwilling bureaucracy. The country's wealthiest were willing to foot the bill for this endeavor, believing that the potential reforms would bring economic ruin.

Given the shared grievance, and the perception that moving outside the

State to repress the enemy was both legitimate and necessary, the hard-liners within each sector aligned with the others who shared their objectives and had access to the resources they had relied upon in the past to fight reformists. These cooperative efforts resulted in the continued reliance on tactics utilized in the past, only outside of the State.

3. *Preexisting Networks.* Even given the opportunity for PMG emergence provided by the shift in institutional power, and the frames that legitimized paramilitary violence for elite hard-liners, any type of political organization requires membership—in this case, foot soldiers. Mobilizing such membership can be particularly challenging for nontraditional modes of political action, and especially so for more radical, violent groups. Movement scholars have found that preexisting social networks, particularly those whose causes or objects are (or were) consistent with those of an emerging social movement, can provide a critical mobilizing base for a new SMO.[10]

As was noted earlier, each of the countries studied here had used armed civilian groups in the past to supplement security forces in their repression strategies. However, in each of the cases, pressures to reform called for the demobilization and disbanding of these groups. Indeed, Chiapas, Colombia, and El Salvador each reversed laws legalizing armed civilian groups. The change in their legal status, however, could not undermine the legitimacy already established by the long-term reliance on these civilian patrols for "national security." Particularly for the wealthy, who had often relied on armed civilians to guard against land reform activists or other peasant movements, the government's decision to disband these defense forces only served to further delegitimize the moderates and further justify the move outside official institutional means. The now-illegal groups served as important mobilization and recruitment networks for the PMGs.

It is important to note that the beliefs and perceptions held by the PMG recruits sometimes differed (to varying degrees) from those of the elite organizers. This will be explored in more depth in the chapters that follow, as permitted by the data. That having been said, certainly one of the legitimizing frames for many of these former civilian "forces" was quite similar to that of the military hard-liners: They had, in some cases for decades, been an important component of a counterinsurgency campaign proclaimed to be critical to national security. The data collected here indicate that their deauthorization by the moderates did not lead to a reevaluation by those civilians of their prior mission, but rather to an evaluation of the moderates in government who came to be seen as sympathizers with the very insurgents the civilian forces had been tasked to defend against. Thus for these recruits as well as for their elite organizers, the moderates were viewed as illegitimate and threatening to the system, and reorganizing outside legal parameters was seen as a necessary and legitimate tactic in furthering the counterinsurgency campaign.

The opportunities, frames, and mobilization networks together help us to understand not only how paramilitaries emerged, but also why PMGS were used rather than some alternative form of collective action. The tools of collection action are likely to be those that can best exploit whatever "leverage" has been afforded by a given opportunity structure (McAdam, McCarthy, and Zald 1996:10), given the preexisting networks that provide mobilizing opportunities and frames that provide justification and motivation for action. The resources brought to bear by the hard-liner factions meshed in an opportunistic way with the mobilization potential of the now-illegal armed civilian groups and the frames discussed above, making paramilitary groups a form of collective action that would be both well resourced and effective.

THUS, paramilitary emergence is likely to occur in countries where:

1. Access to the political system has been limited, permitting exclusive access to the elite and those loyal to their interests for a significant period of time, such that the elite have an entrenched sense of security in and dependence on this system; the influence, identities, status, and loyalties of the country's political and economic elite are protected by the exclusivity of this political system; *and*

2. The political elite, military, and/or political officials have a history of providing arms to civilians loyal to the regime, with a directive to combat other civilians who are perceived as posing a threat to the elite and therefore to the regime; *and*

3. A "new" or "opposition" political or social force, such as a political party (not necessarily a guerrilla force), gains support and demands reforms that would open the political system and therefore potentially redistribute political power and economic resources away from the elite; *and*

4. External or internal pressures prevent the State from using overt State-sponsored force to eliminate the opposition group; *and*

5. The political elite, the economic elite, *and* the military become respectively divided over the issue of reform, usually into a faction of hard-liners willing to rely on force rather than institutions in order to prevent reform at any cost, and a faction of moderates who are willing to make some concessions and minor reforms where moderates have the upper hand in terms of policy making; *and*

6. Factions of the economic elite, the military, and the political elite share a sense of grievance and injustice at their vulnerability to the growing influence of the reform movement, and their potential loss of power and influence at the hands of moderates.

Note that this *causal process* that gives rise to paramilitary groups is one in which the variables' interdependence, the timing, the domestic and international environment, and the perceptions of the actors are all relevant. That is to say, one cannot draw out one specific variable and argue "if you have X, you will have Y." Thus political exclusion, regardless of its longevity or intensity, is not sufficient to explain PMG emergence. Having a divided political elite is not in and of itself enough to explain paramilitary emergence. It is not the presence nor the variance of any of these variables individually, but rather the process by which these variables interact that explains paramilitary emergence. Under *the confluence of* these conditions, paramilitary organization and mobilization is facilitated by a "triad" of allied forces that together offer the resources necessary for PMGs to carry out an underground counterinsurgency campaign against the perceived opposition. The triad is composed of factions of the economic elite, who provide finances, training sites, and other organizational necessities; factions of the political elite, who provide political and legal "cover," ideology, purpose, and leadership; and factions of the military or security forces, who provide arms, training, and leadership.

The following chapters trace the ways in which these variables came together in Chiapas, Colombia, and El Salvador. We begin with Chiapas, the most recent of the cases of paramilitary emergence and the case that has seen the least in terms of formal attempts to resolve the conflict. Chapter 1 discusses the historical and environmental factors that predated the PMGs but laid important groundwork for their emergence. Unlike the other two cases studied here, the conflict in Chiapas is a regional one. Both the proreform movement and the PMGs are particular to the state of Chiapas, thus this chapter also undertakes the question of what makes Chiapas distinct from other Mexican states. Chapter 2 looks specifically

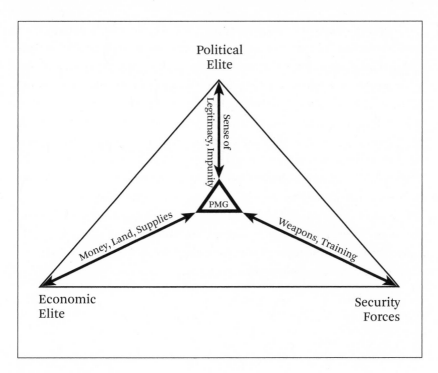

FIGURE 1. Triad Model

at the paramilitary groups in terms of the triad of support that facilitated their emergence and operation, and it looks at the characteristic recruit of the PMGs in Chiapas.

Chapters 3 and 4 then move on to the case of Colombia, where paramilitaries emerged in the 1980s. The Colombian case is the "largest" of those studied here in that the paramilitary groups proliferated in number and have effected comparatively far greater swaths of territory. It differs from Chiapas in that the federal government has made formal attempts at demobilization of the PMGs, but evidence suggests that these have not been an overwhelming success. Chapter 3 presents the history of the country relevant to paramilitary emergence and the contemporary reform efforts that triggered important divisions within the country's elite as well as the formation of the earliest paramilitary groups. Chapter 4 looks at the support network that allowed the evolution, growth, and expansion of Colombia's paramilitary forces, which over time grew to number eleven thousand combatants. This chapter also explores the nascent attempts to demobilize the groups.

Chapters 5 and 6 focus on the case of El Salvador, where paramilitary groups were active from the late 1970s through the early 1990s. As with the previous two cases, Chapter 5 focuses on the stage set by history for paramilitary emergence and looks at the country's initial PMG operations, while Chapter 6 focuses on the triad network. PMGs played an important and violent role in El Salvador's civil war, yet they seemed to fade from the political landscape after the peace accords were signed without any deliberate demobilization efforts. Thus El Salvador allows us to conclude the analysis of cases with a discussion of those factors that may be relevant in the dissolution of PMGs. While eliminating PMGs is not the theoretical focus of this study, it is certainly an important question raised by the findings presented here. Thus, saving El Salvador for last allows us an opportunity to examine the end of paramilitary violence in one country with reflections upon the analyses of Chiapas and Colombia.

# CHIAPAS HISTORY
## SETS THE STAGE FOR
## PARAMILITARISM

In 1994 the guerrilla organization Ejército Zapatista de Liberación Nacional (Zapatista Army of National Liberation), better known by their acronym EZLN or simply as the Zapatistas, began a military offensive against the government of Mexico in the southern state of Chiapas. Attacking early on 1 January 1994, they quickly took four small towns with almost no violence. The guerrillas demanded land reform for the indigenous of Chiapas and the protection of their civil liberties and democratic rights. Their criticisms of the Mexican system and the fraud that plagued it drew international attention and rallied sympathy for their cause.[1]

A cease-fire was declared only days after the initial offensive. The Zapatistas put down their weapons and began using public relations tools to continue pressing for change, rallying even more support (Ross 1995, 2000). Congress passed a policy designed to facilitate talks without further violence known as the "Law for the Dialogue, Reconciliation, and Dignified and Just Peace in Chiapas" in 1995 (CONPAZ 1997:1; Centro 1999:3; AI 1998). The agreement with the EZLN, known as the San Andrés Peace Accords, was reached in 1996.

Subsequent to the Zapatista uprising, at least twelve paramilitary groups emerged in Chiapas; together they are believed to have committed more than 15,000 murders (Hernández Navarro 1998:7), displaced more than 21,000 persons (Arronte, Castro Soto, and Lewis 2000:127; SIPAZ 2000a), burned countless homes and businesses, issued innumerable death threats, occupied communities and committed a range of violations, including rape and the defamation of churches (SIPAZ 2000a:4–6, 2000c; Arronte, Castro Soto, and Lewis 2000; Selee 1999; Ramírez Cuevas 1997a). Despite the trail of corpses and ashes left behind them, and in spite of confirmation of their activities by NGOs, journalists, and academics, the Mexican government repeatedly denied that the PMGs were operating in Chiapas. The debate over the very existence of the paramilitaries consequently allowed the groups to operate like ghosts, below the radar of Mexican law.

The 1997 massacre in the small community of Acteal is perhaps the most internationally known act of paramilitary violence in Mexico. Members of *Las Abejas* (the Bees), a religious group that supported Zapatista goals but denounced the use of violence, were worshipping in their chapel on the morning of 22 December 1997, when the church was invaded. During the ensuing five-hour attack, forty-five civilians were murdered. Coroner reports show that of the forty-five left dead, thirty-two were women and thirteen were men. Nineteen of the victims were younger than twenty-one, and four were over sixty years of age. Nine were shot in the back, among them a two-year-old girl and a sixty-five-year-old woman. More than one-third of the victims suffered cracked skulls due to blows by machetes, among them an eleven-month-old infant ("Chiapas: La Guerra" 1998:8–11), and unborn babies were taken from the sliced-opened wombs of their mothers (Stahler-Sholk 1998:11).

More than five hundred people were victims of PMG attacks in Chiapas in 1997 alone, but Acteal brought unprecedented international attention to the violence. Prior to Acteal, paramilitary attacks had been largely limited to two or three victims, and the circumstances of the attacks had been vague enough to leave the perpetrators' identity and intent questionable. But in Acteal, many of the victims were on their knees in prayer when attacked, the total of dead and wounded numbered seventy, some shot from behind as they were running from the church trying to escape (Stahler-Sholk 1998:12; "Chiapas: La Guerra" 1998).

In addition, the proximity of the army and police and the lack of response to the attack alarmed international observers. As one official I interviewed explained,

> Where the massacre happened in Acteal, there is an army post *right there*, and the murderers — or actors — have to walk, maybe in uniform, for certain together [in a group] and armed, for several minutes to get there. No one saw them? No one heard them? . . . Look, it's a small place. *Las Abejas* was a small, compact group in a concentrated area. And the road goes like this [a road is motioned out on the desk top] through the town. And here [he points to one end of the road] there are police stationed, and here [pointing to the other end] there is the army. And this

group, organized, entered the town, armed, the massacre was . . . hours long, and no one on either end does anything? How? Why?[§2]

Police forces in fact received at least two reports of the massacre *as it was taking place*. As early as 11:30 that morning, one hour into the attack, witnesses notified the local police commander. About thirty minutes later another report reached the police stationed "no more than 500 yards from the chapel," as members of the community escaped and told the same official, Commander García Rivas, what was happening (Ramírez Cuevas 1997b). Still the police did not move from their location. The lack of reaction by the police and military forces inevitably causes one to wonder whether the attack was sanctioned by authorities, or whether there was a degree of outright complicity in the massacre. The question of collusion is even more disturbing given that calls to government officials for help throughout and immediately following the massacre also came to naught.

> And look, someone made a call for help. And in the Constitution of Chiapas, as in all states in Mexico and the federal Constitution as well, it is the law that the governor is the commander in chief of the army in his territory. Did the call not get to the governor? Did no one tell him the army needed to be called in? The process of notification began, the secretary general was contacted. Or did the message get through [to the governor], and still no one called in the army? These are all questions that have to be part of the investigation.[§]

Thus the resonance of Acteal lies not only in the massacre of innocent civilians, but also in the circumstances of their deaths and in the lack of help and protection by state officials.[3] Acteal has become symbolic of the struggle in Chiapas; those five violent hours exemplify the brutality and the complicity that together characterize the conflict in Chiapas. With Acteal, it became clear that the struggle in Chiapas was not solely between the Zapatista guerrillas and the State; it was not a dichotomous movement/countermovement phenomenon. The massacre and the lack of investiga-

---

[§]Confidential interviewee. Due to the violent and controversial nature of the groups under study, this research relied on the ability to protect the identity of a number of sources. While a few interviewees gave explicit and written permission to use their names, most preferred confidentiality. Throughout the rest of the book, the section symbol (§) will be used to indicate a confidential interview.

tion indicated the level of conflict, the impunity of the paramilitaries, and, as we shall see, the strength of the coalition between the then-dominant political party, the Partido Revolucionario Institucional (PRI), and the Mexican military.

### The PRI in Chiapas

In their initial public treatise, the *First Declaration of the Lacandón Jungle* (1994), the EZLN leadership wrote, "We are the product of 500 years of struggle" (Collier and Quaratiello 1999:2). It is true that the Zapatistas are but the latest in a long history of groups to organize against hunger and repression in the region. Likewise, the paramilitaries in Chiapas are the product of the opposing side of the same struggle, five hundred years of the development of and respect for a socioeconomic system, and of putting down the threat of peasant rebellion against that system. The two are only the most contemporary parties of an age-old conflict between the landless and the landlords in Chiapas.

Although Chiapas officially became part of Mexico in the early 1820s, it continues to lag far behind the rest of the nation in economic development and social services. In 1996, the national illiteracy rate was estimated to be 11 percent, whereas illiteracy in Chiapas over the 1990s hovered at 30 percent ("Mexico" 1996; Ross 1995:72). In 1993, 67 percent of the nation's population had access to safe drinking water and sanitation, whereas 90 percent of the indigenous households in Chiapas did not have access even to potable water (Wilkie 1999:196; Ross 1995:72). The infant mortality rate in Chiapas was twice that of the nation, understandable given that nationally the number of doctors per 1,000 patients was 3.7, whereas the same ratio for Chiapas was only 0.54 (Ross 1995:72). And though approximately 20 percent of the country's energy needs come from Chiapas (54 percent of the nation's hydroelectric power, 13 percent of its gas, and 4 percent of its oil), 63 percent of Chiapanecos homes do not have electricity (Collier and Quaratiello 1999:17, Ross 1995:71–72). Chiapas also rates below national averages in terms of personal income. Despite the wealth of natural resources found in the state, the percentage of adults earning at least a "moderate income" (as defined by the Mexican government) in Chiapas is half that of the national level (11 percent in Chiapas versus 24 percent nationally). "Salaries [in Chiapas] are three times lower than the national average; 40 [percent] of the farmers of Chiapas" earn only "half of the Mexican minimum wage" (Ross 1995:72).

Demographically, Chiapas is distinct from other Mexican states in both its indigenous population and religious diversity. In 1990, the indigenous population constituted approximately 8 percent of the national population (Wilkie 1999:139). Some estimates of the indigenous population in Chiapas put it at one-third of the state's total; other measures, incorporating those who cannot speak a native language but have native ancestry, indicate this estimate is too low. The indigenous communities today are primarily descendants of the Mayans, including the Tzotzil, Tzeltal, Chol, and Tojolabal; an estimated one hundred different indigenous languages are still spoken throughout the state (Ross 1995:58, 72). Chiapas epitomizes the mosaic of ethnicities in Mexico revered by some and despised by others.

Prior to the arrival of the Spanish in the 1500s, the area we now call Chiapas was populated principally by Mayan indigenous communities. Resistance against colonization was intense in Chiapas and lasted longer than in other areas of what is now Mexico. The level and duration of indigenous opposition against the Spanish have become an important part of the local history and identity. Tourists taking a boat ride along the Río Grijalva in the Cañón del Sumidero north of Chiapas's capital city will hear the story of the community of Indians who chose to leap from the thousand-meter cliff above the river to their deaths rather than be defeated by the Spanish.

Despite the resistance, Chiapas was conquered and colonized by the Spanish in 1528 and became part of what is today known as Guatemala. Colonial ranches required steady labor, and the Spanish quickly fettered the native inhabitants. As with most other colonizations, the indigenous populations fell prey to both forced labor and to diseases brought by the Europeans, and entire communities were decimated (Collier and Quaratiello 1999:18–22). While the Spanish did establish "Indian Republics," communities for the indigenous complete with communal lands and churches, even these "Republics" were not truly "Indian," as they were both designed and governed by the Spanish. Most ranch laborers lived on or near the ranches and were ruled by the landowner. It was on these ranches where a patron-client system took root in Chiapas.

The roles of the patron and his laborers is at the heart of the broader "patron-client" concept used to describe vertical power relationships characterized by reciprocity between individuals or positions of unequal resources, power, or status. The *patrón* system in Chiapas clearly defines the social and economic order based on one's land (or lack thereof), and thus identified one's "place," one's power or powerlessness. The rancher became the *patrón* to his indigenous laborers, controlling most aspects of their lives (Collier and Quaratiello 1999:22).

During the colonization of Chiapas, the patron system offered an important tool for local control, though resistance against Spanish rule continued. In 1542, an indigenous uprising in the community of Pochotla resulted in the deaths of "priests and taxmen" (Ross 1995:66). In 1712, Tzeltal and Tzotzil communities rebelled against their landlords and subsequently against the Catholic Church, particularly targeting the priests who had been charging high fees for sacraments (Collier and Quaratiello 1999:22). The dispossessed status of the indigenous did not change either with Mexico's independence from Spain (1821) or the annexation of Chiapas to Mexico (1824), nor did the peasant resistance against domination. In 1868, two groups joined forces in Chamula to organize an attack against the elite. Their attack was short-lived, and the bodies of the massacred were left in the city square to "rot . . . as a reminder to those who plotted fresh rebellion" (Ross 1995:67), a tactic that would be used again in the future.

In the years after independence, liberals and conservatives in Mexico fought viciously over the role of the Catholic Church: Conservatives tried to protect the immense landholdings and influence of the church, while liberals worked to redistribute the land and separate the church from the political realm.[4] Under liberal rule in the 1860s and early 1870s, Mexicans experienced an opening in the political system. This period was known as La Reforma, named for the significant reforms undertaken by the liberals as they worked to divorce the church from the State, offer State-centered social services and limited voting rights. Even this "opening" did not question or challenge the distribution of resources and power in Chiapas. Landownership remained the privilege of the few in Chiapas, and this socioeconomic system further strengthened patron-client-type relations.

It was not until the Mexican Revolution of 1910 that the federal government began taking a more egalitarian approach to reform with the three main Revolutionary leaders, Emiliano Zapata, Pancho Villa, and Venustiano Carranza. Though the three differed by degrees on issues of land reform and centralization, all leaned toward a more progressive agenda. In Chiapas, landowners were suspicious of what the Revolution would mean for traditional power holders and landholdings. Though Carranza's ideology was more moderate than Zapata or Villa, even his victory would mean that land reform was at least possible. Landowners' fears proved founded when Carrancistas abolished debt servitude in Chiapas (Collier and Quaratiello 1999:28). Implementation of the law left wealthy landowners and rancheros with no recourse for retaining their peasant workforce. Additional reforms pursued by the new government limited the amount of land that could be owned by a single property owner. Fincas (large estate properties) across the nation began falling victim to the new policies, and the landowners in the highlands were getting nervous (Collier and Quaratiello 1999:28–30).

In an effort to protect Chiapas from the Revolution, local elite formed counterrevolutionary bands called Mapaches (raccoons). Using guerrilla-like tactics and "impoverished peasants who were pressed into joining the cause," the Mapaches fought off the reforms that would have been imposed via federal legislation by fighting the Revolution. The new government eventually conceded and did not enforce the land reform laws that were redistributing properties in other Mexican states in Chiapas. Federal officials "even appointed [a Mapache] to be governor of Chiapas, thus leaving power in the hands of the land owners" (Collier and Quaratiello 1999:28–29; Ross 1995:69; Garcia de León 1985:17). As one scholar aptly describes the fruits of the Revolution, "while the new governor of [the state of] Morelos was a [Z]apatista guerrilla, the new governor of Chiapas was a traditional landlord." (Garcia de León 1985:17). *Los pobres* of Chiapas were already missing out on the promises of the Revolution.

Meanwhile, the Revolution's victors inherited the responsibility of writing a new constitution and designing a new government. Part of that design included the Partido Nacional Revolucionario (PNR), or Revolutionary National Party, a political party claiming to embody the tenets pursued in the Revolution: agrarian reform, democratic government and representation, equality, and prohibitions against the reelection of a president. The "main goal [of the party] was to create a centralized political party controlled by the president that could check the power" of competing ideologues "and force them to resolve their conflicts within an institutional context." The party was redesigned in 1938 and again in 1946 into what is today known as the Partido Revolucionario Institucional, the Institutional Revolutionary Party. The final product was a strong, "[S]tate-sponsored political party, whose function was to mobilize support for the revolutionary elite and ensure that social demands were channeled through the official party" (Council 1993:12–13). Via the PNR and later the PRI, Mexico became the classic corporatist State: unions, newspapers, civic organizations, and professional associations were each incorporated within the party, and therefore within the State. In fact, as early as 1931, a reporter for the *Nation* in the United States concluded that in Mexico, "the PNR is the government and the government is the PNR" (Sherman 1997:18).

Mexico soon became one of the world's noncommunist single-party systems. The PRI was reelected to the presidency by an alleged majority of the population for more than seventy years, periodically relying on the military to quiet opposition and more often on electoral fraud to ensure success. Importantly, the party all but institutionalized a political *patrón* system, similar to the hierarchy established by landowners in Chiapas. The PRI encouraged and enabled political bosses, or caciques, to dole out political favors (often jobs or political positions) to those (clients) whose support would then be guaranteed for the party.

The PNR's continual focus on land reform won it the support of Mexico's masses but alienated many of the landholding elite. Chiapas posed a particular challenge for the new government, and the PNR began working to co-opt the state's elite in spite of their early and determined resistance to the revolutionary project. Beginning with the appointment of the Mapache governor in Chiapas, the PNR began making accommodations with the local powers. In brokering these deals, however, the State actually enabled the local strongmen to continue undermining the ability of the State to establish itself in the rural areas (Migdal 1987). For instance, the party might promise land reform to the peasants and pass land reform packages, while at the same time making concessions with the local elite that undermined the legislation. This cycle of federal-level reforms and local-level accommodations intensified the already contentious issue of land redistribution within Chiapas, but it secured the loyalty of the local elite to the party without sacrificing the support of the poor.

The dynamics of this cycle became more evident in the 1930s, when the federal government began to redistribute "marginal" and generally unused lands to peasants. The land reform provision was filled with red tape and logistical hoops which frustrated *actual* redistribution, saving landowners from large-scale loss. For instance, the law "authorized claims only within seven kilometers of peasant settlements of at least twenty households" (Collier and Quaratiello 1999:48). Thus, when peasants found unused and believed-to-be "untitled, national land" for which they could petition, they often had to move onto the land, "squatting," so that they could *then* petition the government. Despite the lack of real implementation, the federal redistribution plan still antagonized landowners, particularly given the squatting that resulted.

Officials in Chiapas found a way to address the land occupations in 1934 when it began providing "certificates of inalienability" to landowners. The certificates guaranteed large landholders protection from redistribution and went unchallenged by the federal government (HRW 1997:18; Hidalgo 1997:2). The arrangement allowed the party to continue courting the poor by promising and even passing land reform policies, without alienating their elite constituents. Elites who chose to support the PRI soon found themselves with additional benefits, as well.

> *Caciques* became adept at exploiting their profitable relationship with the ruling PRI, working through the state government to fend off land reform in many parts of Chiapas. . . . In exchange for supporting the PRI, local leaders and *caciques* could expect to enjoy the benefits of federal government largesse and to be able to establish commercial interests that often amounted to monopolies in, for example, food distribution or transportation. (HRW 1997:18)

Despite the certificate system, squatting continued to be a problem for landowners. To help deal with the problem, Efraín Aran Osorio, governor of Chiapas from 1952 to 1958, created the statewide Cuerpo de Policía Auxiliar Ganadera, or the Ranch Auxiliary Police. These police were primarily "ranch-hands and peasants working in their spare time" who were hired to remove the squatters (HRW 1997:21). In the later half of the 1950s, landowners also began taking it upon themselves to "deal with" the peasants, using brute force via private security guards to drive the peasants away and punish activists (see Collier and Quaratiello 1999:46; Arronte, Castro Soto, and Lewis 2000:111). Continuing efforts to court both the poor and the wealthy, the federal PRI leadership continued to use the rhetoric of land reform while simultaneously turning a blind eye to the violence against squatters. By doing so, the party again reinforced the regional "strongman" status of local elite, currying their favor, yet retained the support of the peasants with the redistribution legislation.

Despite their early resistance to federal legislation and dictate, the elite within Chiapas became some of Mexico's most ardently loyal priístas. By aligning with the PRI, the wealthy were able to become the "patrons" in the local "patron-client" relationship, retaining not only the regional economic and social influence they had always had, but now also political influence and connections to a national party. Whenever the federal government or party had funds, jobs, or privileges to be doled out, the local priístas became the beneficiaries of these and in turn the patrons of whatever was to be further distributed. The PRI patron-client structure actually institutionalized the local power structure, and connected it via *patrónes* to higher levels of government, thus providing new sources of power and influence for local patrons. As a direct consequence of the PRI's outreach, the elite status in Chiapas soon came to be defined not only by land ownership, but also by position within the party.

## The Guardias Blancas

While the federal accommodation of local strongmen and reliance on the patron-client system strengthened the hand of Chiapanecos elite, it did nothing to mitigate the struggle of the region's poor and indigenous for land and political rights. Indeed, the cycle of uprisings and repression seen during the 1860s was replayed periodically as popular organizations rose to clamor for reform and fell to the local elite reprisals. In 1961, then-governor of Chiapas Samuel León Brindis (1958–64) decided to officially legalize the use of private security forces, who eventually patrolled as many as 225,000 hectares (2,250 square kilometers) (Hidalgo 1997:1–2). The groups, known as Guardias Blancas or White Guards,[5] did much the same of what the Ranch Auxiliary Police did, violently removing land occupiers and repressing activists.

White Guard activity peaked during the 1980s. "During a six-month period between July and December 1982, independent organizers and the groups they represented in Chiapas experienced five assassinations, violent evictions from two ranches, the destruction of an entire peasant town, and fifty-nine kidnappings" (Collier and Quaratiello 1999:80). Violence heightened over the next few years, perhaps signifying a reaction to the increased peasant organizing and activism of the late 1970s. Groups like the Organización de Campesinos Emiliano Zapata (OCEZ), the Emiliano Zapata Peasant Organization, led finca occupations and challenged the corporatist system seriously threatening the caciques. General Absalón Castellanos Domínguez was governor of Chiapas during the 1982–88 *sexenio* (the six-year term of office in Mexico), governing during some of the more violent repression in the state.

> *Guardias blancas* . . . are believed to be responsible for numerous deaths of peasant organization leaders, land claimants, and religious workers, as well as countless threats, land evictions, and home burnings. It is impossible to know for sure the number of deaths attributable to the *guardias blancas*. (Selee 1999)

At the close of Castellanos's term in 1988, Mexico was negotiating the terms and qualifications of the North American Free Trade Agreement with the United States, and the White Guards became problematic for the Mexican negotiators. Governor Patrocinio González (1988–93) therefore led an effort to implement some land reform and overturn the policies which had legalized the Guardias Blancas (Hidalgo 1997:2; Arronte, Castro Soto, and Lewis 2000:111). Dismantling the White Guards proved to be more difficult than changing their legal status, however, and land activists continued to be victimized (see Hidalgo 1997; and HRW 1997).

While it had been characteristic for White Guards to "depen[d] on the ranchers and landowners that organize and finance them," groups began to be involved with the local Public Security Police (PSP) activity against local squatters (Arronte, Castro Soto, and Lewis 2000:111), and carried out violent attacks with no accountability. Organizations operating outside the PRI umbrella, independent of the party and government, were especially targeted. Groups like the Independent Organization of the Agrarian Workers, and the Emiliano Zapata Peasant Organization were among those subject to both repression by the state and private forces. Reports of attacks between 1992 and 1995 indicate that White Guard units were also "hired to annihilate a certain power group that impeded or competed with them in illicit activities (such as narco-trafficking), or in disputes for local power" (Arronte, Castro Soto, and Lewis 2000:111). Thus the private security guards hired by private landholders were being "rented out" to local police officials and offering their services in return for payment.

The "acquiescence and complicity of state authorities in the activities of white guards" remained a problem for years after their legal status was revoked. One blatant example of this "acquiescence" occurred at the end of 1994, when a group of *ejido* demonstrators were attacked by "approximately 300 white guards" accompanied by "municipal authorities." At least one of the activists was taken by the White Guards to their "headquarters." An investigation into the attack found that "state authorities had had plenty of warning that the attack was imminent, . . . but took no action to prevent it" (HRW 1997:21–22).[6] These increasing connections with the police may have laid the groundwork for a future paramilitary triadic network, though the groups still were not yet paramilitary in nature. While there are similarities between the two groups, they are superficial and disguise essential differences between them. It is more accurate to suggest that the White Guard era bled into the initial stages of paramilitary formation than to claim that PMGs are simply renamed Guardias Blancas, due to two important distinctions.

Paramilitaries are unlike White Guards first in terms of their objective. This distinction is perhaps missed at first observation due to the fact that while the groups' objectives differ, the victims are characteristically the same. Like White Guards, PMGs typically target peasant organizers, land reform advocates, and critics of the established social order and power structure. But while the White Guards targeted such individuals for the direct purpose of protecting their boss (the rancher) and his property, the paramilitary groups targeted such individuals because of the threat they posed to the system, as will be discussed in more detail below. This distinction can also be missed due to the fact that the power hierarchy in Chiapas is still based largely on land ownership and wealth, causing a significant overlap between the political elite and the economic elite.

Second, unlike the White Guards, who were hired and armed by ranchers or landowners, paramilitaries are organized, trained, armed, and "professionalized," simulating military units, by a group of individuals. This "lead group" is generally composed of at least one PRI party member or elected official, and one or two wealthy business owners or ranchers, and usually at least one military or police contact. This triad of leadership, explored at more length below, creates a network used to provide recruitment and leadership, military training, arms, impunity from prosecution, and sometimes even small salaries for the PMGs. Hidalgo highlights the differences between the two, noting that PMGs can be

> distinguished because they are . . . organized with a political-military structure. . . . They are not dependent upon land owners or ranchers, but on the federal Army, Police, and Public Security Forces, the government, and on governmental institutions that finances the projects and development; they therefore are responsive to political interests more than to the defense of land, [and] because of this these groups have links to the PRI. (Hidalgo 1997:2)

Thus while White Guards defended property, paramilitaries defend the PRI party dominance that (a) protects the large property holders from land redistribution, and (b) assigns a status and a power via land. Chiapanecos paramilitaries "affirm, in their own words, that they are PRI militants . . ." (Arronte, Castro Soto, and Lewis 2000:112). Due to the political objective, unlike the Guardias Blancas, paramilitaries are not reactive or defensive in nature; they are proactive and organized for the purpose of offensive attacks. Paramilitaries do not select targets because they physically threaten belongings or property, they strike against those who ideologically and politically threaten the regional power structure. Thus, while there is some overlap between paramilitary and White Guard organizers in landowners and there is a similarity in the types of victims that are targeted, paramilitaries differ from White Guards in key ways. Most importantly, while White Guards were largely property-oriented security forces, paramilitaries have a broader political purpose. The shift from White Guard to paramilitary was largely instigated by the EZLN offensive in 1994. The Zapatistas represented a significant shift in the political landscape of Chiapas, and one that was deeply threatening to the local socioeconomic order and the PRI domination.

## Zapatistas

As the violence against campesinos was rising during the 1980s, some activists argued that squatting, land occupations, protests, and petitions were not enough.[7] *Ejido* communities banded together marshaling their resources against both the government and the Guardias Blancas. In the autumn of 1983, what would prove to be a more significant challenge to the Chiapas power structure began fomenting in the Lacondón Jungle: The Ejército Zapatista de Liberación Nacional. Other rebel groups, guerrilla organizations, and the like had been organizing in the mountains in southern Mexico since the 1970s, but whether it was the timing or the preparedness or the tactics, the EZLN would prove to be a more lasting and internationally recognized challenge to the State and to the status quo.

The rebel Zapatistas spent ten years hidden in the jungle, collecting, "expropriating," training with, and distributing arms ranging from AK-47s to single-shot .22s, purchasing and collecting uniforms from street vendors, and reading up on the war and guerrilla techniques of Mexican Independence and Revolutionary heroes. They even constructed model city squares, exact replicas of their planned targets, to practice proposed attacks (Collier and Quaratiello 1999; Ross 1995; Doyle 2004:9).[8]

Autumn 1991 brought perhaps the most crushing affront to the peasants and the indigenous communities of Chiapas. Then president Salinas de Gortari was reforming the Mexican economy, and the inefficient productivity associated with communal lands was not compatible with Salinas's new game plan. In late 1991, the president convinced legislators to modify Article 27 of the Constitution, the legal provision through which peasants could petition for land. The change essentially ended agrarian reform and, as Subcommandante Marcos of the EZLN put it, "'negated any legal possibility of obtaining land'" for the peasants (Collier and Quaratiello

1999:87–89). On 1 January 1994, the day NAFTA went into effect, the EZLN took four municipalities in Chiapas: San Cristóbal de Las Casas, Ocosingo, Las Margaritas, and Altamirano. The EZLN demanded for Chiapas and its indigenous what the rest of Mexico seemed to have: "work, land, [housing], bread, health, education, democracy, liberty, peace, independence, and justice" (Ross 1995:17; Collier and Quaratiello 1999:87–89).

President Salinas decided not to use the full force of the military against the Zapatistas. A cease-fire was declared on 10 January, less than two weeks after the guerrilla offensive. Salinas offered limited amnesty to members of the EZLN on 15 January, and negotiations began (Ross 1995:165). For more than a year and a half, the government commission and Zapatista leadership debated issues that ranged from the democratic conditions (or lack thereof) in Chiapas to the economic plight of the indigenous. During this time, the Zapatistas made public statements on issues they found particularly important using a massive public relations campaign to rally support. Among their concerns were trade policies like NAFTA and domestic policies that had repressed and excluded the indigenous (Ross 1995; Wheaton 1998). They were also critical of the PRI.

The Zapatista cause became a very sympathetic one. After General Absalón Castellanos Domínguez, a former governor of Chiapas, was kidnapped by the guerrillas in their offensive, even his son claimed that he "'understood' the Zapatista struggle and 'agreed' with their demands, but could not understand why the rebels had taken his father" (Ross 1995:181).[9] The popularity of the movement was problematic for the government, particularly given the extreme unpopularity of the army, which had a reputation for excessive use of force. An intelligence report declassified by the U.S. Defense Intelligence Agency reported that the Salinas Administration originally rejected the idea of negotiating with the guerrillas, but at the same time "urged the army to show restraint in dealing with the EZLN" due to "concern[s] with the public image of the army" (Doyle 2004:12).

In February 1996, the government and the EZLN signed the San Andrés Accord and in so doing agreed to continue the dialogue and involve relevant political bodies in designing a "social pact to establish a new relationship between the indigenous people the society, and the State" ("San Andres" 2006). Yet even during the earliest stages of the negotiations, the Mexican army had begun creating new counterinsurgency units, training at some of the more elite counterinsurgency programs in Central America, and acquiring new equipment designed for intelligence gathering (Doyle

2004, esp. 7–8, 15, 17). By February 1994, the army had successfully encircled the EZLN (Ross 1995:180), and the militarization campaign only intensified thereafter. This seemingly schizophrenic policy reflected deep disagreement within the upper echelons of the PRI over how to respond to the uprising.

In order to not be excluded from the promise of the burgeoning international economy, Mexico began a campaign in the late 1980s to improve its all-too-superficial democracy. Some of the reforms, such as the 1991 repeal of Article 27, dealt with land reform policies. Others dealt with human rights issues, as abuses had the potential to be substantial obstacles to meeting NAFTA and other international association prerequisites. The legislation that had legalized Guardias Blancas in Chiapas was repealed, and the Comisión Nacional de Derechos Humanos (CNDH), the National Commission on Human Rights, was established in 1990.

Responding to domestic and international allegations of election fraud, the PRI leadership also began working on legitimizing the appearance of its elections. The Instituto Federal Electoral (IFE), or the Federal Elections Institute, was created in 1989 and was intended to provide "oversight" and legitimacy to the electoral process. Additional reforms limited the percentage of congressional seats that can be held by the majority party called for new voter registration cards including a photo ID, and required the use of voting booths to protect voters' anonymity.[10]

Despite some policy limitations and flaws, the PRI-dominated government made important reforms during this period. The first visible consequence of these early democratizing steps came in 1989 and 1992 with the elections of Mexico's first non-PRI governors in Baja California Norte and then Chihuahua. Since then, the consequences have become only more blatant: As the government proceeded with more electoral reform, the PRI became less successful electorally.[11] The PRI won 90.81 percent of the Federal Chamber of Deputies vote in 1961, and it continued to win better than 80 percent of that vote until 1979 with the exception of 1973. However, by 1988, votes for PRI deputy candidates had fallen precipitously low, hitting 50.37 percent. The percentage rebounded in 1991, but reversed again in 1994 and continued to drop, falling to an all-time low of 37.8 percent in 2000. Likewise, the percentage of senatorial seats held by the PRI has consistently fallen since the early 1980s, from 100 percent in 1982 to only 47 percent in 2000. The trend was the same at the state level, where the drop in percentage of gubernatorial seats held by the PRI dropped from 100 percent as recently as 1982 to only 67 percent in 2000. The PRI held

97 percent of municipal presidencies in 1982, but only 56 percent in 1997 (Base de Datos Políticos de las Américas 1999; Carter Center 2001).

The electoral reforms and weakened PRI facilitated the growth of alternative parties. The Partido Acción Nacional (PAN), or National Action Party, and the Partido de la Revolución Democrática (PRD), Party of the Democratic Revolution, both started to gain popular support and electoral strength. The PAN is "right of center," with a constituency composed largely of the upper-middle and upper class. The PAN is not a new party; it was originally founded in 1939 but gained notable strength in the 1990s. Some have described the party as "favored by the PRI as a bulwark" against the growing popularity of the PRD (Ross 1995:331, 332), although with the candidacy and election of Vicente Fox in 2000, the PAN became the first party to unseat the PRI from Mexico's executive branch.

The PRD represents the left in opposition to the PRI and all that the old party has come to symbolize. Cuauhtémoc Cárdenas, son of the famous Mexican Revolutionary leader and president (1934–40), led efforts to organize the new party out of a group that splintered from the PRI after Salinas de Gortiari was "anointed" as the successor to President De la Madrid. Cárdenas ran as a candidate of the PARM, the party predating the PRD, in 1988 and was allegedly defeated by Salinas. When clumsily covered-up election fraud was revealed to the public, Cárdenas seized his opportunity to mobilize significant bases of popular support (PRD 2002a; PRD 2002b; Schulz and Williams 1995:17–19, 48–50; Oppenheimer 1996:24, 131–32; Collier and Quaratiello 1999:132–33).

Though some of the PRD support appears to be based on anti-PRI sentiment, there are also more ideological characteristics common to its followers. In addition to advocating for democratic reforms that end corrupt and fraudulent elections, the party also opposed NAFTA and neoliberal economic policies, and it argued that the disparity between the rich and poor was too wide. Its members tended to be "*campesinos*, the urban poor, [and] social activists," including a former leader of the 1968 student protest that was so violently repressed by the military, and former priístas, including Cárdenas and former PRI president Porfirio Muñoz Ledo (Ross 1995:332–38; "Declaración" 2001).

On the surface, one might think that the 1990s was a period of serious self-flagellation for the PRI. With the repeal of Article 27 in 1991, Salinas surely knew that he was effectively repealing the guarantee of peasant support for the PRI. After all, the party had devoted nearly forty years to walking the delicate balance of promising land to the peasants while creating just enough red tape to prevent any serious infraction against the land-owners in Chiapas. Then, the administration reformed the election laws so as to curb the PRI's ability to fraudulently ensure its own success. And perhaps more astoundingly, most of the reforms required the approval of the legislature, at least half of which was PRI at the time.

Why did the PRI pursue and ratify such self-detrimental reforms? And how did this contribute to the emergence of paramilitaries?

At the national level, the party was stuck between an international rock and a domestic hard place. As part of the international scene, Mexico had a vested interest in "keeping up with the times," being included in the international market, and in particular, securing NAFTA with the United States. But domestically, some of the reforms necessary to pass the inter-national litmus tests were political suicide for a party claiming to embody the vision of the Revolution while simultaneously propping itself up with the army and stuffed election boxes. While there were those in the party willing to make the reforms in order to strengthen its role as an interna-tional "player," there were others within the party who were more worried about maintaining the domestic party dominance.

Within Chiapas, the electoral reforms passed by the national govern-ment initially had little impact on local processes. Eventually, however, the unflattering reports of human rights observers and election monitoring teams became detrimental to Mexico's inclusion in international markets, and the reforms started creeping from the center to the periphery. Around the same time, the Zapatistas lodged their attack, and it became clear that the PRI leadership in Mexico City was not going to punish the rebels, but was instead willing to talk. The landowners in Chiapas were vulnerable on two fronts. First, political fraud was still prevalent and not necessarily subtle in Chiapas. An *ejido* farmer from Morelia reported that people in his community had "never voted. . . . There is no voting booth here — never has been one. . . . Every election day, the PRI would come and take our vot-ing cards and go vote for us in Altamirano" (Ross 1995:74). New federal election regulations meant that "representatives" voting for entire peas-ant communities could no longer secure preferential candidates. Second, the federal government "negotiating" with the EZLN only twelve days after their attack was a strong indication of additional future reforms. The divi-sion among national PRI leaders created an opportunity structure for local Chiapanecos elite; they now had allies at the federal level among the PRI hard-liners who also opposed the reforms and could provide additional resources to their counterreform movement.

When the Salinas administration agreed to negotiate with the Zapatistas, it delegated the responsibility of representing the federal government to the former mayor of Mexico City, Manuel Camacho. Much to the dismay of many PRI onlookers, Camacho appeared to agree with the EZLN on several issues: not only did he agree to an increase in government-provided schools, hospitals, and social services (things that had been promised by the government before), but also he apparently agreed on the need to strengthen the guarantees of democracy in the region (that is, the right to an anonymous vote) with further political reforms. Splits within the party that had been "papered over" by Salinas's victory and reform agenda became like open festering wounds as Camacho tried to keep the negotiating table open to Zapatista demands (Collier and Quaratiello 1999:6; Golden 1994a, 1994b).

The increasing instability within the PRI became more evident as the reforms went on. Traditionally, it was the right of the Mexican president to choose the next PRI presidential candidate, who would inevitably then become his successor. Officially there were elections, but the ballot included the "anointed" PRI candidate who was guaranteed the victory. Reportedly, the outgoing president originally selected the negotiator Camacho as his successor, but then publicly chose Luis Donaldo Colosio Murrieta instead. But as the negotiations with the EZLN got under way, the rumor mill began working overtime, with suggestions that Salinas might renege and instead go back to Camacho, or that Camacho might break with the party and declare his own candidacy independent of the PRI if snubbed by Salinas. In March 1994, Camacho publicly addressed the rumors, announcing he would not run for the office of president. The very next day, Colosio was assassinated, allegedly by his own party (Kampwirth 1998:15–16; Collier and Quaratiello 1999:5–7).

Ernesto Zedillo Ponce de León, who had been serving Colosio as a campaign advisor, was selected by Salinas to carry on the candidacy, and he eventually won the election. But debate within the party was far from quieted. Camacho resigned as the government's representative in the EZLN negotiations in June, after Zedillo publicly denounced Camacho and the negotiations as a total failure. Shortly thereafter, Jorge Carpizo MacGregor, former Human Rights Commissioner and overseer of the August elections, also resigned, "asserting than an unnamed party was making fair elections impossible" (Collier and Quaratiello 1999:6).

Disagreement within the PRI as to how to address the EZLN became more public as the Zedillo administration took office. Siding with the hard-liners, Zedillo reversed the previous administration's approach, broke the cease-fire agreement, and gave the order for the arrest of the Zapatista leadership. Under his command, the army began an offensive that included seizing land from the Zapatistas, arresting "dozens of unarmed political activists suspected of being Zapatista supporters," and increasing the military presence in Chiapas (Kampwirth 1998:16).

Zedillo's approach, contrasted with that of Salinas, indicates the degrees of separation that had been plaguing the PRI. Zedillo's crackdown probably placated hard-liner concerns, to some extent. The EZLN had been winning public support, with public approval of Zapatista goals (although not necessary their means) up from 61 percent in January to 75 percent in February within Mexico City (Golden 1994a). This support had translated into new movement organizations, NGOs, and political coalitions advocating for various Zapatista issues, ranging from women's rights to indigenous rights to general democratic reform. The ideological pressure against the PRI was building even as the EZLN laid down its arms, leaving some to speculate that Zedillo's new position was largely in response to "this growing political threat" (Kampwirth 1998:16).[12]

Meanwhile, opposition parties were gaining ground in Chiapas, despite harassment and fierce resistance from local priístas. As the climate of change intensified and Mexico began seeing additional political seats at the national level go to non-PRI candidates, the climate of conflict intensified in Chiapas. Members and supporters of the PRD, in particular, faced intense harassment and violence at the hands of PRI loyalists.

Despite this, the party began gaining inroads with voters in Chiapas, largely because of spreading discontent with the military's presence. The militarization issue separated the PRI hard-liners in Chiapas from reformers, as it had at the national level. Pablo Salazar Mendiguchía was a relatively high-ranking priísta who represented the party on the negotiations team in Chiapas. In January 1999, Salazar began challenging the State's explanations for the increasing military mobilization in Chiapas and went so far as to argue that stepped-up military action in the community of Chenalhó was not due to an antinarcotics campaign, as had claimed by the army. Instead, he believed it was an attempt on the part of the military to "justify the repositioning of the army in the state, and to link the Zapatistas with drugs." He left the party in May 1999 claiming that the "state PRI apparatus" had been "harassing" him. In October 1999, the PRD announced that Salazar would run as their official candidate for governor, with the backing of several other "opposition" parties. Salazar announced that he would serve as a "governor who is a facilitator of peace, who does not intend to establish counterinsurgency measures in Chiapas" (Arronte, Castro Soto, and Lewis 2000:1–5).

Ironically, while reformers like Salazar felt betrayed by the party, hardliners in Chiapas were similarly frustrated with the PRI. During the 1997 round of elections, some argued that by promoting dialogue with an insurgent force that was so blatantly threatening their way of life and local security, the PRI had deserted them. Members of a paramilitary group spoke out at an election meeting in July 1997, "arguing that 'their ideological positions' were not 'represented' by the local and federal PRI candidates" who were apparently too moderate. More than one "spokesperson for the group reiterated that they [would] revert to violence in order to impede" the vote in the upcoming election (Avilés 1997).

The 1990s were thus a turbulent time for politicos in Mexico, particularly those who felt their own status and security wrapped up in the exclusivity provided by the PRI-dominated system. The tensions underlying this turbulence were generations old, to be sure. But the conflicts had long been repressed by fraud and violence, such that there was reliability and stability in the system, particularly for the elite. The Zapatistas may not have seemed so threatening to the PRI hard-liners were it not for the fact that PRI moderates were willing to talk with them rather than simply eliminate them. The negotiations, the reforms, the limitations put on the military, and the prohibitions on using White Guards all deepened a divide between hard-liners and moderates and contributed to a deep sense of vulnerability among important and resourced factions of Mexico's most powerful groups: the wealthy, the military, and the PRI. The divisions and newly fomented shared grievance brought hard-liners from each of these three sectors together, and it united local- and federal-level hard-liners. Their shared resources became a potent recipe for continuing the repression, despite the reforms.

# PARAMILITARY
# GROUPS OF CHIAPAS
## TARGETS, TRIAD,
## FOOT SOLDIERS

It was during this period of intense political discord within the PRI that paramilitary groups began emerging. As early as 1995, those who feared their interests would be marginalized or ignored by the party began pulling together the resources necessary to launch their own attack against the reform advocates in Chiapas. Over the decade, at least nine paramilitary groups operated in various communities of Chiapas. Desarrollo, Paz y Justicia (Development, Peace and Justice, DPJ) was perhaps the largest and most influential of the groups. Others included Los Chinchulines, which also went by the names "United Front of Ejido Members" or the "Luis Donaldo Colosio Civic Front;" The MIRA, the Anti-Zapatista Revolutionary Indigenous Movement, a highly connected paramilitary that organized in 1997; and La Máscara Roja (the Red Mask), believed to have perpetrated the attack at Acteal. Five smaller groups included the San Bartolomé de los Llano Alliance, Los Puñales (the Daggers), Los Platanos (the Bananas), the Civil Front, and Tomás Munzer (Arronte, Castro Soto, and Lewis 2000).

## Paramilitary Targets

The PMGs are active primarily in the northeast region of Chiapas (See Map 1), where the Zona Norte, or northern zone, was distinguished from the Zona de Conflicto, or conflict zone. While the two areas were alike in that tensions were high and the political situation volatile, there were some critical distinctions (Boletín 1997:1). The northern zone encompassed fourteen northern municipalities including Tila, Sabanilla, Salto de Agua, Palenque, and Chenahlo. The EZLN was relatively weaker in this region, and PMG violence was stronger (Desarrollo 1997:11). Zapatista support and guerrilla-related violence were reportedly higher in the conflict zone. This region included the municipalities of Ocosingo, Las Margaritas, and La Huitiupan, among others.

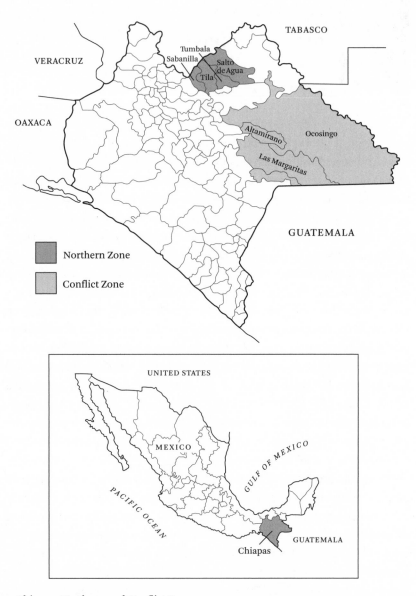

Chiapas: Northern and Conflict Zones

The most frequent victims of paramilitary threats and violence in Chiapas are EZLN activists and sympathizers, PRD members, and officials or communities thought to be PRD or EZLN strongholds. Attacks have also been orchestrated against human rights workers and advocacy groups, as well as civic and religious leaders suspected of being sympathetic to the "leftist" cause. In short, individuals and groups who threaten the dominance of the PRI and the traditional, regionalized political system in Chiapas are PMG targets, regardless of religion or ethnicity.

Human rights groups reported that PRI-organized and supported PMGS displaced several PRD supporters, particularly from "the communities in Usipá, Tz'aquil, Miguel Alemán Valdéz, and others." (CONPAZ 1997). The MIRA reportedly sent numerous "threats to municipal PRD representatives." Similarly, Los Chinchulines focused their attacks "against PRD militants, the Jesuit mission in Bachajón," and an opposition campesino organization (Arronte, Castro Soto, and Lewis 2000:117, 116).

Los Chinchulines is probably most noted for its 1996 assault on Bachajón, a community in the municipality of Chilón. After a local election in which their preferred candidate lost, the PMG attacked the community. The violence continued over a period of days and resulted in the deaths of six civilians. The Catholic school and Jesuit mission were burned, along with the local Center for Indigenous Rights and more than a dozen homes. The leader of the Chinchulines was also killed, along with two of his relatives. The attack serves as an example of the fact that the conflict is centered around very contentious political questions. The threat of change posed by the legal opposition party compelled not only the elite in Chiapas, but also the lower-income citizens who have dedicated their loyalties to the PRI (SIPAZ 1996; HRW 1997:6, 35).[1]

In addition to targeting opposition groups and PRD strongholds, paramilitaries targeted autonomous zones created by the EZLN following the San Andres Accords. The accords provided for the creation of such zones where indigenous communities would have the ability to govern according to their cultural traditions. However, the accords never became part of the Constitution, as promised by the Zedillo administration, and the autonomous zones have since been victimized by PMGS. La Máscara Roja has focused attacks on the Autonomous Municipality of San Andrés Sakamchén de los Pobres (Arronte, Castro Soto, and Lewis 2000:117), and the Civil Front has targeted Tierra y Libertad in Las Margueritas, which was first threatened by the Civil Front and then attacked by the police and "PRI militants" (Arronte, Castro Soto, and Lewis 2000:121; "Military Moves" 1998).

Paramilitary groups in Chiapas have also been extremely critical of the Catholic Church and have launched attacks against its members and leadership. The DPJ is alleged to have organized a 1997 attack against former bishop Don Samuel Ruiz García and Don Raul Vera López. Together with Los Chinchulines, the DPJ has also been suspect in a number of other attacks against communities expecting visits by the bishop and Don Vera and "profaning houses of worship" ("Mexico: Snipers" 1997). Such attacks have allowed some in Mexico to disguise the paramilitary violence as a religious conflict in their rhetoric in an attempt to deny that there is political violence. Indeed, Roberto Albores Guillén, former interim governor of Chiapas, asserted that "since January, 1994, the appearance of intercommunal conflicts of religious or ideological origin has increased, which has facilitated the formation of presumed armed civilian groups, operating illegally" (Arronte, Castro Soto, and Lewis 2000:112). The former governor is correct to acknowledge religious conflict in Chiapas; in May 2000, "more than 30,000 Evangelicals [had been] expelled [and] more than 30 Catholic churches shut down" (SIPAZ 2000d:4). In 2001, communities in and around Las Margueritas were suffering through weekly expulsions. In many cases, squatters and Protestant, mostly evangelical, residents were being ousted from their communities. But his insinuation that the religious and paramilitary conflicts are one and the same is misleading.

The tension between Catholics and Protestants dates back to early days of independence and debates over church-held lands. It only intensified over the decades as Protestantism crept into more and more communities, threatening the social order that had long been defined in tandem with the Catholic Church. In most Chiapanecos communities, and particularly in indigenous communities, "*cargos*," positions of administration and stature within the church, are the stepping stone — the *only* stepping stone — to positions of power within the community. To obtain a "*cargo*" is to have the potential of someday being a cacique — a political boss. Being a cacique entails having already "passed the administrative hierarchy" of the *cargo*, having alternated between service in the ritualistic and civic arenas of the community. Anthropologist Carrasco calls this structure a "civil-religious hierarchy" (Siverts 1981:37, 44), one where religious and civic positions of responsibility, leadership, and administration are intertwined. Thus, in Chiapas, Catholicism was more than just religious doctrine, it is also an important part of how one's personal status within the community is defined.

Protestant churches allowed easy access to leadership positions within the church, even to the poor. Such practices challenged the Catholic Church and, consequently, questioned the traditional power structure (Collier and Quaratiello 1999:55–58; SIPAZ 2000d:5). One anthropologist asserts that "the establishment of the Presbyterian Church . . . implied the formation of a political party. . . . Hence, about 1953–1954 there existed two political parties in [one community]—founded on adherence to conflicting religious institutions. These parties were struggling for power" (Siverts 1981:33). The parties have been struggling ever since, and over generations their religious identity has become intertwined with their political identity.

In 2000, the mayor of Chamula said in an interview, "'Evangelical religion goes against the tradition of the Chamula people.' This affirmation alludes to the fact that members are not allowed to participate in traditional fiestas since they do not buy [alcoholic drinks]. . . . This threatens the power of the local political *caciques* that are often also store owners" (SIPAZ 2000d:5). The suggestion that "religion" and "political party" have become so conflated as to be nearly one and the same in some areas of Chiapas is not to overstate the situation.

Because government officials had publicly tried to link the PMGs to this religious conflict, I often asked interviewees whether the two were related. As explained to me by nearly all of the subjects I questioned on the topic, religious differences do not explain the paramilitary phenomenon in Chiapas. A high-ranking official in Chiapas explained that "the religious conflict has existed since, forever, no? Because the ethnic groups, everyone has a different culture, ways of thinking about internal organization, ways of life. . . . [But] the PMG conflict began fifteen to twenty years ago, with the owners of land trying to protect their land, [their] houses.§ A spokesperson from the Catholic church in San Cristóbal agreed, saying, "the problem here is not religious, it's economic. Social injustice. . . . The government wants people to think it's religious; it's part of their strategy."§

However, the conflict in Chiapas is complex, and even distinguishing between the religious and paramilitary conflict is not as simple as that. "There exists a symbiosis, a mutual use of each other between the government and the evangelical groups. And it seems such also exists between the PRI and the evangelical churches" (Hidalgo 1998). The symbiosis is rooted at least partly in a shared enemy, or a shared perceived threat. Though neither the PMGs nor the Zapatistas have a definitive religious identity, the Catholic Church, via Bishop Don Samuel Ruiz García of the diocese in San Cristóbal de Las Casas, has taken a very clear advocacy role supporting the cause of the EZLN. Thus, those who would like to see the EZLN eliminated share something in common with those who would like to see the dominance of the Catholic Church diminished. Both the hardcore evangelicals and the right-wing extremists in Chiapas share an interest in quieting the voice of the local Catholic leaders. Likewise, while not all EZLN activists are Catholic, they do have an interest in protecting the voice of the diocese as long as it keeps speaking on behalf of their cause. So while the ultimate objectives may not be exactly the same, it is easy to see how the religious and the political conflicts feed off one another.

Within the community, several evangelicals have accused the Catholic church of inciting the Zapatista rebellion. A group of "upper middle class . . . citizens" of San Cristóbal have organized under the name "Auténticos Coletos" (meaning of royal Spanish descent),[2] criticizing Don Ruiz for his outspokenness on the issue (SIPAZ 2000d:57; Hidalgo 1997:3, 4). Others have accused Ruiz and the churches surrounding San Cristóbal of reversing the age-old prejudice against the Indians and discriminating against non-Indians (Iliff 2000:4).

The most outspoken PMG in Chiapas, Desarrollo, Paz y Justicia, is also the most critical of the Catholic Church. Anti-Catholic rhetoric frequently peppers their political statements. Leaders of DPJ have accused the church in Chiapas of "proselytizing for the PRD" and "undermining the value and validity of institutions by calling it 'bad government.'" The group claims that catechists have convinced indigenous communities that Catholicism is part of their heritage and being anti-PRI is part of that belief system, and it criticizes the Catholic Church for intentionally causing conflict by denouncing the party (Desarrollo 1997:17, 20, 24, 47–49).

It is clear from the public statements and publications of the DPJ that the group takes issue with the church not for religious reasons but for political ones. One of their biggest complaints is that the PRD has allegedly worked with the church to conflate politics with religion and turn the indigenous against the PRI and the system.[3] Samuel Sánchez Sánchez claimed in an interview that "the Catholic Diocese under Bishop Samuel Ruiz is trying to destroy the Mexican Political System" (Kern 1998:1). Raymundo Hernández Trujillo, another leader of DPJ, reported in a separate interview that "there was a time when the religious centers turned into recruiting centers" for groups opposing the PRI and the government. They claim that DPJ organized to defend themselves and their communities against those who "incite rebellion" (Desarrollo 1997:42).

While the religious conflict and the Zapatista/PMG conflict may exacerbate one another, paramilitary activity is not based on religious intolerance. There is absolutely no evidence connecting any of the paramilitary organizations to specific churches or ministers or religious groups. There is no evidence of a church or religious leader serving as a pipeline for arms, salaries, or supplies to a PMG, nor is there evidence of any church or religious leader providing leadership or recruiting for a PMG. There are paramilitary organizations that have not intimated any religious leanings. And, just as there are poor, indigenous paramilitary members and poor, indigenous Zapatistas, there are also Catholic Zapatistas[4] and Catholic paramilitary members, and there are evangelical supporters on both sides. Perhaps most telling, religion is not how the paramilitaries identify or define *themselves*.

## The Triad's Political Leg

While none of the paramilitary groups in Chiapas have ties to a religious organization, they each have ties to political, wealthy, and armed allies. Each group maintains contacts that supply salaries, usually through a businessman or rancher; arms, usually through a police or army contact; and leadership, recruitment, and organization, usually through a PRI official. They are often organized and led, even into battle, by established political and military actors and land and business owners. This tripartite support network formed out of the contentious politics of reform that dominated the Mexican political scene in the 1990s.

Within the broader political environment in Mexico, federal-level reforms undertaken by moderates within the PRI tore the party's elite into two camps: hard-liners who opposed any changes that might redistribute economic or political resources, and reformers who saw the changes as a way to encourage Mexico's status and position on the international stage. The wide range of reforms pursued by the government in the 1990s created a shared vulnerability among national-level priísta hard-liners and local elites in Chiapas. This was only compounded by the Salinas administration's response to the rebellion: negotiation. Salinas's approach faced vociferous demands for a tougher response to the rebel group.

Salinas was quite literally caught between diametrically opposed demands from two political realms, and he could not afford to sacrifice support from either. Domestically, his hard-liner PRI cohorts wanted to eradicate the EZLN. Internationally, there was pressure to demonstrate restraint. He attempted to do both, expanding military *presence* in Chiapas while simultaneously perusing dialogue. Salinas's decision to restrain the military was not received well by the armed forces, who, according to a declassified report, "chafe[d] at being prevented from simply 'eradicating' the rebels" (Doyle 2004:12).

Hard-liner members of the PRI and military were not alone in wanting to step up counterinsurgency efforts against the Zapatistas. In early May 1994, the U.S. Central Intelligence Agency reported in a secret intelligence memorandum (since declassified) that Chiapas's more influential civilians were also increasingly impatient with the Salinas administration. "The CIA observe[d] that ranchers and 'other vested interests' in the region consider[ed] Salinas administration tactics 'appeasement of the rebels'" (Doyle 2004:24). Such frustration fueled paramilitary organization and attacks against EZLN supporters and sympathizers.

Given the intense frustration, it is perhaps not surprising that the most consistent variable among the paramilitary groups is the political party identification: PRI. Of the nine paramilitary organizations documented here, eight have identifiable ties to the PRI either through party leaders, PRI elected officials, or PRI unions or organizations. The ninth, the Civil Front, has been alleged to be composed of "PRI militants."

Desarrollo, Paz y Justicia has some of the most visible links to priístas. Most notably, Samuel Sánchez Sánchez, a former PRI state congressman, was president of the PMG and served as one of the "colonels" of the organization. A former municipal head councilman, Marco Albino Torres, who was also an army captain, was also one of the lead members of the organization (Desarrollo 1997; Ramírez Cuevas 1997a; Concha 1997; Arronte, Castro Soto, and Lewis 2000:130). Los Chinchulines is believed to have been organized by former PRI interim governor of Chiapas (1993–94) Elmar Zetzer Marseille, and it had a myriad of contacts among elected PRI officials at the state and local levels. The organization of MIRA has been credited to then federal deputy from Ocosingo and priísta Norberto Sántiz López, and the group's leaders reportedly received a monthly stipend of $1,250 "from the state government" (Stahler-Sholk 1998). The San Bartolomé de los Llano Alliance has been associated with and supported by former PRI federal deputy Eucario Orantes, and Los Puñales and Los

Platanos have both been linked to local-level PRI leaders (Arronte, Castro Soto, and Lewis 2000:115–18; Ramírez Cuevas 1997a:2; Desarrollo 1997; Hidalgo 1997:5).

La Máscara Roja is widely believed to be responsible for the attack at Acteal, and the Mexican National Human Rights Commission further alleges that the attack was led by the municipal president of a local community (Chenalhó) at the time. Former municipal president Jacinto Arias Cruz is also reported to have requested of President Zedillo that priístas of Chenalhó be afforded the right to carry arms to defend themselves against Zapatistas. Reports are that he "initiat[ed] the distribution of arms to *campesinos* in his home town." Individuals from this same town were later implicated in an attack on several "PRD militants and Zapatista sympathizers" in which at least one civilian was murdered and several others displaced (Arronte, Castro Soto, and Lewis 2000:122; Selee 1999:5; Ramírez Cuevas 1997a:2). The group has also benefited from the leadership skills of former PRI federal deputy Antonio Pérez Hernández (Arronte, Castro Soto, and Lewis 2000:115–18; Ramírez Cuevas 1997a:2; Desarrollo 1997; Hidalgo 1997:5).

PRI officials have often been key to recruitment and provided the leadership necessary to pull together an organized paramilitary group. They also provide the ideological identity of the group, associating the members with a cause and organization larger than themselves. The PRI connection links members to a "side" in the conflict, providing them with an identity, a sense of purpose, and a visible "other" or enemy. The PRI connections are therefore crucial to the PMGs in terms of the stature and validity they have in the broader political environment. Their party identification is part of what allows them to remain faceless and invisible to the justice system. Thus, in a less direct or obvious way, impunity is also among the resources paramilitaries enjoy thanks to their PRI connections.

## The Triad's Military Leg

Rather than using political systems, interest groups, ad campaigns, or candidates with high-priced fund-raisers, the elite in Chiapas have long relied on force to protect their way of life. Given the history of circumventing political institutions with grassroots organized violence (such as White Guards and Mapaches), it should not be surprising that when the federal government yet again undertook reforms in the late 1980s and early 1990s that threatened the socioeconomic order, the local reaction was not one focused on GOTV (get out the vote) efforts, but rather on rallying the troops.

A state-level official in Chiapas expressed the value placed by many within the party on stability and longevity, even when secured at the expense of other political aims:

> We are involved in a democratic process. Others look just at the "free vote" and judge us solely on the "free vote" as to whether we are a democracy or not. . . . Democracy is a . . . form of life that cannot be measured with votes, with majorities. Look for example at Mussolini! . . . There are people who hate the PRI, say it's so corrupt, it's so awful. But where else in Latin America in the past seventy years has there been total stability?[§]

On a national level, there is a parallel proclivity on the part of PRI officials to employ and condone military and police force rather than cede to grassroots or electoral opposition. The seven-decade-long dominance of the PRI came at the cost of certain basic democratic freedoms, including the freedom to oppose the PRI vocally, to organize around and speak one's political views. In 1956, the military occupied the dorms at the National Polytechnic Institute in response to student mobilization. In 1968, the institute and the National Autonomous University of Mexico (UNAM) were both occupied by the army in response to uprisings, and hundreds of students were killed in the standoff. In 1971, the army was used against a student demonstration in Mexico City. The municipalities of San Luis Potosí (in 1962) and Juchitán (in 1983) were both occupied when opposition movements surfaced. The state of Guerrero was occupied in 1974, and the governor of Oaxaca was ousted and replaced with a general by the military in 1976 (Anaya 2000:4–10; Arronte, Castro Soto, and Lewis 2000:7). One analyst explains, "As the PRI started to grow old" and its support waned "in various sections and regions of the country . . . the government began to resort to the Armed Forces as a tool of contention and dissuasion" (Benítez Manaut 2000:xvii). The history of using violence to protect the party is a long one, and it demonstrates a high correlation between periods of low popular support for the party and increased use of the military.

In 1988, just as the PRI electoral vote began to drop, the military share of government spending began to rise (see Figure 2). In 1989, the PRI lost its gubernatorial race in Baja California Norte, and military spending reached a percentage of total spending that was higher than it had been since the 1960s. At only 2.8 percent in 1988, it hit 3.0 percent in 1992, 3.5 percent a year later, and was at 5.21 percent by 1995. The Zapatista rebellion contributed to the trend having a cyclical effect: The EZLN embold-

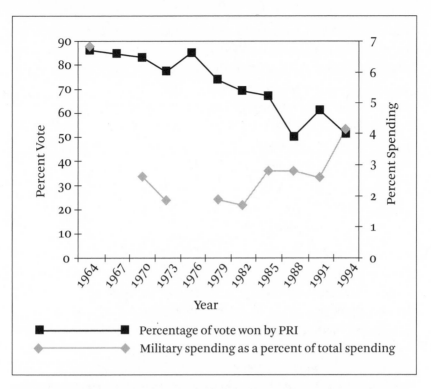

FIGURE 2. PRI Electoral Support and Military Spending (Percentage PRI Vote by Percentage Military Spending of Total Spending). *Sources*: 1964–91, Base de Datos Políticas de las Américas 1999; 1994, Base de Datos Políticas de las Américas 2000; military spending data from Arronte, Castro Soto, and Lewis 2000:xix–xx.

ened vocal opposition to the PRI, and it therefore simultaneously drew increasing demands from within the PRI to augment militarization.

The day the EZLN began its offensive, 1 January 1994, Mexico had 14,000 troops stationed in Chiapas. When the cease-fire was declared, there were an estimated 15,000 troops in the region. Yet six years later, troops stationed in Chiapas numbered between 50,000 and 70,000 — *three* or *four* times the number relied on during the actual conflict (Ross 1995:109; SIPAZ 2000b:4; Selee 1999:1). In 1995, there were 74 troop bases in Chiapas. By 2000 that number had quadrupled to 296 (SIPAZ 2000b:4). This military presence was credited by many with intensifying tension in the region rather than with mitigating the conflict.[5]

Indeed, these figures actually understate the degree of real militarization, as the federal government has also supplemented army troops with immigration officials, antinarcotics squads, and a variety of police forces, including the Public Security Police (PSP) and the Federal Preventive Police (PFP). According to declassified U.S. Defense Intelligence Agency documents, the militarization in Chiapas was undertaken in "prepara[tion] for a protracted guerrilla war." The report concluded that "the army . . . 'would willingly initiate the campaign [in Chiapas] given the opportunity'" (Doyle 2004:18).[6] Certainly the level of militarization has not escaped the attention — nor the criticism — of those living in the area.

> There are a lot of army [personnel] here . . . [and] there are certain military zones, and . . . they are very armed, but there's no war. And this seems odd. Tanks, helicopters, etc. It's an excessive demonstration of strength. It's excessive.[§]

But the army was not given the opportunity. Instead, some of the more hard-line members found an alternative outlet for what they believed to be the better course of action in Chiapas. Military personnel in Chiapas provided significant "cover" to paramilitary groups, providing impunity, support, and material resources like arms. Indeed, most of the PMGs and many of their more atrocious attacks were huddled close to military bases, indicating a parasitic relationship.

Links with specific military officials or battalions are a consistent characteristic of and important resource for paramilitary groups, and those in Chiapas are no exception. The most infamous of such contacts are probably the former military commander Marco Albino Torres, who is among the top leadership of DPJ, and 7th Military Region general Mario Renán Castillo Fernandez, who served as signatory to an economic agreement between the government of Chiapas and the DPJ (Desarrollo 1997; Arronte, Castro Soto, and Lewis 2000; Avilés 1997). Local police have also been accused of assisting with recruiting, training, and providing financial support for several groups, including MIRA and Los Puñales. The Oxchuc police are alleged to have provided around $80 a month to the MIRA paramilitary, and police officials are accused of having murdered local campesinos who opposed the PMG (Arronte, Castro Soto, and Lewis 2000:117). Local PSP and judicial police forces reportedly have assisted the San Bartolomé de los Llano Alliance PMG with attacks (Arronte, Castro Soto, and Lewis 2000:117; Selee 1999; HRW 1997:33–35). Los Platanos reportedly has received training and salaries from the police and the army (Arronte, Castro Soto, and Lewis 2000:118), and the Civil Front has reportedly likewise received assistance from local police forces.

In addition to training and interpersonal connections, a sense of camaraderie may be observed in the willingness of, by at least many units and perhaps the 7th Military Region's troops in general, to permit the organization, activity, and violence of paramilitaries to continue uninterrupted. There is evidence that La Máscara Roja received arms from state police forces, and a military officer who was reportedly "on leave" provided training for the attack at Acteal (Selee 1999:5).

Testimony regarding military complicity at Acteal given by retired army brigadier General Julio César Santiago Díaz, also serving as chief advisor to the PSP and director of the Chiapas Auxiliary Police, was published in the Mexican weekly *Proceso* (1 March 1998). Díaz testified that the paramilitary personnel responsible for the massacre there "were 'accompanied by 40 state police officers . . . [who] for three and a half hours [were] stationed at the entrance to the village [of Acteal], while scarcely 200 meters away, down the hillside, a massacre was committed'" (Arronte, Castro Soto, and Lewis 2000:124). Similarly, DPJ benefited from its relationship with the PSP. DPJ was able to carry out attacks against and displace PRD supporters while the PSP knowingly failed to intervene.

The military connection is also evident in the arms used by paramilitary groups. Witnesses and investigators have frequently found the PMGs to be armed with weapons known to be military issue, and some have reported witnessing the distribution of arms by military or police forces. The army reportedly gave a dozen AK-47s to Los Puñales, and Los Chinchulines were among those carrying weapons known to be used "exclusively by the army" ("Chiapas: La Guerra" 1998:25). Weapons used by several groups were reportedly the "donations" of local police or military forces (Arronte, Castro Soto, and Lewis 2000:117–23; Selee 1999).

> While in prison, retired general Díaz also testified regarding weapons supply to PMGs. Officers from the PSP had gone to a border community (Carmen Xhan, Guatemala) to buy AK-47s, R-15s, and M-16s that were later brought to municipalities . . . principally Chenalhó, where they were sold to paramilitary groups that operate in that area. . . . The same police force assigned to the area, as well as state police officers and ex-members of the Mexican Army, have been the principal suppliers of high-powered arms to paramilitary groups that operate in the region. (Arronte, Castro Soto, and Lewis 2000:124)

A former PSP subcommander, Felipe Vázquez Espinosa, also corroborates the use of PSP and other police officials in the transport and supply of arms to the paramilitaries. Vázquez reported that he himself "escorted a shipment of AK-47s" to a PMG. Vázquez also reported being told by superiors that the "escort" or protection service was "okay" provided that the individuals were "greens," meaning priísta (Arronte, Castro Soto, and Lewis 2000:124, from *Proceso* 1113, 1 March 1998:9).

Official military documents specifically detail the motivation and strategy behind the alliance between the military and paramilitary forces. In October 1994, ten months after the Zapatistas launched their offensive and more than nine months after the cease-fire was agreed to, the Mexican National Defense secretary issued *El Plan de Campaña* (The Campaign Plan) to the 7th Regional Military commander. The primary concern of the directive is to "attain and maintain peace," not surprising given the tension between the EZLN and the army. However, despite the cease-fire, the Defense secretary instructed the commander to establish "a center of operations in Tuxtla Gutiérrez" (the capital city of Chiapas) and to "destroy or neutralize" all guerrilla areas. The directive goes on to instruct the army in the 7th Region to "break the relationship of support between the population and lawbreakers, dismantle the infrastructure of the subversives and their activities among the general population, and provide an atmosphere of physical and psychological safety among populations uninvolved with the conflict" (Marín 1998:1, appendix).

Already reminiscent of the counterinsurgency tactics used in Central and South America in decades past, the directive also charges the army with

- the command and coordination of local public security troops and local ranchers "in the elimination" of the subversives and "the disintegration or control of social organizations"
- "secretly organizing certain sectors of the civilian population, small property owners and individuals with strong patriotism, who will be employed in the support of [these] operations"
- using civilian and military resources to obtain intelligence information, including "counterinformation, combat intelligence, intelligence in support of psychological operations, [and] intelligence regarding the internal situation (political, economic, and social information)"
- working with the "local government and other authorities" to censure the media. (Marín, appendix)

The directive also advises the commander not to "discount the possibility that the EZLN is supported by the political structures of the PRD" indicating that the "opposition" targeted by the army is not to be limited to the EZLN (Marín 1998, appendix). Like other counterinsurgency crusades carried out decades earlier (for instance, in Argentina or Chile), the directive targeted not only militants and violent extremists, but also the moderates, those who perhaps shared some political views with the Zapatistas but who were simultaneously committed to working within the established political system. But the plan went even further, becoming more blatant in its counterinsurgency intent.

> This appendix describes activities of the army in the training and support of self-defense forces and other paramilitary organizations, those that are able to be the fundamental origin of the mobilization for the military and development operations. This would also include advising and support that can be lent/provided to other government functionaries, including local, municipal, state, and federal. In the case where self-defense forces do not exist, it is necessary that they be created. . . . The military operations include the training of local self-defense forces, in order that they participate in security and development programs. (Marín, appendix; translation mine)

One year after troops in the 7th Military Region were charged with the 1994 *Plan de Campaña*, the Sedena, Mexico's Department of Defense, released the *Manual of Irregular War*. The manual has been described as "an almost literal translation of the U.S. Defense Department's *Field Manual Psychological Operations*," used for counterinsurgency training in the United States. The *Manual of Irregular War* was recommended to me in a couple of interviews, particularly when I asked about the creation of paramilitaries and whether there was any link between the PMGs and the army in Chiapas. The manual describes the need — in dealing with guerrilla warfare — to establish a "native" enemy to the guerrilla, civilian or military groups native to the guerrilla's territory, "directed, advised, and coordinated by the military commander of the area" (Aubry and Inda 1998b:1) to cooperate with the military objective of destroying the guerrillas.

As the second leg of the triad, the military and security forces complement the PRI's role in supporting paramilitary activities well. The most obvious benefit of the military connections are resources like training, funding, arms, and intelligence information. But in addition to this, the identity provided PMGs via the PRI is only reinforced by connections to the military, a longtime ally of the party. But the military also adds to the party identity in that it is the acknowledged counterinsurgency force. As such, it can provide a legitimizing aura to the objective of fighting the "subversives."

### The Triad's Elite Leg

As early as 1994, ranchers in the Altamirano region of Chiapas were indicating that they would not wait much longer for federal intervention on their behalf. "The situation is deteriorating. We have no support from the authorities. We're desperate," said Jose Luis Aguilar, the president of the Altamirano Cattleman's Association. "We're giving the government until April 20. If there's no positive solution, we'll adopt other methods" (Scott 1994a:1–2). Feelings of desperate abandonment among Chiapas's landholders fueled their commitment to the paramilitary endeavor. "The lack of government support in the face of the [land] invasions obliged us to act" and to "organiz[e] actions to protect what's ours," explained one Chiapas rancher after EZLN rebellion (HRW 1997:21). This third leg of the support network provided the funding and other material resources necessary to organize and pay for the PMGs in Chiapas.

Most of the paramilitaries in Chiapas have been linked to at least one large landholder; some have links to several rancheros, and others also appear to have links to local businesspeople. For instance, Los Chinchulines have been reportedly trained on the property of a large estate-holder, and a local cattle rancher has been identified as "aiding and arming" the group (CONPAZ 1997; Arronte, Castro Soto, and Lewis 2000:115). Likewise, the origin of DPJ is traced back to a meeting held on the property of a local rancher, which may also have been used for training exercises (Marín 1998; Arronte, Castro Soto, and Lewis 2000:114). San Bartolomé de los Llano Alliance has been linked to "landlords and large landholders, [as well as] merchants" (Arronte, Castro Soto, and Lewis 2000:118). Los Puñales are allegedly led by a local business owner (who is also a local PRI leader). Tomás Munzer has also reportedly benefited from the support of local landholders (Marín 1998:2).

The finances, weapons, and training and meeting locations are among the most important of the material resources provided to the paramilitaries in Chiapas. The local elite ease the job of recruiting by providing salaries to those who join, and they make attacks possible by providing training grounds. Like military hardliners and loyal, conservative priístas, they also have a vested interest in maintaining the system of regional power, now rooted in the PRI, that has protected their land from redistribution for decades.

Chiapas is not unlike other regions of the world where politicians not only are the political elite, but also are often among the economic elite. And for many of the paramilitaries, this has translated into dual roles for some of the individuals involved in the support networks. High-ranking political and military officials worked their connections with the state government to procure financing for the paramilitaries in the region. A "development financing" scandal in 1997 allowed journalists and human rights teams in Chiapas to uncover some of these connections and begin tracing PMG financing. The "Development Package" serves as a useful example of the partnership in complicity between the PRI, local elite, and the military to fund PMG organizations and activities.

In July 1997, as elections were nearing, negotiators for the state of Chiapas and the Paz y Justicia paramilitary group were tying up loose ends on a financial agreement. Signed 4 July, the agreement turned 4,600,000 pesos (US$450,000) over from the state to the PMG for "production development." Samuel Sánchez Sánchez signed the agreement and accepted the money on behalf of DPJ. This Production Development Agreement cited agricultural and fishing development as suitable uses of the money, and it also outlined the state's willingness "to assign an annual budget to promote infrastructure and production projects for rural development for the communities within the municipalities named." Signatories of the agreement included Paz y Justicia members (among them Sánchez Sánchez), as well as then-governor of Chiapas, Ruiz Ferro, and the 7th Military Region commander in 1997, Mario Renán Castillo Fernandez.[7] In this case, the political connections Sánchez Sánchez had been able to establish as a state politician and PRI leader translated into funding support for the PMG (Selee 1999; Avilés 1997).

### The Foot Soldiers

Generally speaking, the foot soldiers of Chiapas's PMGs are young, poor, indigenous PRI members. They are recruited by party and security officials from local communities such as San Quintán, La Trinidad, Agua Azul, Santo Tomas, and Monte Libano (Balboa 1998). The characteristic that is most consistent across recruits and leaders of the PMGs is the strong party identification with the PRI. Survivors of attacks at Bahajón, Venustiano Carranza, Acteal, and several autonomous zones, among other locals, have identified their attackers as known PRI militants and affiliates. Investigations by human rights organizations support these victim reports, as did my interviewees.

In the interviews I conducted, one of the questions that received the same answer time and time again was "who are these paramilitaries?" Regardless of the respondents' party or opinion of the Zapatistas or paramilitaries, they affirmed "todos, todos TODOS son priístas." (ALL paramilitaries are priístas.)§ Others have found that "The principal nucleus [of San Bartolomé de los Llano Alliance] lies in *campesinos* from Paraiso el Grijalva." The press reports on Los Platanos report that the group's membership includes almost entirely "Tztozil youths of the PRI" (Arronte, Castro Soto, and Lewis 2000:117, 119). Residents of areas where PMGs recruit and have been active support these reports, claiming that paramilitaries are composed of "priísta hijos," or "jovenes, indigenous, priístas" (priísta youths, or young, indigenous priístas).§

In addition to the party identification, many of those who join the paramilitaries are likely drawn by the relatively good salaries, prestige, and a chance to escape the cycle of poverty. Others who join PMGs are simply young men living in poverty, hungry and jobless, who cannot foresee any improvement in their quality of life. Often they have waited for the fulfillment of promises made by the PRI — promises for jobs, for homes, for land — to no avail, and they blame the Zapatista rebellion for the economic stagnation.[8] There are also reports of people who are coerced into joining (Ramírez Cuevas 1997a:2), and those who escape the training camps have to avoid those searching for "deserters" by hiding in larger cities (Balboa 1998; Aubry and Inda 1997; §). The DPJ paramilitary group asserted that their members support the group because of its patriotism and commitment to development (Desarrollo 1997:52).[9]

It is important to note that the socioeconomic status of these PMG members is not characteristic only of paramilitaries. Zapatista members are also generally poor. Indeed, the characteristics of members of both groups are eerily similar, excepting the fact that PMG members are consistently PRI, and Zapatista members consistently oppose the party.

### Power of Denial

The case of paramilitary emergence in Chiapas differs from the other two cases studied here in two regards. First, the Mexican government has denied the very existence of paramilitary groups. This is important particularly given the argument made by some that paramilitaries are a means by which the State can "privatize" violence — continue a counterinsurgency campaign while denying its own culpability and placing the blame on uncontrollable, renegade paramilitary groups. Mexican officials did not take this route but rather denied (publicly and in interviews with this researcher) any paramilitary activity in Chiapas. This has a slightly different strategic benefit from the one postulated by "privatization" scholars. By denying the existence of paramilitary groups, the Mexican government was able to continue its military engagement in the region (allegedly in response to guerrilla activity), the military can prolong its relationship with and support for the PRI (because the PRI cannot be connected to nonexistent PMGs), the indigenous communities remain under the thumb of the elite, and the elite remain the rulers of their domain.

What was sometimes surprising was the skill with which the Mexican government continued to avoid the paramilitary issue altogether. In 2001, after the inauguration of Vicente Fox and his proclamation that he could easily resolve the conflict in Chiapas (Murphy 2001), the Mexican government rounded out debate on the indigenous rights bill. The policy proposal prompted debate on the situation in Chiapas not only within Mexico but also abroad, as it muted much of what the Zapatistas had demanded but did manage to acknowledge that an issue existed. In just such a debate in the United States, a panel including Rodolfo Stavenhagen, president of the Verification Commission for the San Andres Accords, and Mario Chacón, a representative from the Mexican Embassy to the United States, debated the "Prospects for Peace in Chiapas" in June 2001. The two speakers addressed an audience of academics, journalists, solidarity groups, representatives from international NGOs, and the Organization of American States (OAS), and in more than an hour of analysis they failed to address the question of paramilitary violence in Chiapas. Stavenhagen seemed to broach the issue when he suggested that Mexico "is not Colombia — *yet*." However, when asked by a member of the audience to expand on his comment, Stavenhagen did not reference the ongoing conflict or the paramilitary violence; instead he repeated the overused official phrase of the Mexican government: "other, non-institutional civilian groups" (Stavenhagen 2001). It is this type of avoidance, this general sense that the Chiapanecos reality is "taboo," that empowers the paramilitaries by staving off accountability.

The second difference between Mexico and the other cases studied here is the regionalized focus of the conflict. Though they enjoyed nationwide and even international popularity and support, the EZLN are the offspring of Chiapas. Likewise, the paramilitaries are local groups with local objectives. This is not to say, however, that similar dynamics are not fomenting in other southern states of Mexico. A small guerrilla band known as the Ejército Popular Revolucionario (EPR), or Popular Revolutionary Army, emerged in Guerrero in 1996. Civilians of the state had been suffering violent repression at the hands of the military and police forces, including attempts at targeted extrajudicial executions, at least one massacre (in 1995), and rapes (Peters 2002; "En Guerrero" 2004). The EPR entered the scene in late June 1996 and later told journalists it wanted to "replac[e] the government with a Marxist proletarian dictatorship" (LaFranchi 1996a, 1996b). Two years later, a report was released alleging that paramilitaries were operating in Guerrero. Armed and composed of members of the PRI, the groups were allegedly harassing indigenous civilians and were accused of issuing death threats and then carrying out the threats in multiple assassinations. The paramilitary was also alleged to be working in collusion with the Mexican army ("La Actuacion" 1998).

Like Chiapas, Guerrero is a poverty-ridden state that has been largely excluded from the economic development of northern and central regions of the country. The state has also suffered extreme political tension that has erupted in violence more than once. A rebel group surfaced in the 1970s (Scott 1994b); in 1990, several PRD supporters "were killed in confrontations over electoral fraud" (Bussey 1990); and by 2002 there were reports of as many as ten "rebel groups active in the remote mountains" (Peters 2002:2).

Despite the apparent similarities, both the leftist, guerrilla movements and the right-wing paramilitary groups operate as separate, regional organizations in each state. And the groups operating in Chiapas, both left and right, seem to enjoy broader support, and broader coverage by human rights groups and journalists, than those in Guerrero. Both may be attributable to the fact that the military presence in Guerrero has outweighed that in Chiapas for some years, perhaps due to the narcotics smuggling that has been rampant in the state (Peters 2002). One might expect that the proclivity for repression and active presence of the military in Guerrero would create a different opportunity structure for a pro-democracy movement than the opportunity presented to the Zapatistas in 1994, and consequently create an environment differing from that which fosters paramilitary organization. In discussing the variability of the political opportunity structure, McAdam, McCarthy, and Zald suggest that "it may be that the form as much as the timing of collective action is structured by the available political opportunity" (1996:10). Thus it is possible that the specific elements of the political environment in Chiapas, differing from that in Guerrero particularly in the presence and methodology of the military and from other states in terms of development and political access, was ripe for paramilitary emergence.

Despite these two distinctions, paramilitary emergence in Chiapas shares similarities with the other cases studied here. In Chiapas, the evolution of the one-party PRI system and its reliance on patronage established a closed economic and political system that favored the elite. This entrenched system of hierarchy was threatened not only by the rise of the PRD and Zapatistas, but also by the political reforms undertaken by a Mexican government trying to court international actors. Laws providing for the White Guards had established a history of armed security forces operating outside the formal structures of the official security apparatus, which served to legitimize such activities even after the laws were reformed. Attempts to reform such laws caused deep rifts within the PRI, the military, and the elite, many of whom had relied on the White Guards and the patronage system for their wealth and status. Thus the hard-liner factions of each of these three shared not only a sense of vulnerability to reforms and new political actors, but also a sense of grievance toward the formal structures of the state for "abandoning" their cause. As we shall see in the coming chapters, the specific actors are different in each case studied here, but the dynamics of paramilitary emergence are exceptionally similar.

# PRECURSORS TO COLOMBIA'S *AUTODEFENSAS*

During the 1980s and 1990s, the people of Medellín, Colombia, lived in an environment so permeated with violence that nearly every facet of life was affected; people suffered not just the loss of loved ones, but also the economic and social repercussions brought on by endless civil conflict. Homes were burned or looted, cattle and land stolen, and whole communities displaced. One woman admitted that she "could not lift her family out of poverty because she was forced to spend a significant portion of her earnings on funerals and burials of family members who were killed" (IACHR 1999aI:10).[1] And while Medellín has been among the most violent areas in Colombia, it was by no means unique. The daily lives of civilians around the country, from the capital city of Bogotá to the most remote areas of the mountains, were affected on a regular basis by the roadblocks, kidnappings, "taxes," massacres, murders, and forced displacements that characterized the conflicts between the State, guerrilla groups, PMGs, and drug lords.

The internal conflict in Colombia dated back more than four decades, with State security forces (including the police, military, and intelligence units) pitted against several insurgent guerrilla groups. During the late 1980s and 1990s, more than one hundred paramilitary groups organized and entered the fray, aligned with the State in the goal of eradicating the leftist guerrillas. Adding to the violence were the drug traffickers, who served as an important ally and source of financing for various parties in the conflict at various times, including, most recently, paramilitary groups. In the late 1990s, the conflict became so widespread and the parties so entrenched that the subversion of institutional order was total. Kidnapping and forced conscription became nearly unavoidable, driving many parents to send their children out of the country on student exchange programs rather than risk their children's safety in a hopeful wait for a visa.[§]

Colombia's paramilitary groups shared several characteristics with those in Chiapas. They targeted their victims for political reasons, generally because they were believed to be guerrillas or guerrilla sympathizers, or to pose a threat to paramilitary objectives. Some of the paramilitary "troops" were civilians, others retired or off-duty military officers. The groups often had allies within local military and/or security forces. They were armed and trained, and committed military-style "attacks" against villages and groups that generally involved multiple slayings (or massacres) and often theft and destruction of homes or property. PMGs also kidnapped, disappeared, and displaced victims, employed tactics including rape, theft, and torture to terrorize, and used forced conscription to inflate their own ranks and shrink the pool of potential guerrilla recruits (see USDOS 2000; and HRW 1999c, 2001a, 2001c).

Unlike those in Chiapas, the paramilitary groups in Colombia became some of the most significant political actors on that country's national stage. They controlled vast swaths of the country and had allies at local and national levels of government. Despite this, Colombia managed to maintain a democratic system of government complete with elections, constitutionally guaranteed civil liberties and human rights in accord with most major international treaties and documents, and enjoyed economic growth and relative stability (IACHR 1993).

While Colombia boasts one of Latin America's longest-running periods of democratic elections uninterrupted by coup or military regime, it simultaneously languishes as a country with one of the most violent histories in the region. Political differences have been dealt with via partisan armed conflict for nearly a century, notwithstanding a two-party system and democratic political institutions that date back to independence. Despite the generations of bloodshed, very little has been resolved in the way of the fundamental issues plaguing the country.

Some have suggested that the seemingly unending violence in Colombia has been sustained by a "body politic [with] a predisposition to violence that may express itself in different ways at different times, but never has been far beneath the surface" (Bushnell 1993:12). In fact it is not a predisposition of individuals or ethnicity, but characteristics of the "informal" political system in Colombia that explain the cycles of violence. There are two elements of this informal system, both designed to make the political process as exclusive as possible. First, the patron-client system, as in Chiapas, has served as a tool of social control and manipulation, protecting the political system (and consequently the elite) from the unpredictable influence of "the masses." This vertical system of exclusion limits political access to the elite while incorporating the masses only under elite control.

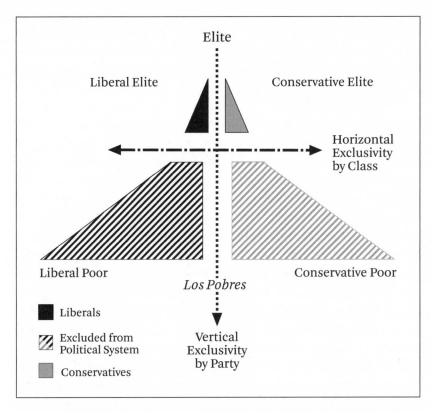

FIGURE 3. Political Access by Party and Class (Model of Political Exclusion under Liberal Party Hegemony)

Second, the two-party system has long been a means of excluding the losing party. Little value has been placed on bipartisanship, and compromise has been viewed as failure. Party competition has been intense and violent from the beginning, and it quickly developed into a horizontal system of exclusion that limited active political decision making to the stronger party.

Consequently, access to the political system is restricted. For the lower classes, as in Mexico, the only ways to make use of the political system are to be a party loyalist to a patron or to use force. Likewise, for whichever party has minority status within government, there is limited ability to influence policy, unless force is used to regain majority status. The informal system of patronage and the formal system of democracy are completely at odds, achieving the paradoxical democratic transfer of power from incumbent to elected official alongside the constant and consistent use of violence to manipulate the balance of power. This long-established informal political system, inherently contradictory to democracy, underlies one of the critical explanatory variables in the emergence of paramilitaries in Colombia.

## Independence Put Asunder

In 1824, the region then known as New Granada finally won its independence from Spain, thanks in large part to Simón Bolívar. Known as "the Liberator" throughout Latin America for his role in leading anticolonialist efforts, Bolívar was the first to govern independent Gran Colombia[2] (Bushnell 1993:50). The celebratory period following independence did not last long, as the new leadership was quickly embroiled in deep disagreement. Issues ranging from the appropriate relationship between State and church to the degree to which government should be centralized in Bogotá were complicated by regional animosities, causing deep rifts between New Granada and adjoining Venezuela and Ecuador.

The oft-absent Bolívar and his vice president, Francisco de Paula Santander, envisioned two different futures for Colombia, and it was not long before each had established his own base of popular support, effectively dividing the country into two camps: the Santanderistas and the Bolivarians. Bolivarians, or Conservatives, supported a strong church role in the state and in education and a centralized government established in Bogotá. Bolívar and his followers also viewed the military as a government ally and supported maintenance of relatively robust forces (Bushnell 1993:61–67; Bergquist, Peñaranda, and Sánchez 1992:25; Safford and Palacios 2002:130–31). Santander led a more progressive, Rousseauian movement that argued for separation of the church from the State and a less powerful central government (Safford and Palacios 2002:140–56), and he developed a strong following among the Liberals. Liberals advocated stricter government control over military budget, size, and behavior (Bushnell 1993:24, 58–64, 81, 95; Safford and Palacios 2002:131, 140–56).

By 1828, it was clear that the Bolívar/Santander dispute was insurmountable. Opposing sides were led by Bolívar and Santander at the Constitutional Convention (1828), where the talks broke down without resolve. Bolívar took over Gran Colombia as dictator supported by the church and most of the military, and he eventually exiled Santander (Bushnell 1993:70–71; Safford and Palacios 2002:130–31). The failure of the Constitutional Convention to reach compromise foreshadowed much of what was to come for Colombia. The ideological split between Bolívar and Santander served as the beginning of the two main political parties in the country, and the parties have been no better at negotiation and compromise since.

The continued inability—or unwillingness—to reach a negotiated compromise in the new republic was evident in the policy swings from left to right (and back again) between 1826 and 1832. While vice-president, Santander had managed to implement some liberal reforms (for instance, the reforms limiting the church's stature), only to see them repealed during Bolívar's dictatorship. Bolívar resigned his rule in 1830, opening the way for elections, the results of which were negated when the elected administration was overthrown. Santander was then elected to the presidency (in absentia), and by 1832 the original liberal reforms were in place again, the constitution had been amended, and Gran Colombia became New Granada (Bushnell 1993:82–84).

The hostility between the two parties was not at all based in class identity; in fact, the popular base of each drew from essentially the same socioeconomic group. Regardless of which camp one was in, one had to have relatively substantial financial resources to be there. Even with the liberal constitutional reforms in 1832, "the right to vote was . . . limited by economic requirements (a minimum amount of property or yearly income) that excluded the great majority" (Bushnell 1993:84). Thus, the masses were not brought into the political arena via modes of participation, but via relationships established with members of the oligarchy. The patron-client system evolved such that lower-class individuals might identify themselves as liberal or conservative only to reap the benefits from a corresponding patron; there was very little if any ideological affinity or popular "demand" placed on the system, political participation, by the clients (Bergquist, Peñaranda, and Sánchez 1992:27; Bushnell 1993:84–86).

While president, Santander adapted the patron-client system so that it would benefit the majority party. Santander saw that the party in power had the upper hand, and he used that to his advantage, controlling patronage so as to exclude rather than work with the Conservative Party. In effect, Santander used the liberal majority status to create the *horizontal* patron-client relationship based on political resources, modeled after the vertical patron-client system based on economic resources. "He . . . showed a streak of vindictiveness that precluded any serious effort to conciliate the Bolivarians. They were not physically harmed, unless charged with conspiracy, but they remained generally excluded from civil and military positions and political influence." With regard to the military, in particular, the president used "governmental exclusivism and denial of patronage" to punish dissenters (Bushnell 1993:86).

The remainder of the nineteenth century was characterized by the two parties periodically swapping roles: one holding political power and excluding the other from any political office, the other rebelling in an attempt to gain dominance. Elections were generally fraudulent, though the presidency was typically turned over to the winner peacefully. Coup attempts were frequent but rarely successful. Despite the relatively systematic postelection transition of political offices, partisan hostility persisted at the popular level via the informal political system. The ruling party used its dominance to replace all minority party officials with their own, completely excluding the opposition. Rebellions by the minority party were frequent and violent. Both parties armed civilians (including those who were not enfranchised), intensifying both the level of violence and party identification. In 1899, the tension peaked with a Liberal rebellion against the ruling Conservatives that was not put down as quickly as in previous years (Bushnell 1993; Safford and Palacios 2002).

The "Thousand Day War" began as an anti-Conservative uprising in 1899, but developed into a full-fledged civil war from there. With no completely reliable records of the toll the war took on the population, most historians estimate 100,000 dead, or about 2.5 percent of the population (Bushnell 1993:151; 1992:15; Bergquist, Peñaranda, and Sánchez 1992:x). Colombia's Thousand Day War has been noted as being "the greatest of Latin America's nineteenth-century civil wars," and "Colombia's most intense period of violence" (Bergquist, Peñaranda, and Sánchez 1992:x).

The Liberals failed in their prolonged and bloody attempt to regain political dominance, though they did gain a small concession in the peace negotiations. In an agreement known as the "National Union" (Sánchez 1992:84–86), or what historian Bushnell refers to as "the principle of guaranteed minority representation in Congress and other deliberative bodies" (1993:160), the Conservatives agreed to include Liberals in some areas of governance. The agreement ended the Thousand Day War with the initiation of a new trend in Colombian politics: a calculated and intentional inclusion of both parties in governing, to the exclusion of others. In 1904, Conservative Rafael Reyes was elected president of Colombia, and he led the first administration that rejected total political exclusion of the opposing party. Reyes initiated an agenda of reform intended to close the divide between the two parties and encourage use of the political system rather than weapons (Bushnell 1993:158), though clientelism continued to be the sole connection of the poor to the political system.

As the country grew economically, increasing political mobilization and activism around labor issues and land tenure made the poor more difficult to ignore. Conservatives continued to use repression against more leftist, marginal groups, including unions. Strikes were broken up by force; demands and concerns of labor organizations went unanswered. During the 1920s as frustration was rising, leftist interests found inspiration in successful popular revolutions abroad. The Partido Socialista Revolucionario (PSR), or Revolutionary Socialist Party, organized in the mid-1920s, labor groups organized and went on strike, and the extreme disparity between the very few rich and the very many poor slowly became part of the political conversation (Bushnell 1993:163–79).

The organization of these previously excluded sectors was worrisome, even if too marginalized to influence any election. Poor and working-class activists made demands on the historically nonresponsive government. Liberal president Alfonso López Pumarejo began a strategy of facing the problems head-on, openly acknowledging the economic disparity and widespread poverty that were antagonizing political contention. López initiated land reform, legalized unions, and even "tolerate[ed] Communist leaders" to head some of the most important labor organizations. But in his efforts to appease Colombia's unions and popular demands, López sent the country's elite into a "nearly hysterical" frenzy (Roldán 2002:17, 18). The prospects of an open political system riled opposition to the administration, and López was ousted in 1945; to replace him, his own Liberal Party offered up a candidate who would reverse the *aperatura*. President Eduardo Santos (1938–42) did just that, but the heightened politicization and López's reforms left a mobilized population needing a leader. Jorge Eliécer Gaitán filled the gap, winning political prominence by denouncing the elite hegemony in policy making and the co-optation of unions. In fact, he so frequently and vehemently denounced the ways in which the elite had marginalized the *pueblo*, one historian recognizes him as "the man who made the term *oligarchy* a household word in Colombia, and a bad word at that" (Bushnell 1993:198; Sánchez 1992:77).

Gaitán became a political force with his efforts to rally the disenfranchised poor and working classes around his populist agenda in the 1940s; his leadership was pivotal in bringing the masses into the official arena of politics and giving them a voice. Opposition to the oligarchy's means of control was, according to some analysts, the essence of his entire political platform (see Bushnell 1993). Regardless of whether his agenda had more substance or not, it gained popular support with great momentum, inviting participation from groups previously either excluded from or closely directed in their political activity. Gaitán was mobilizing outside the patron-client system. The Liberal Party would not back Gaitán's bid for the presidency in 1946, but the charisma and symbolism of the outspoken leader empowered his campaign even without the "Liberal machine" (Bushnell 1993:200). His candidacy was strong enough to split the Liberal vote, giving the Conservatives victory in 1946.

Under the leadership of President Mariano Ospina Pérez and his strong arm Laureano Gómez, known to Liberals as "El Monstruo" (the monster), the Conservative Party moved to reinstate itself. The new party in power repressed Liberals and initiated reprisal attacks against them, and it mobilized Conservative support (furtively among the poor in rural areas, where Gaitán was becoming quite popular). But the violence of 1946 would exceed previous election conflicts. Whereas historically postelection conflict had "petered out" with Colombians settling old scores and adjusting to the new — or reversed — party roles, the cinder pot was continually stoked by leaders sharpening the partisan divide after the 1946 election. Gaitán was breaking all the rules, working directly with the "underclass" workers and peasants rather than with the oligarchy or leadership of co-opted organizations. The Conservatives, meanwhile, were in the process of reminding rural communities about the maltreatment of their own local leaders under Liberal rule and encouraging retribution. Most well-known were groups organized by Gómez in his efforts to "influence the dynamic of rural confrontation [to an] increasingly . . . partisan character." After firing all Liberal police forces, Gómez mobilized Conservative peasants, known as the *chulavita* police, to replace them. Soon resembling death squads, they "[won] a reputation among Liberals as bloodthirsty criminals" and instigated the mobilization of guerrilla forces to defend the Liberals and organize counterattacks (Sánchez 1992:79). The *chulavitas* were perhaps the more formal organization of what had been customary in Colombian politics: armed partisan groups asserting party dominance in peripheral areas. But that formality carved out a new and more legitimate place for such groups in the broader political struggle.

Under these conditions, it was not long before the situation exploded. On 9 April 1948, Gaitán left his office, walked out onto a Bogotá street, and was fatally shot. The assassination immediately set off massive rioting and partisan violence in Bogotá and around the country. One historian described the subsequent two weeks as an "inversion of institutional order" (Sánchez 1992:83; Green 2003:261–62). Peasants and the landless ruled the roost; the powerless suddenly became the powerful. It should not be misunderstood as a period of chaos; it is better described as the previous "order" turned on its head. The fact that rioters set fire to Gómez's home and newspaper offices (*El Siglo*) is illustrative of a symbolic type of order that gave definition to what only appeared to be anarchy (Sánchez 1992:82).

Gaitán had a profoundly polarizing effect on politics in Colombia in that he awakened, empowered, and perhaps legitimized the political activity of impoverished Colombians, and he simultaneously threatened, antagonized, and delegitimized the politics of the elite hegemony. While it may be accurate to say that the *leadership* of the two main political parties had very few ideological differences, the events following Gaitán's assassination indicate the existence of genuine and sharp differences among the people of Colombia. The civil war continued unabated until 1957 and was so gruesome, destructive, and deadly that it earned the appropriately simple and weighty epithet La Violencia — The Violence.

The assassination quickened an initially subtle but consequential evolution in Colombia. The repression and violence began to take on some aspects of class conflict, rather than being solely about traditional, inherited partisanship. The popular uprising, looting, destruction of property, and "institutional inversion" left a shaken oligarchy and changed the nature of Colombian political competition. The elite of both parties found a common ground in their fear of the masses.

Gómez's strategy put elite Liberals between a rock and a hard place. The extreme violence targeting Liberals created a great deal of opposition to Gómez. At the same time, memories of 9 April 1948 were still very fresh, and the oligarchy, even if Liberal, did not trust the masses. Thus the Liberal party took what amounted to a nonaligned position, causing a deep fracture within the Colombian "left." The guerrilla groups approached party officials more than once, attempting to build a coalition against Gómez, but to no avail. The party proper outright rejected guerrilla advances, highlighting a shift in prioritization of competing collective identities. For many peasants, party identity was taking a backseat to the economic and political interests of the poor (Sánchez 1992:84–94; Bushnell 1993:192–207). The Liberal leadership essentially collaborated with Gómez via their quiescence and in doing so opened a window of opportunity for Conservatives that dramatically changed the tenor of the war (Sánchez 1992:90–95; Bushnell 1993:204).

Particularly after being elected president in 1950, Gómez spared no resources; his offensive against alleged insurgents ran the gamut in terms of repression. Unions were dissolved, striking was prohibited, and activists were arrested. The church was used quite effectively as an ally of the government's anti-Liberal crusade, organizing a network of peasant antiguerrilla informants who served "as a *cordon sanitaire* in zones of convergence between the guerrillas and the government forces" (Sánchez 1992:87). Liberal leaders were targeted, attacked, and some successfully assassinated. In rural areas, the *chulavita* police were clearing the way for Conservatives. Massacres left hundreds of peasants dead, communities deserted, and livelihoods destroyed.

The extent to which utter despair had enveloped the nation is evident in the fact that Colombians across the political spectrum breathed a collective sigh of relief at the military coup that finally ousted Gómez, who fled the country. General Gustavo Rojas Pinilla overthrew the Conservative regime in 1953 and began implementing a series of reforms intended to end the violence, deal with the humanitarian issues, and bring politics off the battlefield and back to the bargaining table. Rojas began with a broad amnesty offer for the guerrillas, initiating a dramatic shift in the relationship between the State and civil society. Where Gómez had approached the guerrillas as insurgents, criminals, and threats to the State, Rojas chose to approach them as a warring party, credible partners in negotiation and eligible for amnesty—conditioned on surrender (Sánchez 1992:100–104).

Initial hope in the promises of the Rojas regime was short-lived. The general reverted to military repression and shifted away from resolving the basic problems underlying the civil conflict, leaving all sides unsatisfied with the military rule. In particular, Rojas was neglecting the land issue, which, for rural populations, was easily the most pressing point of contention. Large landholders in Sumapaz were facing communist organization and peasant activism regarding land tenure, with residential peasants demanding ownership, and the wealthy ranchers claiming "official" ownership rights. Rojas eventually moved in to assist the *latifundistas*. The military was again called to "pacify" the activists, resuming the former government's tactics of mass murder and terrorizing entire communities. Over the next two years, the military continued its assault on the region, while former guerrillas regrouped to fight what they viewed as the broken promises of the Rojas regime (Sánchez 1992:110–14).

In 1957, Rojas attempted to extend his presidency, much to the chagrin of the country's oligarchy. Liberals and Conservatives united in an anti-Rojas coalition and forced him to resign. The bipartisan negotiations—which included the ousted Gómez—resulted in a plan to reconstruct the oligarchy's hegemony known as the National Front. The Frente Nacional was essentially an improved version of the earlier National Union agreement, strengthened with a bipartisan security clause written into the Constitution itself intended to prevent another civil war. The front was designed to ensure at least two things: first, that both parties would have equal representation in all elected offices at all levels of governance, and they would alternate terms in the presidency; second, to exclude any third party from a part in official politics, unless running under the guise of one of the official parties. It institutionalized structured power sharing between the two main parties, excluded alternative parties, provided for "the autonomy of the military branch in the management of internal public order," and weakened the legislative branch (Pizarro 1992:174). Referring back to Figure 3, the National Front essentially overcame the vertical divide while simultaneously reinforcing the horizontal divide by ensuring that the Liberal and Conservative parties remained the *only* political voices. Meanwhile, the guerrilla reorganization campaign (which had begun while Rojas was in office) continued, and activism around the land issue only intensified.

In hopes of establishing peace, the National Front addressed the discontent and conflict around the country by including an amnesty provision for all combatants who agreed to give up their weapons and rejoin mainstream society. However, there was still deep skepticism among workers and peasants that the oligarchy would eventually provide poverty-relief legislation and genuine democracy. Some groups, for instance the Communist party, registered their dissent through conference notes or party votes but remained committed to a "peaceful revolutionary struggle through the progressive democratization of the country," rejecting the resumption of armed conflict (Pizarro 1992:173).

Others chose to reject the offer of amnesty. By the early 1960s, some of the guerrillas who had originated as Liberal defenders during the civil war had evolved into more sophisticated and widespread organizations militarily engaging the State. Like the nascent groups, the modern guerrillas had anti-oligarchy political agendas including land redistribution and political reform. But where the Violencia groups had been primarily Liberal loyalists who perceived themselves as defensive organizations against the Conservative oppressors, the post-Violencia groups were more class conscious and less loyal to their traditional party identity. Somewhere between Gaitán and the National Front, the underclass—the poor workers and peasants, the landless—developed an anti-system ideology that rejected the oligarchy's hegemony and the traditional two-party loyalties and hatreds (Bergquist, Peñaranda, and Sánchez 1992:xiii; Safford and Palacios 2002:323; Pizarro 1992:175–77). This shifted the nature of politics in Colombia; the oligarchy could no longer establish peace simply by lining up their party loyalists and saying it was so. Increasing numbers of the excluded lower classes were realizing their lack of access to the system regardless of which of the two main parties was in power. The "peace" conceptualized by the Front's authors was one characterized by a hegemonic oligarchy, rather than by a pluralist, competitive democracy. The undermining of the Front was written into its very structure; by closing the political arena to any third party or social movement, the elite effectively facilitated the mobilization efforts and popular support of the guerrilla organizations.

### Los Guerrilleros and Las Autodefensas

The Fuerzas Armadas Revolucionarias de Colombia, or the "Revolutionary Armed Forces of Colombia," better known as the FARC, is generally viewed as Colombia's oldest guerrilla organization. Able to trace its roots back as early as the 1940s, the group espouses a socialist/communist ideology and has found its support base largely among the peasants in rural areas of Colombia. Among the chief concerns of the FARC are the distribution of land and financial resources, reforms that address the high percentage of the population living in poverty (67 percent in 2002) and the apparent inability of any political candidate, party, or organization to make inroads in a political system dominated by the traditional oligarchy (USDOS 2003:1; Ruiz 2001:7; Pratt 2000:5–6). In recent years, the FARC has expanded its areas of concern, which now also include ending "Gringo military aid; . . . impositions from the International Monetary Fund; foreign debt; interference from the United States in the internal affairs of Colombia . . . [; and] peasants without land or credits," and downsizing military spending (Pratt 2000:5).

The FARC is renowned for its kidnapping, and for good cause. Of the thousands of kidnappings each year in Colombia, about half were attributed to guerrillas (HRW 2001a:5). Political leaders were sometimes kidnapped in an attempt to influence policy or to force prisoner-exchange negotiations, but more frequent were kidnappings for ransom. The FARC was especially known for its "fishing expeditions." In these operations, members of the FARC waited at "checkpoints" along roads and highways, temporary roadblocks they constructed, for potential kidnapping victims. Using a laptop computer, the guerrillas would check out the bank records of those they stopped, sifting for those "worth" kidnapping (Wilson 2002c:3; Guillermoprieto 2000:1; USDOS 2003:22).[3]

Monies collected from ransoms were supplemented by war taxes demanded of business owners, landowners, and other wealthy residents of guerrilla territories. Otherwise known as *"vacunas,"* or vaccinations, these taxes provided an estimated 6 billion pesos for the FARC in 1991. Drug cartels were treated similarly: Landowners growing coca were charged a *"gramaje"* (additional tax) by the guerrillas, in addition to a "percentage of the profits of coca processing and shipment." For 1991, income generated by these war fees was estimated at "between 20 and 25 billion pesos" (IACHR 1993:X.13). Converted into 2002 U.S. dollars, in 1991 the guerrilla group acquired nearly $2.25 million from *vacunas* and almost $7.5 million in taxes on drug crops, processing, and shipping.[4] "Ley 002" was particularly useful for the FARC. Implemented by the FARC in areas under their control in 1999–2000, the "law" required "persons with more than $1 million (2.95 billion pesos) in assets to volunteer payments to the FARC or risk detention" — that is, pay the tax or risk being kidnapped (USDOS 2003:11; HRW 2001a:5).

The Ejército Liberación Nacional (ELN), or National Liberation Army, is second in size to the FARC and was "created by FARC dissidents influenced by the ideas exported by the Cuban Revolution" (IACHR 1993:II.4) in 1964. The ELN used tactics somewhat similar to the FARC and was actually "credited" with introducing the use of "mass kidnappings" for political and/or economic gains to Colombia. In 1998, the UC-ELN (Unión Camilista-Ejército de Liberación Nacional) commandeered Avianca flight #9463, kidnapping all forty-one individuals on board. One month later, the group conducted a second mass kidnapping, entering a church in Cali and taking 140 worshippers. Following this incident, the guerrilla group busied itself with "increas[ing] its pace of kidnapping by 217 [percent]." Over the next three months, 463 individuals were victims of ELN kidnapping. During that same time, the guerrilla leadership issued a statement regarding the Cali church incident. The group "apologized not for the Cali kidnapping itself, but for failing to wait until mass was concluded to carry it out" (HRW 2000a:3).

By 1968 the guerrilla forces were significant, and the Colombian government found itself unsuccessfully trying to wage a counterinsurgency campaign. In an attempt to supplement its military capabilities, the State legalized civilian self-defense units. Decree 3398 of 1965 authorized the government to organize civilian groups and arm them with military weapons typically prohibited from civilian use in peacetime as a provision of the state of emergency declared that year. The plan was to organize civilian forces that would supplement the official military. Law 48 was passed in 1968 in order to broaden the prerogative of the civilian patrols by permitting the groups to remain organized and armed after the state of emergency expired (IACHR 1999aI:3; 1993:II.5).

The groups formed by Law 48 had a structural relationship with Colombia's security forces. Initially the relationship was limited to arms provision, but the relationship evolved as the State redesigned its military doctrine toward the "National Security" principles espoused by the West during the Cold War (IACHR 1999a:I.4).[§] The doctrine was based on the thinking that "subversive activities were international aggression orchestrated from abroad and planned and executed from within" (IACHR 1993:II.6). Groups such as unions and student organizations were suspected of being "infiltrated" by insurgents who threatened the Western traditions of liberty and freedom. Under this doctrine, the mission of the military was to "search-and-destroy," and since the threat was perceived as festering domestically, military attention was turned inward rather than focused externally (IACHR 1993:II.6).

The consequence of implementing the National Security doctrine through a structural alliance between civilian patrols and the military was a legalized team effort between the two aimed at flushing out the guerrillas and their support networks. Initially, the two groups operated cooperatively, for instance in "fumigating" areas of guerrillas. "Fumigation" was the groups' response to the guerrillas' *vacuna* (vaccination) campaigns, and it involved "driving out all subversives" (IACHR 1993:II.6–7). The *vacuna* campaigns, kidnappings, and violence led by the guerrillas enraged *hacendados*, who were popular targets. Consequently, the fumigation efforts found a natural ally in *latifundistas*, who needed — and were willing to pay for — protection against the guerrillas. Bands of farmers joined forces to protect their land and their families and began providing the armed civilian groups with resources beyond the arms provided by the military. In a statement to the Inter-American Commission on Human Rights, Father Adolfo Galindo Quevedo explained the logical and inherent nature of the relationship that developed between landowners and civic patrols: "The owner of a ranch says to himself: 'well, if I have to pay 20 million in ransom for every kidnapping, then I'll pay a million for protection and save 19 million in the bargain.' If a hundred people think that way, then there's a hundred million for self-defense groups" (IACHR 1993:II.6).

The antisubversive campaign continued in this vein, still unable to overcome a stalemate with the guerrillas, until Amnesty International released a scathing report on Colombia's human rights situation in 1980. The NGO reported having evidence of wide-scale political imprisonment, military courts trying civilians, severe repression, and imprisonment of labor organizers, indigenous and peasant organizers, and political protestors practicing rights clearly protected in the Constitution. According to the report, the Colombian government was using excessive power in order to maximize control over not only true subversives, but also any political organizer or activist (AI 1980). Evidence also suggested that members of police forces and the army had committed extrajudicial executions, and in a 1981 special on-site investigation, the IACHR found that the State had done little if anything to discipline and prevent such abuses by its own agents (see IACHR 1981).

Leading an administration that took office nearly two years after the release of the AI report, President Betancur took a radically different approach to the guerrilla conflict. Rather than using the military to try to subdue the rebels, Betancur worked to subdue the military and control the police. And adding insult to injury, the president's focus on ending the military excesses was closely followed by efforts to negotiate with the guerrillas. Both landowners and members of the military felt a sense of impotence against insurgents and resentment, even indignation, toward the new executive policies. The shift away from military counterinsurgency efforts and toward cooperative peace building proved incendiary. The new approach made the idea of *las autodefensas* increasingly popular, particularly among ranchers, landowners, and frustrated military troops.

President Betancur's strategy of curtailing the military and negotiating with the guerrillas infuriated those who had been victimized by the FARC or other groups and left them with a sense that the government was knowingly ignoring their security needs. The total frustration and feeling of abandonment defined the shared grievance that mobilized the country's landowners and ranchers into localized grassroots organizations (Gomez 2004:1; Wilson 2001a; Valencia 2002:1). This period proved to be critical in the formative stage of paramilitary emergence, a time when potential and former guerrilla victims mobilized critical resources for their would-be self-defense groups ("Historia de la Autodefensa" 2003; IACHR 1993:II).

By the early 1980s, the armed groups were supported and organized not only by the military, but also by wealthier civilians under the guise of the 1965 and 1968 laws. In this transformation away from a strictly state-sponsored (and therefore state-controlled) type of organization, the groups exercised some autonomy in their activities, in their support base, and in their ideological purpose. Some groups became involved with drug cartels and secured their autonomy and financial independence by trafficking in illegal substances. Through maintaining contact with military units and landowners, the groups grew more powerful than the government had intended. Still legal under Law 48, they carried out attacks against villages, suspected subversives, politicians, and government officials with impunity. Eliminating subversives and suspected guerrilla sympathizers broadened their support and territorial control (IACHR 1993:II.7; 1999a:I.4). A Colombian official described this process to me as one that was used to solidify "social support" for the transformation into paramilitaries. For one group in particular, the strategy of moving into a small town, identifying guerilla supporters, removing or eliminating them, and then providing protection and support for the remaining civilians proved very successful.[§] That nascent paramilitary group was led by Carlos Castaño.

Castaño provided the leadership and authority necessary to build what would become a highly sophisticated paramilitary organization in Colombia, the Autodefensas Unidas de Colombia (AUC), or Self-Defense Forces of Colombia. He was to the paramilitaries what Pablo Escobar was to the drug cartels — the most wanted and feared man by some, the most revered and emulated by others. Castaño was born in Antioquia department in 1965 and was raised on his family's two-hundred-hectare farm with eleven siblings. When he was in his early teens, Carlos's father, Jesus Castaño, was kidnapped by the FARC and held for $7,500 ransom. Carlos and his family raised what money they could, mostly contributions from "friends, and from a loan," amounting to about half of what the FARC was demanding. But his father was killed anyway; his body has never been recovered, nor was the roughly $3,000 the family paid in ransom (Valencia 2002:2; Wilson 2001b:4.1; Wilson 2001a).[5] In his memoirs, Castaño is clear in identifying this as the pivotal point in his life, the moment that he determined to end what he saw as the guerrilla reign of terror. "I could forgive all that has happened in these past twenty years of war, but the death of my father, no." He adds, "This period of my life," fighting the guerrillas, "will not be closed until they return my father's body to me" (Aranguren 2001:12, translation mine; IACHR 2000a:1.7).

Determined to avenge his father's death and join the counterinsurgency, Carlos and his younger brother Fidel both initially trained with the army's 14th Brigade, in the Bombona Battalion (Wilson 2001a:4). Carlos was resolute. He killed his first guerrilla at the age of sixteen, targeting those specific guerrillas he believed to have murdered his father. Nonetheless, he was quickly disillusioned with the State's counterinsurgency campaign. His frustration with what he perceived to be a losing strategy grew. He explained in a later interview that while in the military, "'we invoked justice, we trusted justice, but when it did not respond, we felt we could take justice into our own hands. And I'm not ashamed to say we did it for vengeance'" (Wilson 2001a:4). Indeed, when Castaño "turned the person responsible [for his father's death] over to the police, he was released in three days" (Wilson 2001b:4).

Soon Castaño and his comrades took their mission outside of the military. They were quickly transformed in the process of the hunt, moving from an unwavering focus on retribution for a specific murder to a widespread and organized campaign for what Castaño calls justice. "During the first year, we were an organization whose exclusive purpose was vengeance, and when we had executed most of those who had assassinated my father, we began to be enforcers of strict justice. We were the only . . . group whose cause was justice. It's that simple" (Aranguren 2001:12, translation mine). The level of frustration with State institutions did not wane with time. Castaño claimed in a 2001 interview that regardless of the accusations made against the AUC in terms of violent human rights violations, the organization "exists because . . . [the] Armed Forces have not done their institutional duty of guaranteeing Colombians their lives, property, and honor. . . . We are doing a patriotic duty" (Wilson 2001b:2.1).

Like Carlos Castaño, many paramilitary leaders and foot soldiers began their antiguerrilla crusade via the institutions and structures of the State. An early crusader against guerrillas and later commander of the Metro Bloque paramilitary, a man who goes by the nom de guerre of "Rodrigo 00," initially served as a lieutenant in the armed forces in the Magdalena River region. At the time, popular support favored the guerrillas, and Rodrigo 00 "began forcing young men who had avoided Colombia's obligatory military service to work as guides [for his troops] or face jail time" (Wilson 2003:2). He was subsequently suspended from service but wanted to continue fighting the guerrillas. Rodrigo 00 joined up with Fidel

Castaño in 1989 (Wilson 2003:2) and joined what the Castaños called their self-defense forces.

Others became involved with the paramilitaries after first having been active in less-militant but strongly anticommunist civil society groups. Iván Roberto Duque became an elite member of Colombia's PMG leadership who went by the war name of Ernesto Báez. He related in an interview that as early as his university days, 1980–81 at the Caldas University, he felt a strong indignation against what he perceived to be the domination of the political left over campuses and education. He specifically loathed the popularity and influence of the guerrilla group known as the M-19 on campus, and he began his own countermovement, the "Movimiento de Unidad para la Resatauración Acadêmia" (MURA), or the Unified Movement for Academic Restoration. Báez recalled that his organization was "immediately branded an ultra-right movement" ("Historia de la Autodefensa" 2003:2; translation mine). Undeterred, he continued to pursue involvement with nascent anticommunist groups that were organizing in Puerto Boyacá. Pablo Guarín, one of Puerto Boyacá's prominent antisubversive activists and a member of the national Congress, had a particular influence on Báez's early involvement with the first *autodefensas*, inspiring Báez (among many others) to rally forward and fight against the "vultures of the FARC" ("Historia de la Autodefensa" 2003:2; translations mine).

President Betancur's move to negotiate with the guerrillas became a watershed moment for Báez and the organizational efforts of the early *autodefensas*. Báez recounted a headline in a local newspaper catching his eye. The article focused on the talks and featured a photo of the three top FARC leaders as peace negotiators. "These are the bloodthirsty of Uribe, more dangerous as criminals armed with guns than as pacified negotiators of peace. . . . [The article] impacted me" ("Historia de la Autodefensa" 2003:2; translation mine). The FARC and ELN had terrorized families, kidnapped loved ones, and demanded payment of illegal taxes, and the only hope for justice for many Colombians had been the military and security forces. For those who held this hope, the thought of the government treating the guerrillas as good-faith political negotiators was nothing short of repulsive.

In 1982, an organizational meeting was called to bring together a variety of individuals committed to fighting against the guerrillas. Among those in attendance were more than two hundred landowners, ranchers, and business owners. In an interview, Carlos Castaño explained that the meeting was held in the city of Medellín because "70 [percent] of those in the city could not return to their fincas" ("Historia de la Autodefensa" 2003:2; translation mine), suggesting that guerrilla activity had driven the anticommunist activists to the city, effectively stealing their land.

The ACDEGAM, the Asociación Campesina de Ganaderos y Agricultores del Magdelena Media (Association of Rural Ranchers and Farmers of Magdelena Media), mobilized and armed themselves, determined to end their own victimization at the hands of guerrillas. Part of the plan was to form "brigades" to go out into communities to help with basic survival, including meeting the health needs of the civilians; but the organization was more than philanthropic, it was antisubversive. The group teamed with members of the armed forces, using Law 48 to organize self-defense patrols (IACHR 1993:introduction, 4), and began funding forty-two training facilities ("Historia de la Autodefensa" 2003:3; Pearce 1990:xvi).

Meanwhile, the ACDEGAM was also working to build a network of support throughout various sectors of society. The lobbying efforts paid off in the capital, where the group found a number of political officials, including a former cabinet member and some members of Congress, who were staunchly opposed to the guerrilla cause and lent support to the *autodefensas*. As was later documented by the AUC, "the self-defense group was already functioning as a political project" ("Historia de la Autodefensa" 2003:3; translation mine). It is important to note that, as *legal* organizations, these groups were state-sponsored and had not yet evolved into paramilitary groups.

During the same period of time, the Medellín drug cartel was establishing a private justice organization to fight off guerrilla kidnappings and extortion. Drug cultivation and narco-trafficking began its "boom" in Colombia in the late 1960s and early 1970s. Cities along the Atlantic coast became centers of marijuana production and exportation, primarily to the United States. But the combination of eradication efforts in Colombia and an increased level of marijuana production within the United States undermined the viability of the Colombian trade, and it eventually declined. In the meantime, Medellín was becoming a popular site for the illegal processing of coca plants brought in from other South American countries and then exported north. Cocaine eventually replaced marijuana as the illegal export of choice and provided a profit margin large enough to finance powerful cartels that managed, protected, and expanded the industry (IACHR 1999a:I.4; Bushnell 1993:260–61).

The illicit drug industry is an inherently violent one, in part because of the fact that it is illegal and in part because of the competition between cartels. Very early in Colombia's cocaine boom, the Medellín cartel and the Calí cartel became powerhouses competing with each other for control of the market, vying for territory and control. Territorial expansion was relatively easy: "People who made fortunes in the drug trade began to buy up landed estates, which ordinary landowners, tired of guerrilla extortion, were eager to sell" (Bushnell 1993:265). Control was more difficult. While the cartels could bribe many of the local — and even regional and national — authorities into doing their bidding, guerrilla groups were a different matter altogether. The new narco-*hacendados* did not take kindly to the guerrilla domination, nor to their war taxes. The drug cartels had no interest in seeing the guerrillas gouge their profit margin, and they had the resources to create their own defense squads (Bushnell 1993:265). So what may have seemed like an inevitable collaboration between illegal groups became an antagonistic relationship and, in parts of the country, out-and-out competition for territorial control (Bushnell 1993:265; IACHR 1999a:I.4).

The group known as Muerte a Secuestradores (MAS), or "Death to Kidnappers" was founded in 1981 in a cooperative effort between high-level Medellín traffickers, including Pablo Escobar, and private ranchers. Carlos Castaño's brother Fidel was one of those who contributed to organizing the group after a sister of one of the cartel members was kidnapped by the M-19 guerrilla group (IACHR 1999a:I.4-7; Bushnell 1993:265; Commission for the Study of the Violence 1992:268-69; HRW 2003:4).

## Internal Division, External Repudiation, and Growth

According to Carlos Castaño's account, this association with drug traffickers severed the early self-defense supporters into two deeply divided camps. While his brother Fidel cavorted with the Medellín traffickers, Carlos maintains that from the very beginning he disapproved. Of course, his brother being so heavily involved with the cartels made the situation difficult. "Behind the back of my brother Fidel, who still maintained a good friendship with Pablo [Escobar], I began in a discrete manner to oppose Escobar, and during more than three years I maintained a cold war against Pablo" ("Historia de la Autodefensa" 2003:6; translation mine). Carlos was not alone in quietly shunning the drug trade; the dynamics and repercussions of this division among the paras would eventually cause an important reshuffling in alliances and leadership.

Within a few years of his work with MAS, Fidel Castaño became heavily involved in trafficking, "amassing a fortune . . . and becom[ing] one of northern Colombia's most powerful ranchers" (HRW 2003:4; Valencia 2002:1, 3). His assets allowed him to leave MAS in the middle 1980s and, together with brother Carlos, to initiate a new group, a well-trained and armed organization known as Los Tangüeros (HRW 2003:4–5). Carlos describes this period as one in which he and his brother laid the groundwork for what they hoped would be a growing and influential power to counter the guerrillas. Their initial efforts focused on accumulating land and financial resources and securing their territory from guerrilla activity. They began compensating ranchers for land they had deserted when fleeing guerrilla encroachment, and then they pushed the guerrillas out of the area. The first "zone they liberated" was a ranch in Córdoba known as "las Tangas," from whence the group created its name Los Tangüeros. They fought this and other early battles with approximately one hundred troops, first identifying guerrillas and their sympathizers and then eliminating their influence via executions. The group became "the most notorious death squad in north Colombia, blamed for more than 150 murders in the late 1980s and early 1990s" (Wilson 2001a:4).

Eventually, Fidel began making money outside of the narcotics industry. He would buy land for nearly nothing from the farmers and ranchers who were desperate to avoid further extortion and wanted to move to more urban areas, and then he defended it against the guerrillas. He recruited and trained others interested in fending off the guerrillas and eventually secured regions against FARC and ELN attacks. Fidel then made returns on the land, selling to ranchers who now felt safe enough to move back (Dudley 2002). Thus the Castaños became living proof that the guerrillas *could be* repelled, and they continued to win supporters.

Carlos claimed that even throughout this period, Fidel maintained a strong relationship with Pablo Escobar, visiting him in his home regularly, despite his brother's distaste for the capo. Carlos, in fact, recalls an incident in which they were both visiting Escobar's home, Santa Helena, in Medellín. Escobar was asleep, and Carlos immediately saw an opportunity and said to Fidel, "'Brother, we are here alone, armed, and with this man who is so dangerous and so bad, upstairs sleeping . . .' Fidel said to me, 'Calm down, he is who will help us after we win the fight against the guerrilla.'" Carlos continued to distrust Escobar but acknowledges that his brother's association with the capo brought power and financial support to their organization ("Historia de la Autodefensa" 2003:8; translation mine).

Despite Carlos's widely proclaimed distaste for the capos, drug traffickers allegedly continued to contribute financing to paramilitary properties, including a "fortress," or safe house, near Nudo de Parmillo in Córdoba. The ranch was a sort of "home base" for Castaño himself, among other high-ranking leaders (Ruiz 2001:29). Yet Carlos's strong opposition finally won out and the brothers united against the capo. The two later worked in tandem with government officials to end Pablo Escobar's reign as drug kingpin (Wilson 2003:2; Valencia 2002:2; Castro Caicedo 1996:39–40; Dudley 2002).[6]

Even such decisive action on the part of the Castaño brothers did not end paramilitary involvement in the drug industry. The early progress of the paramilitary project was interrupted, according to Carlos Castaño, when the leadership again divided over involvement in the drug trade. "El Mexicano," the war name of Rodríguez Gacha, became very influential in Magdelena Medio's self-defense group and very involved in the drug trade. Gacha reportedly became so tied to the cocaine industry that his organization became a rival with other, more established groups, competing particularly with the FARC. On at least one occasion, El Mexicano accused the FARC of stealing hundreds of kilograms of cocaine. According to Castaño's version of the story, this ignited an apolitical conflict between the FARC and El Mexicano's *autodefensas* ("Historia de la Autodefensa" 2003:3–4). It was also a continuation of a deep division within the paramilitary countermovement, which would continue to plague the group and undermine its ability to function politically as a unified voice.

Even as the paramilitary groups were organizing and strengthening, President Betancur was making headway in his negotiations with the guerrilla groups. One of the significant concessions made by his administration was to grant amnesty to guerrillas who agreed to turn in their arms and rejoin civil society. In order to facilitate this demobilization, Betancur also agreed to the creation of the Unión Patriotica (UP) in May 1985, an organization designed to serve as a "political vehicle of guerrillas in transition." The idea was not just to give guerrillas amnesty, but also to allow former guerrillas to join the political conversation via this new party organization. The FARC and the two smaller guerrilla groups, the Ejército Popular de Liberación (EPL), or Popular Liberation Army, and the M-19 each agreed to a one-year cease-fire with Betancur's administration and supported the formation of the UP. Efforts were continued under President Barco (1986–90), and by 1986, the organization was defined and structured enough to offer candidates in elections at all levels of government. As a party, the UP won "9 seats and 3 alternate seats in Congress, 10 seats and 4 alternate seats in departmental assemblies and 350 seats on town councils," and earned 14 mayoral seats that year (IACHR 1993:VIIc.10). The party's presidential candidate, Jaime Pardo Leal, took 4.55 percent of the presidential votes cast (see IACHR 1993:VIIc.10; and Bushnell 1993:292).

But becoming a member, candidate, or elected official of the UP soon proved a life-threatening decision. Between 1984 and 1993, an estimated 1,163 members of the UP were executed, at least 123 members were disappeared, and at least 43 individuals "survived assassination attempts." Another 225 individuals received threats due to their activity in the UP. Mirroring violence against the PRD in Chiapas, a report released by the Colombian Ombudsman for the People concluded that "the greatest numbers of violations of human rights committed against the Patriotic Union coincide with those areas where the Patriotic Union has achieved the greatest electoral support, [and] that the greatest violence against the members of the Patriotic Union occurred during periods of electoral activity" (IACHR 1997c:5). The UP essentially fell apart, as some members returned to guerrilla organizations and many lost faith in the State's negotiations and overtures. Though some candidates continued running under the UP name, the influence and potential of the movement was totally undermined by the assassinations.

There is no doubt that some of the violence waged against the UP was the work of the "self-defense" groups. Carlos Castaño and Ernesto Báez contend that it was El Mexicano who declared war against the UP, led the massive eradication campaign against UP members, and put out the hit on UP presidential candidate Jaime Pardo Leal ("Historia de la Autodefensa" 2003:3–5). As with the narco-trafficking, El Mexicano's activities did not meet Guarín's approval. According to Báez, when Guarín heard about El Mexicano putting out the hit on Leal, "[Guarín] said to me, 'this death is lamentable and will bring many negative'" things ("Historia de la Autodefensa" 2003:4; translation mine).

Prompted by the attempt to eliminate the UP wholesale, the Colombian government took the bold step of recognizing the mass elimination of individuals who share common membership in a political organization as "political genocide" in 2000 (USDOS 2002a:11). Regardless of such symbolic moves, the utter lack of accountability for those who committed hundreds of human rights violations against members of the UP drew intense criticism of the Colombian government. The fact that the State did little if anything to protect, prevent, or punish the violence against the UP brought the complete disintegration of the Betancur peace initiative, and it perhaps had the lasting effect of undermining future attempts at negotiation. A leader of the M-19 explained, "the problem is that the oligarchy does not want to give up anything because they think that the solution for this country comes from [the] submission and silencing not only of the guerrilla movement but also of the democratic sectors and of the new forces that want a different life" (Ruiz 2001:169).[7] And for those members of the oligarchy who did indeed hold this position, the slaughter of UP members made clear the PMG ability to undermine federal efforts to negotiate an end to the guerrilla conflict.

For Colombia's self-defense groups, the late 1980s were a period of dangerous fluidity. El Mexicano's involvement with the drug capos created a deep division that quickly developed into a type of internal war. Castaño's group continued to look disparagingly on El Mexicano's actions, believing they were tainting the public image of the self-defense cause. Báez lamented in an interview that in "the eyes of the country, the Self-Defense Group of Puerto Boyacá was a group of paramilitaries, managed by the narco-traffickers," and, he said, the public did not know just how bad it really was. That might have been the case, until April 1989, that is, when *La Semana* broke a story about the narco-paramilitary link in Puerto Boyacá. The article was viewed as a huge public relations win for the FARC, and a black eye for all paramilitaries ("Historia de la Autodefensa" 2003:5; translation mine).

It is significant that El Mexicano and his faction's entanglement with drug processing and transport succumbed to a stronger, more ideological element, personified by Carlos Castaño. Perhaps it is this fact, this moment in paramilitary evolution, that is most telling: Just when the power structures around them were collapsing, when the cartels had fought each other to the point of causing their own demise, and when El Mexicano's power and organization were withering away as paper tigers in the fallout, it was the small, regional *autodefensas* who were the unlikely survivors. The durability of these small units is indicative of two important characteristics. First, these regional groups were not dependent on the major cartels; they had some degree of autonomy or even independence. Second, the regional groups were founded on something other than the competition and business of the capos. They are not patsies to the narco-traffickers but in fact make use of the drug growers, processors, and traffickers to finance their own purposes. Analysts who "dumb down" the Colombian conflict to a drug war, or misinterpret the paramilitaries as profiteering drug-traffickers, are blind to the political character and nature of the paramilitary.

The self-defense initiative emerged from the growing pains of the 1980s with two critical components of any movement's mobilization: political purpose and relevance, and leadership. Báez recalls his surprise upon his release from jail (for a murder Castaño admits his own involvement with) when he found that Castaño had "achieved what was most difficult, to create collective solidarity among the self-defense groups" ("Historia de la Autodefensa" 2003:5–7; translation mine). The local groups had survived as what AUC negotiator Hernán Gómez described as "fiefdoms with armed power" (Gómez 2004:1; ACCUBEC 2003c:9) largely due to the relevance they had and purpose they served for local communities. This perception of self, and the frame of legitimacy the groups projected to the public, was critical in their shift from legally armed civilian groups to illegal paramilitary organizations. The networks of support, the mobilizing structures, and the subjective perceptions of self and reality were all in place when the State rescinded their legality.

During his administration, Barco undertook reforms to reign in the military and "impose legal restrictions on [the] activities" of the armed civilian groups (IACHR 1999a:I.4). In terms of the state security forces, Barco's administration attempted to create stronger executive "checks and balances" over the armed forces, creating the office of the Presidential Advisor for Human Rights and a Civilian Prosecutor for the Military and Police Forces. In addition to these, the Office of the Attorney Delegate for Human Rights was formed and tasked with investigating and prosecuting crimes against humanity (IACHR 1993:v).

In 1989, the government implemented legislation to revoke the 1965 and 1968 laws that had legalized self-defense groups, taking a first step in outlawing the future organizing of non-state armed brigades. Armed civilian groups were finally banned outright when Law 48 was found unconstitutional by the Colombian Supreme Court in 1989. Members of groups were, by law, required to disband and return their weapons to the army (IACHR 1993:II.7). In reversing the legal status of the units, the Barco reforms affected nearly every aspect of the conflict. The armed groups became illegal PMGs and were thus officially stripped of any international recognition as a legitimate combatant in a civil conflict. This instigated a new line of paramilitary discourse, as it became necessary to defend their very legitimacy. This effort was facilitated by the government itself, which did not simultaneously act to fill the security void that had "necessitated" the *autodefensas* in the first place.

In passing the legislation in 1968, the Colombian government had effectively relinquished a portion of its "monopoly over the legitimate use of violence" to a sector of civil society. Law 48 played the same role in Colombia as the legalization of the Guardias Blancas did in Chiapas: the State did the legwork of distributing resources like arms and training for the civic patrols, and therefore for their progeny the paramilitaries. But the implications of the law were more profound than this. The law also initiated the organization of previously unorganized individuals and provided them with a common identity and purpose: to fight guerrillas. Thus, and perhaps most importantly, the State gave the civic patrols legitimacy and purpose in the counterinsurgency objectives of national security. The repeal of Law 48 was simply not enough to nullify or invalidate the collective identity that now mobilized groups previously mobilized by the law. The paramilitary groups were unwilling to comply with legal restrictions, and the State was apparently unwilling to genuinely enforce the law.[8]

## Mobilization and Expansion

León Valencia compared the self-defense groups prior to 1994 to local "paramilitary gangs." During the mid-1990s, Carlos Castaño led the groups through "a time of unification and configuration as a national political and military force . . . a time when the character of the self-defense units transformed from eminently defensive to an organization with grand offensive potential" (Valencia 2002:1). What Valencia recognized here is that as local "gangs," the self-defense units did not have ambitions of grandeur or expansion; they were doggedly committed to protecting what was theirs from the guerrillas.

Even prior to their legal alienation with the repeal of Law 48, the Castaño brothers envisioned a broader campaign of actually gaining ground against the guerrillas, rather than simply preventing further loss. Los Tangüeros was an early indication of their commitment to expanding the cause. After Fidel and Carlos Castaño helped defeat drug kingpin Pablo Escobar, they returned to their ranch and focused on building paramilitary support. They had already won the loyalty and support of their "natural" allies, the landowners and ranchers who had stayed all these years and tolerated the guerrillas, or who were now moving back and counting on the likes of the Castaño brothers to protect them. But there were still many more campesinos in rural Colombia than landowners, and it was people from among this much larger population who had supplied the guerrillas with recruits and safe haven for decades. The vast tracts of land that Fidel had amassed, reportedly twenty-five thousand acres, became a key part of winning the support of the poor. "He began parceling out property to peasants in an effort to build a bridge between the region's small economic elite, who supported the fledging paramilitary groups, and the far larger pool of rural poor, many of whom supported the guerrillas" (Wilson 2003:2).

Substantial resources had already been mobilized, thanks to military and landowning allies. But Fidel was right in identifying the need for support from *los pobres*, particularly if self-defense groups were to have any significant influence beyond their individual private properties. The Castaño brothers demonstrated particular skill in combining a few different strategies to maximize mobilization. First, they responded to the desperate poverty faced by so many Colombians and redistributed some of the resources from their elite supporters to the poor who joined their forces. Second, the fear of guerrillas ran rampant, particularly in rural areas where civilians were much more vulnerable to the violence. Thus the PMGs offered a sense of personal security, winning the loyalty of those they protected.

Fidel Castaño is believed to have been killed, allegedly by the Ejército Popular de Liberación (EPL) in 1994.[9] After his death, Carlos continued the efforts by establishing the Autodefensas Campesinas de Córdoba y Urabá (ACCU), or the Self-Defense Peasants of Córdoba y Urabá. Castaño made clear in several interviews that his intent was to accomplish what the military had failed to do — wage a definitive and conclusive war against the guerrillas (see Valencia 2002:4).

As Castaño's ACCU organization expanded, he began reaching out to other regional paramilitary leaders to discuss the idea of a coalition or federation, one that would respect the autonomy of the groups but strengthen their antisubversive capabilities. According to Castaño's memoirs, the organizational effort took about two years, from 1995 to 1997, and was assisted by Báez and Salvatore Mancuso among others. By 1997, the inter-paramilitary organization the Autodefensas Unidas de Colombia (AUC), United Self-Defense Forces of Colombia, took form and included four regional member organizations (in addition to the ACCU, these were Las Autodefensas de Puerto Boyacá, Las Autodefensas de Ramón Isaza, and Las Autodefensas de los Llanos Orientales); it was modeled after the organizational structure of the ACCU and headed by Castaño (Gómez 2004; Valencia 2002:3). Estimates are that when the AUC first organized, they numbered around only three thousand armed members. Nonetheless, some involved felt that the consolidation in and of itself had effectively secured inevitable paramilitary success against the subversives. "When the self-defense groups converted to a national force with one direction, in my mind, this is when they won the war against the guerrilla" (Gomez 2004:2).

After the AUC consolidated, it expanded from a coalition of four regional groups into a powerful organization of 8,000–10,000 troops (Valencia 2002:4). The paramilitary part of the AUC eventually was organized by region into seven "*bloques*," known officially as the Bloques Norte, Central Bolívar, Centauros, Calima, Pacifico, Sur del Cesar, and Élmer Cárdenas. The seven were formally known as by their "autodefensas" titles, which perhaps gave more recognition of their autonomy, and at times they are still referred to by these probably more familiar names. The *bloques* were accompanied by a complementary political organization. In their founding documents, the AUC defined itself as a "National Movement" dedicated to countersubversive efforts against the guerrillas. Though the scope of the AUC began small, the organization did eventually meet the objective of being national. Tracking reported attacks attributed to the AUC (by the PMGs themselves or investigators) suggests that by 2004 or 2005, they maintained some presence in nearly every department. In addition, the organization itself became very sophisticated in its internal structure. The PMG began holding annual national conferences in 1997, established bylaws and later a constitution, and published an array of papers and communiqués on various political issues, all of which were made available on the group's Web page. The PMG had a tight hierarchical organization despite the regionally "autonomous" units and evolved into a sophisticated political machine.

As mobilization and recruitment efforts continued to succeed under a centralized command structure, the AUC became the unquestionable nucleus of paramilitary activity in Colombia. The hierarchical structure of the paramilitary network provided the strength and organization necessary to efficiently and effectively take advantage of their impunity. Though there was division, infighting (particularly over narcotics, as noted earlier), and some degree of autonomy exercised by regional leaders, the AUC enveloped most if not all of Colombia's individual paramilitary groups within its federation, with the more criminal and less political groups remaining outside the massive PMG structure.

Castaño's rise to the status of senior "strongman" of the organization was quickly solidified. Though the AUC was a "federation" that was to respect the autonomy of its organizations, its leader showed no mercy when members fell out of step with AUC protocol. Camile Morantes headed the self-defense group in Santander. Though he signed with the AUC, his brigade continued to use some of the tactics prohibited by the AUC; he was killed by Castaño and replaced (Gómez 2004:2). Hernán Gómez explained the commitment of many of the AUC leaders to a strong, centralized union of paramilitaries, rather than regionalized, autonomous groups, saying it was "for the same reason that Moses prohibited the worship of gods other than Yahweh. . . . The monotheistic religions were designed so that they could manage everyone with one God, it's easier" (Gómez 2004:1; translation mine). Following the Morantes assassination, there could be little doubt that Castaño and his loyalists were serious about the "one leader" structure of the AUC.

As head of the AUC, Castaño "described himself as the 'fighting arm of the middle class'" (HRW 2001a:3), specifically framing the organization as "anyman's" security force. Indeed, recruitment was facilitated in part by the economic hard times faced by many Colombians and by the continuing threat of guerrilla violence. Economic challenges in rural areas of Colombia run the gamut; many rural civilians live in extremely harsh conditions, with 68.9 percent below the poverty line in 2001 (UNHCHR 2002:26–27). The PMGs used this environment, offering not only jobs but also opportunities for people to earn money while avoiding the cartels and the guerrillas. Particularly after Castaño organized the ACCU and then the AUC, paramilitary soldiers were better compensated than those working in legal positions. Members of the AUC received arms and uniforms and were reportedly paid between $300 and $400 per month in 2001 (Reid 2001b:2). Military soldiers who "spent their vacations moonlighting as paramilitaries to obtain extra cash" reportedly were paid $500 per month (HRW 2001c:38). Comparable positions in the military during the same year paid only $200 a month (Reid 2001a:4). According to a former bookkeeper for the AUC, "fighters in rural areas got a minimum of US$275 per month, which included money for food. In urban areas, they got US$350 per month, increased if they were promoted" (HRW 2001c:23).

Expanding their network of support among individuals with more "official" capabilities, the PMGs similarly doled out financial resources and provided other sorts of privileges to members of the military serving in their areas, to local police officials, and to civilians. One Human Rights Watch informant, a former employee of the AUC accounting office in Putumayo, described several such transactions.

She explained that the requests for cash were constant. "Dario [the local AUC 'financial chief'] once told me that he was exhausted, completely sick of all of these people from the army and police who thought he was the milkman (*lechero*), if it wasn't asking for their U.S. $100, $150, then it would be for airline tickets. I never learned the name of this one officer, but I know he belonged to the police, and he was asking for U.S. $20,000 so that he could buy some real estate in Bogotá." (HRW 2001c:16, 23)

The AUC also exploited the fear of Colombians in their efforts to mobilize support. For instance, when a woman relocated to a paramilitary zone, members of the PMG visited, welcomed her, and told her she was now safe. The welcoming committee "gave her the cellular telephone number of the local AUC commander to use in case of emergency, much like a police hot line. 'They guarantee that they will react within fifteen minutes if she reports unusual activity,' her son-in-law told Human Rights Watch" (HRW 2001c:14). In using such tactics, the PMGs accomplished several things. First, they presented themselves as "the good guys" to newcomers and established popular support, while simultaneously portraying the guerrillas as the dangerous enemy. Second, they undermined local police, because in introducing themselves as essentially "first responders," they simultaneously painted the police as "bad guys" at worst, and useless at best. Third, the paramilitary created a sort of informal network, should people like the woman in the account use the cell phone number and report anything suspicious. Finally, the PMGs had an advantage they could easily exploit to boost their numbers: They were armed and operated free of legal constraint. Forced conscription became an effective means of recruiting even the unwilling.

The Constitution and Discipline Code of the AUC, agreed upon by federation members in 1988, specifies membership and recruiting standards. Among the prerequisites, members had to "certify that they [were] at least eighteen years of age; enjoy a past history and family of honest and hardworking people; be a resident in the same region [of the bloque into which] they wish to be inducted; [and] may not conduct themselves in an antisocial or undesirable manner before the public" (AUC 1998:6; translation mine). Individuals with a wide range of backgrounds agreed to join the paramilitaries. Some were young adults, just out of school, who faced a future without many options; if they wished to earn money and contribute to the family's living expenses, the paramilitaries paid well. Others were former members of the military, some had achieved a high rank and left or were dismissed, and others retired and joined the PMGs. In one interview, Castaño reported having more than 1,000 former Colombian soldiers and at least 135 former officials from the military (Reid 2001b:2).

The AUC also counted former guerrilla fighters among its ranks (Wilson 2001a; AUC 1999:1). According to Castaño, at one point the AUC forces boasted more than 800 defected guerrillas. Castaño and other paramilitary leaders touted the number of former guerrillas among their ranks, indicating that the AUC welcomed former FARC or ELN combatants, probably in the hope it would lend credibility to their cause. For instance, a 1999 document noted, "guerrilla fronts . . . joined the *autodefensas* abandoning the guerrillas and . . . combat subversion" (AUC 1999:1). Nonetheless, there was an obvious vulnerability in welcoming the enemy to their ranks. The AUC rules included a specific regulation for former guerrillas who wished to change sides: They were required to provide evidence "to prove their social reincorporation and acknowledge the error of their previous conduct" (AUC 1998:6).

# COLOMBIA'S PARAMILITARY TRIAD

As Colombia's paramilitaries became more organized and centralized, their objectives were made increasingly clear to the Colombian people. Initially, the PMGs communicated their interests and demands primarily through their attacks. In 2000, the AUC member organization the Calima Front began a major para offensive through Valle and Cauca departments. In a formal letter announcing their plans, the AUC warned "local mayors and ... the governor" that "any citizen or civil authority who gives any type of assistance to subversives after our arrival in the department of Cauca will be declared a military target" (HRW 2001c:43). Castaño was pressed on this conceptualization of a "subversive" in a 2001 interview:

> Collaborators are defined in three categories: In group one you have the collaborator for obligation, the one who gives food or shelter to the guerrillas. They were an objective the first three years of the conflict, because we were entering the war and because if it hadn't been that way we would not have survived. Then there is the collaborator out of convenience. We tell them to leave the territory until someone is in complete control. If he does not leave, he becomes a military objective. And last is the subversive in civilian clothing. He is always an objective. (Wilson 2001b:1)

Beyond the circles of guerrillas and their support network and sympathizers, Colombian paramilitaries used threats and attacks to discourage and frustrate attempts at organizing even unarmed civil society groups whose agendas ran counter to the paramilitary agenda. As early as 1988, international organizations were reporting that among the primary targets of paramilitary violence were "trade unionists, civic movements, and supporters of legal opposition movements" (AI 1989:1). As it turned out, this list would fall far short of covering all of the would-be targets of the AUC. As has been noted, members of the UP were particularly and heav-

99

ily targeted. In addition, unions, indigenous rights leaders, human rights and NGO workers, journalists who spoke out against the PMGs, teachers, government officials, and people within the justice system who followed through in investigating PMG crimes were frequent and regular targets of the paramilitaries.

According to data from the International Labor Organization (ILO), "300 trade union members" were murdered between 1995 and 1998, allegedly by paramilitary agents (USDOS 2000:46). Attacks against labor organizers continued as the PMGs became more sophisticated and organized. In 2000 alone, 112 union activists were assassinated (UNHCHR 2001c:¶175). A subsequent report issued by the ILO declared that "there has been 'an increase in the number of murdered trade union officials and members.'" Barranquilla was home to the "regional branch of the National Association of Hospital Workers of Colombia (ANTHOC)," before paramilitaries drove many of the members out of town and threatened so many others that the union eventually disbanded altogether (UNHCHR 2002:56, ¶290–91).

Journalists were also heavily victimized, despite the AUC's need for friendly news outlets. For instance, Hernando Rangel Moreno was killed in 1999. "He occasionally had written reports critical of the paramilitary groups for the El Plato, Magdalena local newspaper" (USDOS 2000:33). In May 2000, a reporter from the Colombian newspaper *El Espectador* was kidnapped by a paramilitary group and "beaten, tortured, and raped by four men who accused her of being a guerrilla sympathizer." She was eventually freed, with the warning that additional journalists would be targeted, apparently a message to her coworkers (HRW 2001a:5). The following May, a car bomb went off in Bogotá "outside the offices of the weekly newspaper *Voz* and the Unión Patriotica headquarters. . . . [The] AUC claimed responsibility" (UNHCHR 2002:33).

Like journalists, those who spoke out against paramilitaries became targets. The community of La Granja, Ituango, in Antioquia department came under attack in 1996, apparently the repercussion of outspoken opposition to the close proximity of a paramilitary group. People in the area had reported PMG activity to officials in the past, and at least two individuals who had "repeatedly denounced" the PMG had been specifically threatened. In what the Inter-American Commission on Human Rights described as a "pre-announced incursion," one of those individuals, a priest, escaped, while the other, an attorney, was killed. The attack lasted five hours, during which the paramilitary group went to specific homes or establishments in search of specific individuals, who when found were executed. Bodies of those killed in the attack were further mutilated and decimated with chainsaws, and the remnants were thrown into the river (IACHR 2000a:1–4).

Witnesses reported that "before leaving the district of La Granja, the armed men . . . threatened the local residents, saying: 'Guerrilla sons of bitches, this town and Santa Rita are ours, we'll be back.'" The survivors who later gave official statements about the attack had to leave the country due to death threats. After the witnesses fled, the prosecutors were threatened and also had to relocate. One prosecutor who worked in the regional antiparamilitary unit and had functioned as the "prosecutor Delegate," was assassinated on 3 April 2000, nearly four years after the attack (IACHR 2000a:1–5). Paramilitary "follow-up" like this was not uncommon. Attacks that were investigated and pursued by the justice system extended as the paramilitaries then pursued witnesses, investigators, prosecutors, and even judges.

Human rights advocates were also frequently threatened, harassed, and attacked (UNHCHR 2002:22). In 1999, paramilitaries announced that rights workers would thereafter be treated as legitimate targets in their war against subversion. The announcement was preempted by the abduction of four of Colombia's better-known activists. Castaño publicly acknowledged responsibility for the attack in a letter, identifying the four who had been abducted as "three parasubversives and a guerrilla." In this initial letter and one that followed, Castaño claimed that human rights activists were "'façades' for the guerrillas" and that they were therefore marked as "military objectives" of his paramilitary troops. Eleven days after the abductions, two men announced that as members of the AUC they were specifically declaring the Peace Brigade International and Popular Women's Organization, two human rights groups, as official "military objectives" (Lobe 1990:2).

Paramilitaries likewise attacked "peace communities." Civilians weary of constantly running or watching their friends, families, and neighbors being victimized organized to protect themselves from the violence by declaring their communities zones of neutrality. In some cases, peace communities were established by groups that had been displaced and resettled in a new area; others were the result of grassroots efforts by noncombatants to declare their communities off-limits to all armed groups. The "28 communities forming San José de Apartadó in the Urabá region of Antioquía decided, in April of 1997, to publicly sign a declaration demanding respect for their neutrality and an end to war" (IACHR 1999aVI:12). The community was subsequently attacked on multiple occasions by paramilitary groups, at times reportedly with support from the military's 17th Brigade. ("Paz y Justicia" 2001:2; IACHR 1999aVI:12). In June 2001, the peace community at Nueva Esperanza (New Hope) "was burned to the ground by a group of paramilitaries" (UNHCHR 2002:59; USDOS 2002a:6). The following month, the peace community at La Union was raided by paramilitaries, who "killed one resident and drove out hundreds of others." According to one report, military officials did "not accept the declaration of neutrality, because they consider[ed] it a declaration of alliance with the armed dissident groups" (IACHR 1999aVI:12).

Given this broad range of targets, it is probably not surprising that in 2001 the Colombian government "calculate[d] the AUC now kills more civilians than the main guerrilla army it was founded to combat" (Wilson 2001a:2). And despite PMG rhetoric proclaiming its dual-dedication to the war against guerrillas and to protection of the middle class, "attacking the civilian population [was] the main strategy employed by the paramilitary groups" (UNHCHR 2002:32). Nonetheless, Castaño denied that the AUC attacked noncombatants and rebuffed horrific accounts of AUC attacks given by survivors. He did, however, explain that many times subversives "disguise themselves as *campesinos*" or hide among noncombatants (Collado 2001:3). Insinuating that such guerrilla tactics may fool some, he asserted that the AUC was not duped by the false front.

That the paramilitaries were not interested in filling a "power vacuum" or taking over the State, as some theorists propose, was made clear in the statements of their leadership as well as in their targets and behavior. At the First National Conference of the AUC in 1997, paramilitary leaders outlined the organization's preliminary Constitution. According to Article 3, the organization was "a political-military movement, a countersubversive armed force that has a legitimate right to defend itself, to reclaim the state, but not to replace [the state]" (AUC 1997:1; translation mine). Regardless of how strong the paramilitaries became, how well armed they were, or their level of sophistication, regardless of how weak the State was, and regardless of the AUC dissatisfaction with the government, the paramilitaries did not make any effort to overthrow the State.

## The Triad in Colombia

Like the PMGs in Chiapas, the AUC and its subunits relied on certain types of support from certain sectors of the population. The political supporters in Chiapas were PRI loyalists and militants. The two-party system made for a different environment in Colombia, but both systems are based on an exclusivity that benefits the elite. In Colombia, political support for paramilitaries emanated from those who felt most threatened by the guerrillas and the reform compromises, and it was these politicos who served as advocates of and sometimes leaders within the paramilitary network. Financial support in Colombia came from the same sources as in Chiapas: ranchers and landholders. Added to this group in Colombia, however, were the narco-traffickers, who shared with ranchers and landholders not only access to wealth but also a need to protect their assets from guerrillas and political reform. Finally, access to arms was facilitated in Colombia much as in Chiapas; local police agents, members of the military, and other security personnel provided weapons and sometimes worked directly with the PMGs in Colombia.

### Political Ties

Political support for Colombia's paramilitaries came first in the way of the laws of 1965 and 1968, which even the AUC credits for facilitating the organization and arming of civilians against the guerrillas ("Historia de la Autodefensa" 2003:2). Very much like the Guardias Blancas in Chiapas, Law 48 overtly gave State permission to civilians to do exactly as the early *autodefensas* did: arm themselves and repel the guerrillas from their own properties and communities. And, like in Chiapas, the early "civil patrols" were local and perhaps intended to be defensive in nature, but over time they evolved to enjoy more autonomy and have a broader agenda. The fact that the laws stayed on the books for so long and had to be "phased out" over time is indicative of the degree to which such organizations were viewed as acceptable (and perhaps even helpful) among some legislators, government officials, and their constituents.

Political support came largely from the likes of Pablo Guarín, who reportedly defended the "self-defense" cause and made use of their antisubversive rhetoric even on the floor of the National Congress. In the course of a Congressional debate during the mid-1980s, a member of the UP demanded that the disappearances of members of a guerrilla group be investigated. Guarín accused the member of being "a guerrilla dressed in civilian clothes, enjoying the benefits that the Colombian democracy offers" ("Historia de la Autodefensa" 2003:3; translation mine).

In 2002, Colombia's interior minister Armando Estrada acknowledged that the paramilitaries continued to benefit from political support. "Some [members of the Congress] have reached an accord with the paramilitaries. . . . There are some who are definitely candidates of theirs, and others who are simply more predisposed toward legislation that could be helpful toward them" (Forero 2002c). In the spring of 2005, in the middle of a demobilization process that began in 2002, Salvatore Mancuso asserted that at least one-third of the country's Congress members were "friends" of the AUC (Rivas 2005b). Indeed, in October 2005 the Colombian daily *El Tiempo* revealed that operatives within the country's intelligence agency (DAS) had been planning "the creation of a special intelligence unit for the AUC, which would be funded by the paramilitaries and operate on their behalf" ("Colombia: Don Berna" 2005). Apparently the scheme involved the sale of intelligence information to either still mobilized or reconstituted paramilitary groups ("Week's Top Story" 2005).

Paramilitary political influence was even stronger at local levels of government in regions where the PMGs had a strong presence. In Córdoba, for example, one report concluded that in 2001 "the AUC control[led] the local government. The surveys show[ed] that between 10 [percent] and 15 [percent] of the population approve[d] of Castaño and the AUC," compared to only 3 percent support for the guerillas (Reid 2001b:2).

The use of intimidation and force characteristic of paramilitaries accounted for some of the official political representation at the local level; as has been noted, PMG candidates were successful in some cases because opposition candidates retreated after PMG threats. But this does not mitigate the fact that the PMGs ran candidates and established, through whatever means, a notable level of political influence. In 2001, Castaño gave two televised interviews in which "he cast himself as a protector not of the large landowning class that has helped finance the paramilitary forces, but rather of middle-class workers fearful of kidnappings." After the networks aired the programs, "38 [percent] of those questioned said their image of Mr. Castaño had improved. Seventy-two [percent] said the paramilitary forces should take part in the peace talks" (Forero 2000).

"'Castaño is the only Colombian who has the nerve to attack the guerillas, and that makes him the good guy,' said Luis Jaime Córdoba, a Bogotá teacher" (Forero 2000). A Colombian civilian I spoke with, a young woman, expressed the same sentiment. When asked about the paramilitaries, she responded,

You know what is so sad about that situation? It is so sad, because the people who are wealthy, and the people who work, and the people who have jobs and homes, they organized those [groups] so they would feel safe. Because the guerrillas, they do crazy things. And they kidnap and they take your money, and they do crazy things. And the people just got sick of it. They just got sick of it. And so they created these groups to protect what they have from the guerrillas.[§]

The all-but-total exemption from the law enjoyed by the paramilitaries was also indicative of the stature PMGs attained within the country's political arena. Beginning in the early 1990s, PMGs exercised and demonstrated this strength by kidnapping and/or assassinating guerrillas and noncombatant rural civilians, in massacres that left whole villages decimated, in harassment and threats against human rights and humanitarian aid workers, and in the kidnapping or assassination of journalists, politicians, candidates, and civil society leaders. And despite the thousands of Colombians who were victimized by the paramilitaries, the State's ability to counteract the PMGs was even more pathetic than its failure in dealing with the guerrillas. In 2001, for instance, the State captured 1,623 guerrillas, compared to only 992 paramilitaries, and killed 979 guerrillas as opposed to only 116 paramilitaries (USDOS 2002a:11, 22).

This is not to suggest that the State was working as one cohesive unit in permitting paramilitary activity. In 2000, Human Rights Watch reported that the "Human Rights Unit of the attorney general's office was among the most effective government institutions combating paramilitaries" (HRW 2000a:2). It is unfortunate that this "effectiveness" was in part due to the unit's acknowledgement that there were government officials whose interests were best protected by their own ineffectiveness, and its willingness to work around these other, less-than-effective government agencies. For instance, in 1998, when the Cuerpo Técnico de Investigación (CTI), a human rights unit under the attorney general, arrested a "powerful ally" of Carlos Castaño, Víctor Carranza, the CTI purposefully did not inform local security forces that they were planning the arrest, "for fear they would alert Carranza" (USDOS 2002a). Such tactics allowed the agency to make considerable progress amid a sea of failure. In 2002, the Human Rights Unit "arrested 57 members of the state security forces . . . and filed charges against 25 for a variety of crimes, including murder, torture, kidnapping, and collaboration with paramilitary groups" (USDOS 2003:3).

Its relatively successful campaign against the paramilitaries also made the CTI one of the few government agencies consistently targeted by the paramilitaries. No fewer than nine of their investigators were abducted by the PMGs in 2001 alone (USDOS 2002a:16). Individuals working within the CTI were repeatedly threatened, some to the point of fleeing for their lives. Some of the threats were reportedly "made by military officers being investigated for paramilitary ties." Other CTI investigators were found murdered (HRW 2000a:2).

### Financial Support

In stark contrast to the guerrillas in Colombia, the AUC established a fairly successful financial machine. Expenditures are among the most available evidence of the fund-raising efforts and subsequent AUC expenses. Foot soldiers in the AUC were uniformed, armed, and well paid (relatively speaking) (Reid 2001b:2). Such expenditures contributed to recruitment and retention efforts. In addition to these, the organization incurred expenditures for pay-offs made to members of the State military and security forces and "compensation" payments given to families of murder victims who were mistakenly killed by paramilitary troops. In one such instance, a family was given US$700 after their son had been mistakenly killed by an AUC unit operating in Puerto Asís. The boy had been killed for allegedly stealing a motorbike; once the father convincingly explained that the bike had been borrowed, the local PMG commander compensated the family (HRW 2001c:21–22).

Like compensation payments, payoffs to local officials were at times initiated by paramilitaries not as "hush money" but as a proactive means of obtaining support, and perhaps for securing a debt of loyalty. Gilberto López was working for the local office of the Colombian National Police in Putumayo when the AUC's local military commander offered him "a monthly salary." López testified that the offer was made "without anything required from me and that [they suggested] I should take it as a kind of collaboration and that it was a good sum of money" (HRW 2001c:20). The local *personero* for the Puerto Asís community reported a similar offer made to him by the local paramilitary. This particular *personero* had been in his post for some time and had been collecting and documenting complaints regarding paramilitary activity and human rights violations. He had followed through on notifying police officials, but to no avail. He was eventually offered a "stipend" by the local PMG trying to secure his cooperation, which he refused (HRW 2001c:34).[1]

Such tactics are corroborated by an AUC bookkeeper, who kept records for a monthly budget of approximately $650,000 for the Putumayo paramilitary forces. Among the regular expenses she recorded were monthly payments to local officials, including army majors (US$2,500 a month), captains (US$2,000–3,000 a month), and lieutenants (US$1,500 a month). Some of this money was apparently payment for supplies, according to the bookkeeper, who testified that thousands of dollars were paid to a major of the 24th Army Brigade for "military uniforms" (HRW 2001c:21–23). Other payments were for services rendered, since the paramilitaries used their connections within security forces for intelligence.[2] The AUC members were always notified prior to a military or police action, so they could clear out of the targeted zone before officials moved in. The book-keeper reported that her boss, the financial chief of the AUC in Putumayo, "always knew in advance about military raids, so he could make arrangements so that nothing was found. The paramilitaries had radios and cellular phones, and were in close communication with police agents and their military contacts" (HRW 2001c:15).

In 2001, members of the army's Fifth Brigade stormed a paramilitary stronghold at San Blas, in Middle Magdalena. This hideout had reportedly been used even by Castaño himself, who had allowed journalists to interview him there. In the interviews, published in *Vanguardia Liberal*, Castaño assured reporters that he was in no danger of being apprehended, as he had "clear advance warning" of military raids. This claim appeared to be the case in the 2001 raid, when "not a single paramilitary was arrested" (HRW 2001c:52).

In terms of income, data suggests that sources of AUC financing ranged from local landholders and ranchers who supported the paramilitary activities with donations, to taxes collected from locals living under PMG "governance," to income from illicit activities like narco-trafficking. The percentage of AUC income garnered from voluntary donations versus illegal activities is impossible to confirm; estimates of the breakdown of PMG income vary broadly across sources. Nonetheless, there does appear to be consensus regarding the various sources of PMG funding in general.

A former scout for the Third Brigade in the department of Valle told investigators about the early fund-raising efforts of the military and paramilitary organizers who established the National Front, reporting that the "rich people in the area" were called together for a meeting and to "contribute money to bring paramilitaries into the region" (HRW 2001c:37–38). The U.S. State Department concurred that "legitimate businesses finance[d] the right wing groups," citing evidence collected in intelligence raids and the "seizure of financial documents" by the CTI and Colombian army (USDOS 2002a:22). Another report found financial support for the paras supplied by "ranchers, who [in 2001] reported 25,000 head of cattle stolen and 1,000 slaughtered as a result of refusing guerrilla extortion demands" (Wilson 2002c:2). Thus, there is evidence to support Castaño's claims that at least some portion of AUC income was in fact from ranchers, upper-middle-class entrepreneurs, and business owners.

Despite the evidence suggesting that Colombia's paramilitary groups were funded at least in part by legitimate businesses and wealthy individuals, this "legitimate" financial backing may not be a valid measure of *support* for paramilitary activity. There is inconsistent evidence regarding just how voluntary these "donations" from the legitimate businesses were. In 2002, the UNHCHR reported that the AUC was using death threats to strong-arm payments from civilians within their territories, writing that "in San Carlos (Antioquia), shopkeepers must go to the paramilitary camp in El Jordán each month to pay their 'taxes'" (UNHCHR 2002:32). And reportedly "taxes" *were* paid by businesses and landowners in AUC territories, regardless of what was grown or produced. However, Castaño pointed out in 2001 that the government has created an environment in which voluntary donations must be concealed as involuntary.

> Some 80 per cent of our income comes from contributions. But we had to change our methods. Now we are extortionists because we have to be. We send our contributors a note with the amount of money that they have to give us, because if they do it voluntarily they are put in jail [by the government]. (Wilson 2001b:3.3)

The legal conundrum faced by any would-be voluntary contributor does in fact make it difficult to discern the facts regarding the nature of such contributions.

In an interview in 2000, Castaño acknowledged that his self-defense unit also benefited from funding provided by "the money from coca growers," but he adamantly denied any involvement in the actual production or trafficking of narcotics. "The self-defense forces don't produce drugs, or protect laboratories, or export drugs" (Pratt 2000:6). In 2001, Castaño detailed further, reporting that his organization had garnered about $2 million annually via taxes collected from people in the industry (he estimated this at 20 percent of the AUC's income); he again maintained that neither he nor his organization was directly involved in trafficking (Wilson 2001a:3, 5).

The same Putumayo bookkeeper who relayed the expenditure information also reported that "most of the income" she recorded came from the drug industry, corroborating AUC claims that they benefited monetarily from cocaine production. "Wholesalers paid paramilitaries a fee for every kilo of raw cocaine bought in villages that they controlled. Laboratories where raw cocaine was crystallized also paid a fee. For example, a small laboratory would pay the paramilitaries at least U.S. $3,500 a month" (HRW 2001c:23–24). Castaño reported in 2001 that the organization made approximately $2 million per year from narco-traffickers (Wilson 2001b:3.4).

Despite the consistent claims by AUC leadership to the contrary, the evidence of direct involvement by factions of the PMG in the drug trade were too obvious even for Castaño to continue to deny. In the 2001 raid at San Blas, the array of paraphernalia left behind indicated to investigators that the base had been quickly abandoned: "AK-47 rifles, munitions, and communications equipment. Soldiers also reportedly found five cocaine laboratories, sixteen kilos of raw cocaine, and 22,000 gallons of the chemicals used to crystallize it into export-grade powder" (HRW 2001c:52). Assuming the Fifth Brigade's inventory was accurately reported, this evidence suggests that the AUC was in fact financing itself not only via taxes collected on growers, but also in the processing and distribution of export-grade illicit narcotics.

Some argue that the vast majority of AUC monies came from the narcotics industry, while others reported that the percentage is actually much smaller. In a 2001 interview with the *Washington Post*, Castaño reported that his organization received "80 percent of its funding by collecting contributions from wealthy landowners and businessmen seeking protection from [guerrilla] attacks in zones that the AUC controls or operates in. The other 20 percent comes from the 'taxes' on the drug producers" (Wilson 2001a:5, 2001b:3). Quite contrary to this, however, was a report posted on the AUC Web page in which the author asserts that Castaño himself "has admitted that 70 [percent] of [AUC] resources are provided by illicit drugs" (Valencia 2002:4; Forero 2004:3; Rivas 2004). In actuality, the degree to which the narcotics industry supported paramilitary groups has probably fluctuated over the years, as the top leadership has been very inconsistent in its stance on PMG trafficking.

A 2002 breakdown in the AUC, though temporary, resulted from the deep divide over narcotics involvement, indicating the extent to which drugs were financing some regional AUC efforts. While chief regional leader Aldofo Paz refused to give up his drug connections (and in April 2004 was still described as "closely linked to the cocaine trade" (Forero

2004:1), others stubbornly refused to give in to the drug money and consequently began using other methods of fund-raising. The leader of the former AUC Metro Bloque, which later operated autonomously in Antioquia, began selling black-market gasoline to boost income (Wilson 2003:3). In fact, the U.S. Department of State found that black-market sales of stolen gasoline became "a multi-million dollar criminal enterprise dominated by paramilitaries" (USDOS 2003:7).[3] Police later uncovered a "huge money-laundering network" operated by Ernesto Baez's Bloque Central Bolívar. According to police, "20 businessmen and cattle ranchers were involved in the network" ("Colombia: AUC probes" 2005).

The financial strength enjoyed by the AUC was evident in its expenditures, but its economic vulnerability was equally evident in the controversy surrounding narcotics and diversification efforts. The fact that breakaway but well-established regional paramilitary groups resorted to selling black-market gasoline suggests that the private funders (ranchers, entrepreneurs, and so on) were not sufficient to support PMG efforts. Paramilitaries are products of an intersection of interests, and their financial roots and well-being are no exception. The earliest PMGs in Colombia were established by a mix of involvement with the drug trade and by private upper-middle-class financiers, and despite some efforts to avoid entanglements in the narcotics trade, PMG growth and expansion was funded largely the same way.

### Military Support

In a 2001 interview, Castaño asserted that "the truth is that there is no such thing as paramilitarism. The crime of anti-subversion has not been codified, thus if subversion is a crime, anti-subversion must be a right" (Wilson 2001b). His assertion reflects a sense of justification and legitimacy among PMGs as "brothers-in-arms" of sorts with the official military. Certainly this perspective was among the less tangible of benefits the network of connections PMGs enjoyed within the State security forces provided.

Connections between the official and unofficial armed units benefited the latter in a myriad of ways, both direct and indirect. The most direct support, aside from outright forming a PMG, took the shape of collaboration by providing arms and supplies, assistance in attacks, and/or intelligence and names prior to an attack; erecting roadblocks during an attack, preventing witnesses or medical assistance to get through; and/or taking possession of corpses after an attack. Less direct (but no less important) military assistance included ignoring pleas for help or prior warnings of an upcoming attack, and failing to carry out arrests or to actively pursue and capture suspected paramilitary members; finally, some assistance came in the form of indirect protection, where paramilitaries were permitted to carry out activities at will within startlingly close proximity to significant security force presence. The fact that the army or police were so close obliged the State to protect the safety of said citizens. Nonetheless, the State chose a deployment strategy that left many brigades and bases relatively disconnected from superiors and other units, the assumption being that even without any formal evaluation or accountability, the officers posted would carry out their duties. Instead, the autonomy gave such units a tremendous amount of control within the regions they serve. If they chose to "overlook" paramilitary activity, they could provide a great deal of protection for the PMG against any indictment by the State.

The role of certain military units in establishing PMGs is undisputed. Government reports concluded that "active duty and reserve officers attached to the army's Third Brigade in Cali . . . set up and actively supported the Calima Front" (HRW 2001a:1; HRW 2000b). Indeed, there is evidence from multiple informants that "former officers . . . assumed positions of command" within the Calima Front (HRW 2000b:7; HRW 2001a). An informant for Human Rights Watch who used to work for the Third Brigade reported that he himself witnessed direct cooperation between the Calima Front and the army and that they "coordinated constantly with paramilitaries in the field, using cellular phones and radios" (HRW 2001c:38). According to one account, the Third Brigade organized the Calima Front following the ELN abduction of 140 people from a local church, many of whom were connected to the Cali cartel. The group was allegedly formed to carry out retribution against the guerrillas (HRW 2000b:6–7). When they organized, a member of the Calima Front "told local journalists that [they] had come 'because many people have asked us to be in this area, since they are tired of the attacks by the guerrillas'" (HRW 2001c:38).

After mounting evidence and international condemnations, Colonel Rafael Hani, who commanded the battalion of the Third Brigade most closely identified with the creation of the Calima Front, was arrested under orders of the attorney general's office. "Prosecutors told Human Rights Watch that they have strong evidence showing that Hani set up paramilitary groups, supplied them with vehicles and supplies, and coordinated actions with them. They characterized the evidence as 'extremely strong, and involving direct support for and participation in paramilitary crimes.'

Hani's support for paramilitaries, investigators told Human Rights Watch, 'was flagrant'" (HRW 2001c:50).

In Antioquia, a "private justice group" was allegedly formed by or with the assistance of "Second Lieutenant José Vicente Castro (commander of the police sub-station in Ituango) and Lieutenant Jorge Alexander Sánchez Castro (commander of the military base in the area)." Both were charged with the crime of forming illegal armed groups. The Fifth Brigade, stationed in Librija, Santander, allegedly established "Las Colonias" "without government authorization." Members of this group had been known affiliates of a paramilitary operating in Middle Magdalena (HRW 1999c:5). Elements within the Colombian navy were also involved in the "form[ation], promot[ion], [leadership], and financ[ing of] paramilitary groups in order to carry out dozens of extra-judicial executions," according to the country's Internal Affairs office. Naval Intelligence Network No. 7, in particular, was involved in "dozens of extrajudicial executions in and around the city of Barrancabermeja, Santander" from 1991 and 1993. Eight members of the network were actually tried within the military system for "plan[ning], order[ing,] and pa[ying for] hit men and paramilitaries to carry out these killings." None were found guilty (HRW 1999c:3).

Members of the military were also integral in providing weapons to the paramilitaries. In 1999, the U.S. Department of State reported that "paramilitary forces [found] a ready support base within the military and police," who "provid[ed] them with ammunition" (USDOS 2000:2). The same agency reported that in 2002, army Major Orlando Alberto Martinez was arrested for "his alleged role in trafficking thousands of AK-47 assault rifles from Bulgaria to the AUC. On May 30, Martinez was dismissed from the armed forces based on the discretionary powers of Presidential Decree 1790 of 2000" (USDOS 2003:23). According to United Nations Human Rights Commission findings, the military also provided paramilitary groups with military-issue uniforms and vehicles (HRW 2001c:41).

In some instances, members of the military collaborated with paramilitaries and carried out joint offensives. This was not uncommon in Putumayo, where the army's 24th Brigade frequently worked with local paramilitary troops in fighting guerrillas. One informant reported that while working for the paramilitaries, she was told that "their commanders had been transported in an army helicopter," and that though the military claimed that the army had killed a guerrilla in the attack, it had actually been members of the paramilitary that had killed the guerrilla (HRW 2001c:24).

Military brigades were also helpful to paramilitary efforts by cordoning off the area of an attack, blocking roadways to prevent passage of witnesses or assistance to the victims, or by allowing paramilitary troops safe passage through roadblocks en route to an attack. In one instance, witnesses reported that "a military helicopter hovered" above a paramilitary attack on a peace community where six individuals were murdered; in other cases, local security forces were reportedly in a position to prevent or intervene in an attack but did not act (USDOS 2002a:6–9; HRW 2001a, 2001b). In 1999, a paramilitary offensive against a small community in Valle was possible only after "two paramilitary trucks filled with armed fighters passed right through an army roadblock" (HRW 2001c:38).[4]

During a 2001 ACCU attack on El Salado, Bolívar department, three hundred paramilitary soldiers spent a full two days "tortur[ing], garrot[ing], [and] stabb[ing]" residents, while they reportedly "drank and danced and cheered." Some victims were decapitated, some were shot. There was at least one incident of gang rape, and a six-year-old girl was "tied to a pole and suffocated with a plastic bag." Meanwhile, the navy's First Brigade "maintained roadblocks around El Salado that prevented the International Committee of the Red Cross (ICRC) and others from entering. Thirty minutes after the paramilitaries had withdrawn safely with looted goods and animals, navy troops entered the village" (HRW 2001a:2).

In the case of a massacre in Chengue, local leaders and police took several steps to prevent the massacre, and to get help to the scene as the massacre was taking place. "Months [before the attack], local authorities warned military, police and government officials that a paramilitary planned to carry out a massacre." A government investigator confirmed that government and security personnel had in fact been forewarned, yet they took no action to protect the community or prevent the attack. Furthermore, local police gave "timely information . . . on [paramilitary] vehicles, whereabouts and direction" on the day of the attack, and they still received no assistance (HRW 2001c:9–10). "According to credible accounts," members of the military "provided safe passage to the paramilitary column and effectively sealed off the area while the killing took place" (HRW 2001b:1; Wilson 2001a:7). The attack involved an estimated fifty paramilitary soldiers, who took the lives of twenty-six people.

Elkin Antonio Valdiris Tirado was a member of the PMG that attacked the village and was subsequently arrested by Colombian officials. In the course of questioning, Valdiris "implicated two active duty marine sergeants; one [of whom] was charged and was awaiting trial . . . while the other was detained pending formal charges" in late 2001 (USDOS 2002a:5). The weapons used in the Chengue attack were allegedly provided by a navy soldier, Rubén Darío Rojas, who has been charged with the crime. Brigadier General Rodrigo Quiñones faced a disciplinary hearing after being charged with inaction, in effect allowing the massacre. Both were members of the First Naval Brigade (HRW 2001c:9–10).

In other cases, the military apparently used a different technique, pulling out of established checkpoints just in time for a paramilitary attack and returning to their posts following the attack. In 1996, the military and state security forces had established checkpoints "at the entrances and exits of the highways leading to" Ituango, Antioquia department. These regular checkpoints were "suspended, with no explanation, from June 9 to 11, and resumed only after the massacre" at La Granja, where four victims were killed. The "checkpoints were crossed freely and in the full light of day by 20 men who were visibly armed with F15 rifles" (IACHR 2000a:3, 7). Similarly, in 2001 the massacre of thirteen individuals took place in San Carlos, Antioquia department. Investigation into the massacre by the Colombian Commission of Jurists (CCJ) "charged that police and military troops withdrew from the area of the attack three days prior to the massacre and permitted a truck carrying 15 paramilitary hostages to pass unchallenged through a military roadblock" (USDOS 2003:4).

"Legalization" was another form of cooperation, and another means of protecting the impunity of the PMGs. Legalization involved paramilitaries targeting "those suspected of supporting guerrillas, then deliver[ing] the corpses to the army. . . . The army then [would] claim the dead as guerrillas killed in combat while the paramilitaries receiv[ed] their pay in arms" (HRW 2000a:1). In other cases, the military would engage in allegedly legitimate battle and later report casualties. Later, witnesses reported that certain of the alleged casualties were not killed in the legitimate military battle, as reported by officials, but in off-site events. For instance, "between 26 August and 6 September, in the settlement of Santa Ana, municipality of Granada (Antioquia), as men from the army's Fourth Brigade were engaged in a military operation, several people were killed in incidents that took place, according to those making the reports, away from the fighting" (UNHCHR 2002:21).

Perhaps among the most frequently reported forms of cooperation given by military factions to paramilitary activity was simple inaction and denial. Innumerable witnesses testified after an attack that they had called specific officials for help, or that the military had been informed of explicit threats of an impending attack by a PMG against a specific community, and despite this the attack was successfully carried out unimpeded. In the case of La Granja, Ituango, noted earlier for the military's abandonment of posts just prior to and during the paramilitary attack, one witness who gave just such testimony was later assassinated (HRW 2001c:12). Barrancabermeja, a city which has suffered immense violence, is home to human rights workers with the Regional Committee for the Defense of Human Rights, Comité Regional para la Defensa de los Derechos Humanos (CREDHOS), who told Human Rights Watch in 2001 that they "spen[d] most of their time using portable telephones, receiving detailed information about paramilitary movements and relaying that information immediately to the authorities. 'We pass information constantly,' Francisco Campos said, 'but the violence has not stopped'" (HRW 2001c:57).

A United Nations report found that the State was indeed culpable for human rights violations committed by paramilitaries in its "failure in its duty to provide a guarantee" of protection. The fact that the UN also found that this "failure has been systematic" is not surprising, given that the military and security forces' failure to act on information of a planned paramilitary action has been documented by a variety of international agencies to have occurred repeatedly over the course of years, apparently without due sanction against the offending officers (UNHCHR 2002:18–19; HRW 2000a:2; HRW 2001c).

> In the case of Puerto Alvin, Meta, local officials and the office of the Public Advocate (Defensoria del Pueblo) warned authorities over a dozen times of an imminent attack. Nevertheless, paramilitaries seized the town unhampered on May 4 and reportedly killed at least twenty-one people, including store owners and a five-year-old child. (HRW 1999c:2)

> "When guerrillas attack, the Army responds in less than two hours," said one Cauca *personero* from the region, who asked that his name and town not be used. "But despite killings every three or four days, there was never a response by the Army against the paramilitaries. I can't think of a single clash between them." (HRW 2001c:43)

The fact that paramilitary activity was concentrated in the same areas as military personnel, and that despite this fact the PMGs operated without challenge, is perhaps the most startling evidence of military complicity. Barrancabermeja is one region where this was particularly blatant. A journalist who had been in the city "with a humanitarian mission" noted the presence of multiple AUC checkpoints, even despite the militarization of the area. In one case, the journalist "recognized a Colombian Army soldier wearing an AUC armband" (HRW 2001c:52).

Like in Chiapas, PMGs were frequently located within close proximity to military bases. In 2001, Human Rights Watch concluded that "authorities also received reliable and detailed information about the location of permanent paramilitary bases, often within walking distance of military sites, yet failed to act against them" (HRW 2001a:2). The "Hacienda Villa Sandra" was known to the residents of Puerto Asís, who referred to the paramilitaries as "Power Rangers," as the local paramilitary headquarters. There had been repeated raids on the hacienda, though it was always completely abandoned by the time the military arrived on scene. Nonetheless, corpses of victims from paramilitary kidnappings were found buried on the property, providing evidence that corroborated multiple eyewitness testimonies to the AUC presence. The hacienda was five hundred meters from the 25th Battalion army base, part of the 24th Brigade (HRW 2001c:18–19, 29). Officials from the Colombian Office of Internal Affairs reported in an investigation that another residence used by the paramilitary was "'perfectly' visible" from the army base, "and was less than 500 feet from" the base entrance. In the same report, the investigators "noted that armed and uniformed AUC members were playing pool in full view" (HRW 2001c:29).

The complicity of the military was acknowledged as a major obstacle by other government agencies, including the CTI. Agents sent to conduct investigations or arrests were often hampered by military officers who tipped off the paramilitaries and gave them plenty of time to relocate temporarily. One government agent confessed to Human Rights Watch that "there is little we can do if the military is protecting [the paramilitaries]," noting that the CTI was "not authorized to heavily arm [the investigators] to carry out dangerous operations so [they] must rely on the CNP or military" (HRW 2001c:33). A raid carried out by the Human Rights Unit in Putumayo in 2000 netted one paramilitary fighter, who went by the war name "El Russo." Informants reported that the only reason El Russo "was caught [was] because he failed to understand the hand signals made by the police guarding the Puerto Asís airport entrance. 'Some of the police were sitting in the El Paisa restaurant in front of the airport, and they were trying to signal him to get lost, there was danger, [but] . . . he didn't understand.'" (HRW 2001c:32).

Much of the witness testimony regarding military and paramilitary collaboration was corroborated by Castaño and the State itself. The increasingly frequent warrants and arrests of State security forces for collaboration with paramilitaries, many of which are discussed in the conclusion below, indicated that the State did in fact have knowledge and documented evidence of the connections discussed here. In fact, former Colombian defense minister Luis Fernando Ramirez once acknowledged that "you fire [military members involved with the PMGs], and immediately they are contacted by the paramilitaries" (Wilson 2001a:3), suggesting that eliminating paramilitary collaborators from the military was really a double-edged sword. Castaño corroborated Ramirez's account, reporting in a 2001 interview that of the thirty members of the military who had been retired the previous year for PMG collaboration, twenty-five simply joined the AUC. He also reported there were "some 35 officers, more than 100 lower rank officers, and at least 1,000 professional soldiers or policemen" within the ranks of the AUC (Wilson 2001b:1).

Why would high-ranking military officials willingly delegate or give up the institution's monopoly over the legitimate use of violence? And particularly to a growing, well-organized and efficient body? Times of change make for strange bedfellows. A common enemy can go a long way toward melding new allies and toward redefining what might otherwise be a competitive relationship into a cooperative one. One reporter suggested that "the connection between the two anti-guerrilla forces is a logical outcome of the war" (Dudley 2001). The military was created and defined as the protector of the people, the warrior against the guerrillas. Despite the fact that the past two presidential administrations have moved toward negotiation with guerrillas and ending abuses by the armed forces, defeating the guerrilla is still the primary military objective. And, as a former peace envoy of the Colombian government noted, "For our military, the enemy of my enemy is my friend" (Dudley 2001).

Officials put it slightly differently, emphasizing the fact that the PMGs did not threaten the State, the subversives did. The UNHCHR reported in 2001: "This Office has been witness to statements by high-ranking Army Officers that paramilitary groups do not threaten constitutional security and consequently, it is not the Army's responsibility to combat them" (UNHCHR 2001a:4). In other words, at least sections of the military shared the logic of Castaño: The paramilitaries were simply brothers-in-arms, able to carry out those missions that the military itself could not.

The relationship between the PMGs and the Colombian military was not static over the course of paramilitary emergence and evolution. In many cases, members or entire brigades of the armed forces were integral in the formation of small, regional paramilitary units. But particularly in the later 1990s and into the turn of the century, there was some strain between the military and some paramilitaries as the government tried to crack down on what was, after the repeal of Law 48, illegal cooperation with unauthorized armed groups. This is not to say that all military/paramilitary cooperation ceased—far from it. Though domestic and international pressures demanded that the Colombian government shut down the PMGs, Castaño asserted that the military still were "are like brothers. . . . Our enemy is the guerrillas and that has not changed" (Wilson 2001a:3).

## Transformation to Legitimacy?

It is clear that, like the paramilitaries in Chiapas, the AUC was driven by a political agenda, one that it shared with a triad of supporters. Early hints of the group's political roots were evident in documents from the second meeting of the AUC (1998), where the group outlined its "ideological platform." The subsection on political objectives planned the "construction of a political project, of national scope and dimension," comprising political and military structures that could evolve and serve as a legal and democratic political movement in the postconflict era (AUC 1998:3; translation mine). Among the priorities listed were the protection of private property, specific political development strategies, and an outline of democratic principles (AUC 1998). In a document written the following year, "Origen, Evolución y Proyección de las Autodefensas Unidas de Colombia," the AUC demanded that the State open a national debate on specific issues, including

> political and democratic reform, a model of economic development, agrarian reform; urban reform; politics of energy and hydrocarbons; decentralization and territorial order; sustainable development and environment; judicial reform; the armed forces, the State, and society and rights; narco-trafficking, the conflict and [our] international relationships; and international human rights. (AUC 1999:3–4; translation mine)

The environment within which the paramilitaries were making such demands shifted dramatically in the late 1990s during the administration of Andres Pastrana. In 1997, the administration began committing resources to fighting the PMGs, organizing "a specialized search unit" specifically tasked with taking PMG leaders into custody. Pastrana also created the office of the Human Rights Ombudsman to work alongside the CTI under the attorney general's office. Both became rather unique state agencies in their persistence and success in pursuing the paramilitaries (IACHR 1997a:9–10). In 1999, in a speech before the National Peace Council and in subsequent speeches and statements, Pastrana was blunt and harsh in his reproach of the PMGs: "I have been clear in affirming that they—the paramilitaries—do not possess a naturally political character. The only viable option for these groups is to immediately cease their operations and dismantle their military structures" (Valencia 2002:5).

Pastrana's reversal of the State's previous policy of ignoring or abetting the PMGs was essentially announced with a single word. When Pastrana used the word "paramilitary," he communicated a clear message: these groups are illegal, are illegitimate, and do not have the support of the State. "Self-defense group," the self-appointed characterization of the country's PMGs, implies a defensive posture against victimization, a legitimate last-resort effort. The use of *autodefensas* represented the AUC assertion that they "did not initiate the armed conflict . . . but had to become involved in order to defend what is essential: life, dignity, and liberty" (Mancuso 2002:2; translation mine). "Paramilitary" implies a belligerent effort that is illegitimate and illegal. In using the term, Pastrana proclaimed their illegitimacy. The president later reiterated the illegality of non-state armed groups, saying "I want to reaffirm that the defense of the State and the exercise of force is incumbent only upon the legitimate authorities. . . . The criminal action of groups known as the '*autodefensas*' can not be tolerated through action nor through nonaction by any government agent" (Valencia 2002:5; translation mine).

Pastrana was simultaneously intensely pursuing peace negotiations with the FARC and ELN. The administration laid out a plan for negotiation known as the Common Agenda, based on the assertion that the guerrilla motives were rooted in very real social and economic inequalities that had to be addressed. Invitations to discuss the issues of contention were extended to the guerrilla leadership but were flatly denied to the AUC. In 2001, Castaño was asked about his thoughts on the new governmental "Anti-Paramilitary Commission," and he offered an interesting assessment: "I think the honest Colombians ought to be attentive as the government combats all of the organizations on the margin of the law. Unfortunately this includes the *autodefensas*, which, while legitimate, are not legal" (Utria 2001:3; translation mine).

Trying to bring more centralized leadership to their political strategies,

Carlos Castaño stepped down from serving as the director (military and otherwise) of the AUC in May 2001 to found and manage the political arm of the group. Named the "National and Democratic Movement," the organization was intended to run candidates for office and politically pursue the goals of the PMGS (USDOS 2002a:22, 30). The AUC eventually chose a presidential candidate to endorse, one who reportedly had paramilitary sympathies and perhaps personal connections. As former governor of Antioquia (1995–97), Alvaro Uribe Vélez "created groups of *campesino* security forces, then known as 'CONVIVIR' [Servicios de Vigilancia y Seguridad Privada (Special Vigilance and Private Security Services)] . . . who were accused of 'being connected to the [local] paramilitaries'" ("Redacción Judicial" 2002). There had also been rumors during his administration regarding his personal links to PMGS, including reports of Uribe's failure to respond to pleas for help from those under threat of paramilitary attack. The PMGS in Antioquia were incredibly powerful during his term as governor and had cooperated closely with local military units. While president, Pastrana had dismissed two of the local generals (Rito Alejo del Rio and Pernando Millan) for violations committed under their command, and he was criticized by Uribe for having done so (Forero 2002a:2).

Uribe ran for president on a right-wing, hard-liner, countersubversive platform as a member of a new independent party he called "Colombia First." His promise to take a heavy-handed approach against the guerrillas appealed to many Colombians, including the AUC (Forero 2002a). "We appreciate the emphasis that Pres. Uribe has put to make known before the UN, and the governments of the US, Spain, and France, his policy of re-establishing the authority of the state" (Mancuso 2002:1). Uribe won the election, and he immediately began implementing his plan to stop the guerrillas.

Despite the failures of Law 48, CONVIVIR licenses, and previous states of emergency, President Uribe undertook similar hard-liner policies. On 12 August 2002, Uribe announced that he was declaring a "State of Internal Commotion" ("Colombia Authorizes" 2002; "Colombia Steps Up" 2002; Forero 2002a, 2002b). Implemented after the FARC announced an offensive against mayors and governors throughout the country (Gutiérrez 2002), the decree was described as less severe than a state of emergency. Instead of giving the government broad powers to restrict civilian rights and movement, this step granted security forces slightly expanded authorities. Detainees could be held for twenty-four hours without official charges or being brought before a prosecutor, search warrants were no longer requisite for police searches of homes and business, and phone conversations could be more easily monitored.

Uribe also announced a new tax on the wealthy, 1.2 percent on all assets over $60,000, to fund the expansion of the military and police forces. Despite the economic challenges facing those affected, the measure had popular support (Gutiérrez 2002; "Crecerá" 2002; Forero 2002e; "Colombia Declares" 2002). Uribe found additional funding for his agenda by currying the favor of U.S. president George W. Bush. Previously, military aid from the United States had been limited to antinarcotics efforts; President Bush lifted these restrictions in 2002, allowing Uribe to use the support in other aspects of the conflict (Forero 2002d).

The tax revenues and newly unrestricted resources were used by Uribe to expand the State's security apparatus in a plan eerily reminiscent of Law 48. Uribe called for the addition of a "new network of 100,000 civilian 'police auxiliaries'" and a "million-strong network of civilian informers" ("Colombia Declares" 2002; "Se creará" 2002). In essence, the government began recruiting and arming rural civilians as makeshift soldiers. Referred to by U.S. print news as "civilian informants" and by Colombian papers as "*soldados campesinos*" (rural soldiers), the informants would serve as reinforcements in the counterinsurgency campaign ("Reclutarán" 2002; "Gobierno" 2002; "Colombia Authorizes" 2002; "Colombia Steps Up" 2002). Guerrillas dubbed it a "network of snitches" (Wilson 2002c:1).

These groups of civilians were recruited, organized, and armed by various brigades within the military. They had military-style uniforms and military-issue weapons. Members of the civilian patrols were paid by the State and permitted to serve within their home communities and carry their weapons at all times. "Control Agents," civilians who were in charge of collecting "intelligence" from civilian informants and then reporting to the authorities, were reportedly told they would be receiving $75 a week (Forero 2002f). Those who were recruited for "undercover" positions in intelligence gathering were not provided with weapons and were paid per piece of valuable information (Wilson 2002c:1). The new troops were to provide security for the poorer Colombian communities where regular security forces were in short supply, and they were to use their weapons only in response to a guerrilla attack or in self-defense ("Redacción Judicial" 2002; "Reclutarán" 2002). When asked about the new civilian patrols, one interviewee replied plainly, "well they remind me of the 1960s legislation — especially with them carrying arms."[§]

In completing his reversal of Pastrana's approach to the conflict, President Uribe then agreed to negotiations with the paramilitary groups. Despite the deep divisions over narco-trafficking, which had caused a rift within the AUC in 2002, Castaño managed to hold the group together and begin negotiations. Castaño "urged the U.S. to suspend the extradition orders [against many PMG principals for narco-trafficking] and give the leaders a chance to prove they can behave like regular citizens" ("Colombian Government, Rebels" 2003). Despite continued worries about extradition, the AUC leaders and the government agreed to the Peaceful Disbanding Agreement in November 2003, which provided for the immediate cease-fire between the government and the AUC, and a commitment by PMG leaders to completely demobilize their forces before 1 January 2006 ("1200 Colombian" 2005). The demobilization began on 23 November ("Undemobilized" 2005), and the two sides began hammering out the legal ramifications for the AUC leadership, particularly extradition, once demobilization was complete. As the negotiations continued, division within the AUC leadership deepened.

The government rejected AUC demands for a guarantee that leaders would not face prison time nor be extradited to the United States. The PMG leadership began to factionalize, making the talks increasingly difficult. Castaño "broke his silence and said in an anguished tone of voice that he predicted a bad future for the talks if some way to disentangle them was not quickly reached." The Peace Commissioner agreed to try to "seek alternatives," but the AUC remained divided ("Colombian Peace Commissioner" 2005). Carlos Castaño was particularly having problems with other high-level leaders, including his brother Vicente, who were unwilling to make a clean split with the drug industry ("Colombia: Vicente" 2005; "Colombia Not Pursuing" 2005). Over the next two weeks, Castaño was persuaded by his colleagues to resign his position as a member of the AUC negotiation team, a move allegedly forced by Ernesto Báez ("Undemobilized" 2005). The Peace Commissioner received a letter of resignation, allegedly from Carlos Castaño, on 31 March. The AUC also restricted Castaño's access to the AUC Web page, preventing him from writing his editorials or making public his stance on the negotiations. In an e-mail to the Peace Commissioner dated 12 April 2004, Castaño "expressed his willingness to demobilize immediately and submit to court proceedings as established by Colombia's government and laws" ("Colombian Peace Commissioner" 2005). Four days later was the last confirmable time Carlos Castaño was seen alive.

Rumors abounded over Castaño's disappearance, with allegations that he was in hiding in the United States, perhaps in a witness protection program, or that he had been killed by one of the PMG leaders over drug trafficking, or that he had simply gone underground. In 2006, the Colombian government insisted that they had DNA evidence confirming that recovered human remains were those of Carlos Castaño and alleged that he was murdered by his brother, Vicente Castaño (Romero 2006). In the years between his disappearance and the alleged discovery of his remains, the AUC nonetheless continued to proclaim its political intentions . . . and prowess. Ivan Roberto Duque (a.k.a. Ernesto Baez) took over as political director of the AUC in Carlos Castaño's absence and announced in 2005 that the demobilization process, by then two years underway, did not mean the termination of the AUC but its "transform[ation]." "We have permanently penetrated the political process, building power structures at [the] local and regional level. . . . This will not cease with the peace process. [The AUC] will transform itself into a democratic movement offering the voters an alternative." ("Colombia: AUC Probes" 2005). There were also reports that former AUC commanders expressed interest in running for Congress themselves (Forero 2005c).

The peace negotiations continued under the leadership of Vicente Castaño, assisted by Báez and Mancuso. Demands for guaranteed protections from jail and extradition continued. Later, Castaño added the demand that all demobilized PMG leaders be protected from any trial before the International Criminal Court (Colombia is a signatory to the court, and human rights groups had been calling on the court to act against the paramilitary leaders for crimes against humanity) ("Colombia: Paramilitary Chief" 2005; Vieira 2005a). He also emphasized the importance of legal changes that would allow President Uribe to run for a second term, as "many of the paramilitaries would only agree to demobilize if [Uribe] was still in charge after the 2006 election" ("Colombia: Paramilitary Chief" 2005). The rules were successfully changed, and Uribe secured the right to run for reelection.

In June 2005, the new "Justice and Peace Law" was passed by the legislature, securing many more of the AUC demands. Those paramilitary members who were not accused of crimes against humanity would be pardoned and reintegrated into civilian life.[5] Those few who were accused of crimes against humanity (an estimated two hundred individuals), would be given certain legal guarantees and mitigated sentences in return for their cooperation. The law included two key provisions that in principle met the demands of the PMG leadership. First, "all charges brought against para-militaries [would] be dealt with collectivity, rather than on a case-by-case basis." This meant that all crimes related to narco-trafficking or crimes against humanity would be treated as part of the paramilitary involvement, not as separate crimes. Second, membership within a paramilitary group was defined explicitly as a "political crime." Under Colombia's "1997 ex-tradition laws, political criminals cannot be extradited" ("Paramilitaries Gamble" 2005).

In order to be eligible for these provisions, applicants were required to provide a full and voluntary account of their illegal activities; prosecutors were given sixty days to investigate the veracity of the confessions.[6] They would then be found guilty of their crimes, but the punishment would be reduced to a sentence of five to eight years. It was also within the court's power to sentence those convicted to serve their time on a farm rather than in a prison. Those who were found not to provide a full account in their confession could see their sentence increased by 20 percent, "provided the omission [was] not intentional." Those omissions found to be intentional would vacate the applicant's eligibility under the Justice and Peace Law, and they would be subject to the normal sentencing guidelines. The law also required that former paramilitaries turn over their "illegally acquired goods," which would then be used for reparations to victims ("Between Peace" 2005; "Shameful" 2005; Forero 2005b).

Most criticism of the law focused on the lack of any structured follow-up on those who claimed to demobilize. For instance, there was no confir-mation process to force paramilitary leaders to "disclose the location of their hidden bank accounts and drug processing labs, or reveal the names of their arms suppliers and financial backers" (Vivanco and McFarland 2005). Colombia's delegate for Human Rights to the United Nations ex-pressed deep concerns with the lack of "truth" likely to be volunteered.[7] In addition, members were not required to "reveal the inner workings of their organizations . . . essentially permit[ting] the underlying structure . . . to remain" (Forero 2005a, 2005c). Human Rights Watch called the law a "get out of jail free card" (Forero 2005c). A member of the Colombian legisla-ture forecasted such consequences when the bill was passed, saying, "this is a law that brings no justice, no peace. It should be called what it really is, a law of impunity and immunity" ("Forero" 2005a).

The government insisted that demobilized paramilitary members would not be permitted to retain any illegally gotten wealth ("Colombia: Demobilization" 2005) and massacres, kidnappings, and homicides were dramatically reduced (Vieira 2005b). Despite this, reports indicated that "demobilized" paramilitaries were in fact reconstituting under a new guise. Paramilitaries murdered at least two thousand people between the time of the cease-fire and 2005. There were also reports the same year that the paramilitaries were still collecting "taxes" from landowners in their territory ("Colombia: AUC Calls" 2005). In October 2005, reports were that a "significant number of the ten thousand who ha[d] disarmed so far . . . [were] continuing to commit crimes, often alongside their former comrades" ("Colombia: Government" 2005).

Despite the criticisms, the number of demobilized paramilitaries was incredibly high. By February 2006, 22,300 paramilitaries had been demobilized and disarmed ("World News" 2006). The political future of the paramilitaries remained unclear — the Constitutional Court recommended in the fall of 2005 against former paramilitaries being permitted to run as legitimate candidates in the 2006 elections ("Colombia: Paramilitary Demobilization" 2005). Nonetheless, Vicente Castaño claimed that the AUC still enjoyed support from a third of congressional members ("Colombia: AUC Chiefs" 2005), and the Constitutional Court upheld the constitutional reforms allowing President Uribe to run for reelection in 2006 ("Colombia: Court" 2005).

While Colombia's paramilitary groups were considerably larger and far more national in scope than those in Chiapas, the parallels between the conditions of PMG emergence in the two cases are significant. Negotiations with the guerrillas, the legalization of alternative political parties that proved competitive, and additional reforms undertaken collectively threatened to democratize a country whose system had long been defined by both horizontal and vertical exclusivity. These changes caused deep divides within the political and economic elite, some of whom saw the reforms as a means of finally ending a violent insurgency and securing approval on the international stage, others of whom saw them as threatening Colombia's system of wealth and power distribution. As with Chiapas's White Guards, the country had a long history of arming civilians to promote party and State prerogatives, such that a mobilizing structure was already in place when Colombia's hard-liners began to unify and move outside the official confines of the State to continue their own, unofficial "counterinsurgency." Paramilitary emergence shares this same opportunity structure and mobilization networks with Chiapas and Colombia. However, while Colombia has undertaken a demobilization of questionable success, El Salvador's paramilitary groups quite decisively dissolved at the end of the country's civil war. El Salvador thus presents us with a case of important similarities and consequential divergence with which to close the analysis.

# EL SALVADOR

## THE RISE OF
## PARAMILITARIES

Traffic in San Salvador looks like utter pandemonium to an outsider. Red lights appear to have no meaning at all as drivers whip right through them; intersections are a mishmash of speeding, overcrowded cars, loud public buses, pedestrians, bicycles, and mopeds. The taxi driver taking me to the National Assembly building in 2004 did not hesitate or look before darting out into a main intersection of the Boulevard Los Heroes right through a red light, crossing four lanes of traffic. "¿Estoy seguro?" "Am I safe?" I asked, half-jokingly. He assured me that I was. "No one stops for red lights here," I said. "Do you know why?" he asked, smiling. "Because during the civil war, if you sat still at a red light, you got shot. . . . And now, that's just how we drive."

When I arrived at the offices of legislators from the Alianza Republica Nacional (ARENA) party, or the National Republican Alliance, I was greeted by a woman who exuded the preelection fervor that was in the air of the capital city. It was less than two weeks until the Legislative Assembly elections, and she excitedly talked about the ARENA campaigns. She gave me butter cookies imprinted with "ARENA" and wrapped in foil wrappers with the ARENA flag across the front. She gave me a beaded necklace and matching bracelet, also white, red, and blue. She said that she had a videotape I would be interested in seeing; it was about the history of ARENA; she promised I would love it.

The video was a series of clips of Roberto D'Aubuisson, founder of the ARENA political party, making speeches at public rallies and giving interviews during the civil war. D'Aubuisson was a charismatic military intelligence officer who had risen through the ranks, repeatedly proving his loyalty to and leadership skills within right-wing factions. During the middle 1970s, he had achieved the rank of captain within the armed forces and was one of the regional campaign managers for right-wing presidential candidate Colonel Arturo Armando Molina. By the end of the decade, he

127

had been promoted to major and was serving as the assistant chief of Intelligence (Stanley 1996:88).

Showing what some have called his "neofascist" stripes, D'Aubuisson was dogmatic in his determination to eliminate all leftists in El Salvador. By the time he was assistant chief of Intelligence, he had taken a prominent role in organizing the far-right-leaning Frente Amplio Nacional (FAN), the Broad National Front (Dunkerley 1982:145; Stanley 1996:164). The FAN pulled together members of the country's oligarchy, who then could coordinate their "financial and logistical support" for D'Aubuisson's death squads (Stanley 1996:189). Using the FAN in conjunction with allies within the military and the 1979 governing junta, D'Aubuisson served as a political entrepreneur, pulling together all of the elements necessary to coordinate an effective and impervious network of paramilitary troops (known as death squads in El Salvador) capable of taking out the left. He was known to have ties to at least one paramilitary group, the Unión Guerra Blanca (UGB), or the White Warriors Union, and was suspected of organizing others.

D'Aubuisson became a central figure in the war when he used his intelligence files to guide the "death squad" operations that would be responsible for countless assassinations and disappearances during the 1980s. Unabashed in his determination to rid the country of "communists" by whatever means necessary, D'Aubuisson ran for president in 1982 and rallied supporters with his theme song, which promised "El Salvador will be the tomb where the Reds end up" (Dunkerley 1982:203).

The video I was watching in the ARENA offices provided no hint of D'Aubuisson the assassin, but it demonstrated what a gifted public speaker he was. Charismatic and passionate, he was surrounded by throngs of people cheering for him. The woman behind the desk was filing her nails and said, "Isn't he handsome? Isn't he gorgeous? He is the father of our party! He was so smart." Her face was glowing as she watched the tape. I remember a particular a clip of him standing in an esplanade on a makeshift platform. He was smiling broadly yet speaking forcefully, giving an impassioned speech to hundreds, maybe thousands of people shouting their support.

I was finally escorted into the office of an ARENA legislator who had a poster of D'Aubuisson hanging in his office. The poster read "Father of the Party" below the picture of D'Aubuisson, his fist in the air, energy and passion in his face, surrounded by a captivated crowd of supporters. The party slogan *"Dios, Patria, y Libertad"* (God, Country, and Liberty) was printed along the bottom. Such admiration of D'Aubuisson was not unique to the one legislator. He remains an icon, representing the party's roots in the countersubversive militarism of the 1980s. Another high-ranking member of ARENA I interviewed explained proudly that D'Aubuisson was

> such a charismatic leader, and had a lot of support. But he didn't want to be president. He could have been, many people wanted that. But he said the country needed a more *tranquilla* [calm] leader. He was very *dura* [strong] and said the country needed another.§

Acclaimed journalist Tina Rosenberg visited El Salvador during the elections of March 1989, exactly thirteen years before my visit. Her account of her work in San Salvador is eerily reminiscent of my own experiences in the city. Reading the journalist's description of conversations and experiences she had in 1989 felt like déjà vu. Recounting an experience at an ARENA rally in San Salvador in 1989 where D'Aubuisson spoke, Rosenberg writes,

> There were plenty of upper-class teenagers and women in red, white and blue ARENA T-shirts and sun visors. . . . Three blond girls wearing too much perfume called his name. He looked at them, put his hand over his heart, and pretended to throw it to them. They screamed the way girls scream at rock stars. (Rosenberg 1991:264)

At another point, Rosenberg was traveling with the twenty-year-old son of one of the country's wealthier families. He had moved to the United States when guerrilla kidnappings began to increase and had returned to El Salvador for a brief visit. "'I like it here,' Manuel said. 'Life is much more relaxed than in the States.' I asked if he'd noticed a change in four years. 'People have no respect for traffic laws,' he said. 'Every time I come back it's worse'" (Rosenberg 1991:233).

The legacies of the civil war clearly run the gamut — from seemingly innocuous traffic habits to more subtle and perhaps more consequential loyalty to political icons and intolerance and disdain for the political "other." The war has ended in El Salvador, but the schism and hostility between the left and the right in El Salvador seems not to be have been bridged by the war, nor the peace process. There is little trust and less cooperation between groups at opposite ends of the political spectrum, whose agendas remain fairly consistent with what they pursued during the 1980s and for decades before that. Years of repression, conflict, and negotiation have brought little consensus in terms of reconciling their collective past or of mapping out a collective future.

What has changed in El Salvador is that groups now compete to implement their agendas via electoral competitions and political institutions, rather than with weapons. Though my interviewees revealed a limited tolerance for each other, they also revealed a solid commitment to democracy and a general consensus around the idea that "you have to fight communism with democracy, not with repression," as one insisted.§ I asked several individuals from a variety of political and socioeconomic perspectives whether they thought another conflict or heightened political violence was likely, particularly if the Farabundo Martí Front for National Liberation, Frente Farabundo Martí para la Liberación Nacional (FMLN), were to win a presidential election. An academic who has written prolifically on the evolution of democracy and civil society in El Salvador replied "No, No, I don't believe [the right would use force against the left]. Today, over these last twelve years, we have been committed to democracy and using the system. I don't believe there would be violence."§ It seems that despite the hostility and distrust that remain and the economic disparity that has worsened, El Salvadorans have indeed determined to win by "the pen and not the sword."

Thus El Salvador differs from the other cases studied here in that it has successfully transitioned out of a conflict characterized by extreme levels of paramilitary violence. During the 1980s, at least eight PMGs, known in El Salvador as "*escuadrones muertes*," or death squads, operated in tandem with an eighty-thousand-member right-wing organization that supported paramilitary activities and served as the hub of the death squad network. El Salvador's paramilitary phenomenon is rooted in the same confluence of factors as Colombia and Mexico. The PMGs targeted the same types of individuals as Colombia's AUC and the PMGs in Chiapas. They enjoyed the same level of impunity, the same connections with choice military officials, and the same spoils of an upper class that was primarily on their side. How, then, did El Salvador transition from a country suffering extreme paramilitary violence to a functioning (if still consolidating) democracy? What shifted in El Salvador that has not changed for Mexico and may be beginning to shift in Colombia? What is the critical variable that opens — and subsequently closes — the political opportunity structure for paramilitary groups?

The organization, mobilization, and longevity of El Salvador's death squads were in part dependent upon the country's long history of economic disparity and violent repression and exclusivity. Like Chiapas and Colombia, paramilitary groups were one in a long string of violent mechanisms used by the country's wealthy to protect their ability to exploit and suppress their cheap labor force, but one which also depended on the socioeconomic and political structures and collective identities that were established along the way. Transitioning away from the use of PMGs required the successful use of a new mechanism.

## Coffee and Class

In El Salvador, as in the other cases, land is the traditional source of wealth and the foundation of the country's traditional oligarchy. Not long after independence, the oppressed indigenous population began organizing and rebelling against the system of landownership and distribution that prohibited their socioeconomic upward mobility. Despite the hostility between ethnic oppressor (those of Spanish decent) and ethnic oppressed (indigenous groups), the conflict over land became a unifying force among campesinos regardless of ethnicity. Indigenous rights advocates and peasant activists have consequently rallied together around the call for land reform and redistribution of resources several times over the country's history.

Over the later decades of the nineteenth century, political rivals came to agree on matters of interest to El Salvador's oligarchy, a remarkably small group of individuals who controlled the majority of El Salvador's wealth. El Salvadorans today still refer to "Los Catorce," the fourteen families who were the elite of the elite,[1] owning the vast majority of the country's land and wealth, and not without a hint of hostility. In 1931, after the Catorce had at least doubled in size, U.S. military attaché Major A. R. Harris commented that "roughly 90 [percent] of the wealth in the country is held by about one-half of one [percent] of the population. Thirty or forty families own nearly everything in the country" (Skidmore and Smith 1992:333).

During the 1860s and 1870s the oligarchy redistributed traditionally indigenous communal lands to the elite. The "*ejidos*," or communal properties, were made illegal in 1880 (Lauria-Santiago 2004:17) and were sold to those who could afford to buy property. Thus the economic endeavors of the State during the latter half of the nineteenth century were clearly designed to benefit the country's wealthiest. With the State protecting their interests, the elite could focus on what one historian called their "ideological hairsplitting over Liberal and Conservative doctrines" (Cockcroft 1989:128). Competition between the two was often fierce and bred political instability.

It was in the midst of this intraparty conflict that the government created the first nationwide security forces. In 1895 the Rural Police and the Mounted Police were established. Neither fully replaced the private militias most of the wealthy used to protect their haciendas, and some of the private forces were involved with the new official agencies. The Rural Police would later evolve into the National Police, still not entirely replacing the privately armed organizations. Instead, the National Police supplemented the private forces in pursuit of a shared purpose: the prevention of organizing or other activities by the peasantry that threatened the distribution of wealth and influence. Private security troops protected property and kept a watchful eye for troublemakers, while the National Police focused on intelligence gathering and urban centers (Montgomery 1995:30; Dickey 1983:18).

Despite some agreement over protecting elite interests, violent competition between the two primary political forces continued until 1903, when the country implemented a system of appointed succession for the executive office. The new system, of course, did not allow for ideological competition or genuine political turnover. Instead, the presidency was passed from one member to another of a single family between 1912 and 1927. During these years, the percentage of land dedicated to coffee expanded exponentially, and the value of coffee exports tripled between 1915 and 1928. Meanwhile, the coffee elite organized and promoted their interests via La Asociación Cafetalera, an extremely powerful interest group. The growing cooperation between the State and the oligarchy institutionalized the socioeconomic stratification and political distribution of power that had informally been evolving since independence (Anderson 1992:20–21, 25).

The State security forces were further expanded during this era, beginning with the establishment of the National Guard, commonly referred to as "Las Guardias," in 1912. Las Guardias were established with the express intention of replacing the private security forces. "But, in a demonstration of how entrenched the social stratification had become and how important the local forces were perceived to be in protecting that system, [the president] was assassinated by the landowners. Within a few years the National Guard gained the reputation for being the 'most cruel, barbaric security force'" (Montgomery 1995:31–32; Wood 2000:226–27).

The shift in labor force from sharecropper to migrant worker that accompanied the shift to coffee (a crop requiring only seasonal labor) posed a significant challenge to the landowners, as the number of landless and therefore activists increased. Despite the ferocity of the National Guard, the private militias were not disbanded, and they continued to operate under the guise of the landowners in response to continued organizing and demands on the part of the working peasantry, many of whom had begun "squatting" in order to obtain access to land (Montgomery 1995:30; Wood 2000:226). Thus the National Guard was essentially co-opted by the oligarchy to work in close collaboration with their private forces (Cockcroft 1989:127). Despite the repression, the poor continued advocating for their rights and organizing.

In 1917, future president Alfonso Quiñóez Molina established the "Liga Roja," or the Red League. The Red League may be seen as an early and ultimately failed attempt at corporatism. It operated somewhat like the PRI in Mexico; it was nominally pro-labor with "a red flag for its banner [and] vague socialist sentiments for its programs," the idea was to use these appearances to win support of the poor without actually following through in policy. Revolutionary icon Farabundo Martí, who would later lead the 1931 peasant revolt, "denounced the formation of the *Liga Roja* as a petit bourgeois attempt to sidetrack the working class" (Anderson 1992:54). Martí's assessment was not off base. "The government's decision to permit such organizing was probably rooted in a corporatist impulse: they sought to recruit 'auxiliary classes' to supplement their thin political bases, while keeping them from becoming a potential base of opposition" (Stanley 1996:44).

Provided with total impunity from the justice system, the Red League ran its own security force composed mostly of poor laborers at the behest of the ruling oligarchy. The troops were used to strong-arm election turnout to guarantee results, to disrupt political organizing, and to provide intelligence on "subversive" activities (Dunkerley 1982:20; Anderson 1992:40). This early experiment with armed civilian groups proved a successful one overall, and it meshed well with the social hierarchy and preestablished system of order maintenance. The league and its sidearm militia were the start of what became routine in El Salvadoran politics: a two-pronged strategy to maintain the socioeconomic hierarchy. The government, first, made a meager attempt to co-opt or preempt opposition organizing by paying lip service to reform measures and, second, used violent repression to terrorize the more militant into submission.

Thus the security forces were substantially expanded over the first decades of the twentieth century, all without replacing the private security guards. Foundations for the eventual messianic self-image of the military were being laid during this period (see O'Donnell and Schmitter 1986:31), as were, however implicitly, the "national interests" as they would be later defined by that military. By designing a national security structure focused nearly entirely on the protection of the country's elite, the leadership was creating a military that would define any threat to the elite and system of exclusion as a threat to the nation.

The relationship between the security forces and the oligarchy was strong, especially at the local level. The experience of Mario Zapata, a young Salvadoran man, visiting the campo serves as an illustration.

> On vacations, he took to visiting the *fincas* of wealthy friends to find out what he could about social conditions. At [the] house of a friend he found the table richly laid for lunch with beer, chicken and meats. He thought it was for the lunch of the *hacendado* and his family, but then some *guardia* came in and fell to. On asking about this he was told, "They are our salvation, without the *guardia* we could not operate." (Anderson 1992:100)

Like the relationship between the oligarchy and the military, the strength of the socioeconomic hierarchy was also strong and influential at the local level. It was so strong, in fact, that "political life revolved around the making, breaking, and maintaining of patronage alliances." Particularly in terms of election outcomes, the patronage system allowed full control of the process. Until 1950, El Salvadorans cast their votes orally and publicly, one at a time, before an election *directorio*, a board of election officials. Citizens would gather and file by the *directorio* speaking their vote as they passed. The opportunity for fraud is obvious, but interestingly the fraud was not, for the most part, conducted through falsely recording votes but through patrons controlling who voted and who did not. Clients loyal to the patron's network (the patron's patron) were permitted access to the election and were able to cast their vote. As with Colombia's earliest political alliances, the patronage in El Salvador called upon clients to be militant in their loyalty. And "when politics and elections turned violent, which occurred often, patronage demands turned to the human and material resources needed to wage battle" (Ching 2004:55, 56).

Despite the liberal and conservative factionalism and strong regional patronage, poverty served as a powerful coinciding cleavage rooting a collective identity. International organizing around labor issues intensified during the 1920s, and El Salvador's workers and now landless campesinos began cooperating with regional and international groups to organize locally. The first formal labor organizations surfaced in the early 1900s, as did political student organizations and early communist organizations (Anderson 1992:41, 56; Dunkerley 1982:20).

Romero Bosque was appointed to the presidency in 1927 and introduced a period of moderate *aperatura*, an opening in the political system. He addressed some labor concerns, carefully tiptoeing around the coffee sector so as not to upset his base. In 1928 and 1929, he supported labor reforms by "regulating the hours of work in some industries" (excluding the agricultural workers) and implementing a worker compensation program (Anderson 1992:61; Stanley 1996:45; Dunkerley 1982:21). By the spring of 1930, activism was rising. A communist parade in San Salvador boasted eighty thousand participants (Anderson 1992:42). The protests continued over two months, with chants of "We demand work; we have no way to live" (Anderson 1992:46; Dunkerley 1982:22).

The *aperatura* proved limited, however. The labor reforms were perhaps negated by the repression used against organizers, many of whom were imprisoned (Anderson 1992:56). "A 'white terror' reigned as security forces detained protestors and activists. In one case, an estimated 600 were arrested for signing a petition against a Presidential decree that had outlawed 'agitation and workers' rallies'" (Anderson 1992:61; Stanley 1996:45; Dunkerley 1982:22). In October, President Bosque issued a decree that "forbade all demonstrations of peasants' or workers' organizations against stores, individuals, or the authorities" (Anderson 1992:62), and repression increased. By February "about twelve hundred persons were imprisoned for left-wing activists or labor agitation" (Anderson 1992:62; Stanley 1996:45; Montgomery 1995:36).

Despite this, in 1931, President Bosque broke the tradition established in 1903 and held the first free and fair democratic elections in El Salvador. For the first time, the patronage networks were irrelevant, and the elite were not guaranteed an electoral victory, and in fact they did not achieve one.[2] Instead, Arturo Araujo, "a wealthy renegade landowner," was elected thanks to the support of the organized left (Diskin and Sharpe 1986:51; Ching 2004:52). The victory seemed promising as Araujo pledged to make reforms that would expand the political opening and deal with the maldistribution of wealth (though he rejected a socialist or communist discourse). But Araujo underestimated the strength and importance of the coffee elite, who were inevitably threatened by his proposals, and the determination of the military to protect the elite. He also underestimated the breadth of reforms that would be popularly demanded, and the fervor with which the left would demand them. Protests became increasingly frequent. In May a leftist protest drew violent repression by the National Guard and police. A student protest in July seemed threatening enough to some that the National Guard was again called to get control (Anderson 1992:103, 77; Stanley 1996:47).

The oligarchy were already feeling waves of insecurity and uncertainty about the direction of the country when Araujo announced that the coming local elections would be free and fair, open to even Communist Party candidates. Most historical accounts note this decision as the breaking point for the traditional power holders. Only ten months after winning the election, Araujo was overthrown in a military coup. Some witnesses, historians, and Araujo himself believed the coup was led by his vice president and minister of defense (and former competitor in the presidential election), General Maximiliano Hernández Martínez (Anderson 1992:71–88; Stanley 1996:47; Montgomery 1995:35).

### La Matanza

The Bosque and Araujo reforms fell by the wayside as Martínez limited political access to his allies and repressed those who opposed him. Despite the repression, the left refused to be shut out of the political process and continued organizing. Determined to use political routes before resorting to violence, the opposition ran candidates in the municipal elections of January 1932. It would later prove telling that the regime required citizens to register their names and their party of membership in order to vote (Anderson 1992:119). The elections were held as promised, but the government refused to certify results where communist candidates won, or cancelled the election altogether in "western parts of the country where the Communist party was considered strong" (Anderson 1992:120; Dunkerley 1982:26).

Rebel leaders then attempted to negotiate with the administration. Refused by the president, they were permitted to speak only with an administration representative. "The group offered to halt illegal activities and confine the movement to peaceful protest if the government would make substantial contributions to the welfare of the peasants." Legend has it that the official was warned, "The peasants will win with their machetes the rights you are denying them," and he answered, "You have machetes; we have machine guns" (Anderson 1992:123). The revolt was on.

Of course the attempted negotiation tipped off the administration. A series of bungles and misfortunes for the rebels undermined whatever potential the plan had, and the result was utter disaster. Farabundo Martí, leader of the movement, was arrested on 18 January, just days prior to the scheduled uprising. On the 19, one group of rebels began the revolt far earlier than planned and tried to attack the barracks at the First Cavalry. The officers were ready and forced the rebels to retreat. The early start "g[a]ve the government ample cause to proclaim a state of siege," which it did in the western departments thought most likely to rebel, while "martial law was proclaimed for the entire country." The rebellion was conveniently proving the legitimacy and necessity of the military's role as defender of internal order (Anderson 1992:129, 130).

Incredibly, despite Martí's arrest, the early start and the state of siege, the rebels did manage to pull off an uprising and had nearly twenty-four hours in some areas before any counterattack came. Half of the twelve municipalities captured by the rebels remained occupied for four days (Ching 2004:52). The "official" attack began on 22 January 1932. Allegedly Martí's orders had been to kill the wealthy on sight, that hesitation was unacceptable, and to "spare only the children" (Anderson 1992:124–25). Despite the ordered bloodbath, none occurred. The rebellion spread over three days as the leftists, armed primarily with machetes but also with some small arms, moved from town to town. They burned buildings associated with the oppressors (businesses, homes of the wealthy, and the police and National Guard buildings) and looted homes. There were reported cases of rape, and members of the oligarchy and Guardias suffered capture, torture, and murder (Anderson 1992:131–42; Stanley 1996:41), as did some *mayordomos*,[3] or "farm foremen" (Dunkerley 1982:27). At the attack's end, "the rebels [had] killed about 35 civilians and local police. . . . Nine National Guardsmen were killed and 10 wounded, and the regular army lost between 20 and 40 soldiers" (Stanley 1996:41).

The aftermath of the rebellion was far more violent than the uprising itself. Martínez acted swiftly and definitively. The full power of the security apparatus was brought to bear, so much so that "at least 10,000 people [were killed] in less than three weeks" (Ching 2004:54). Though the response may have far exceeded the threat posed by the mostly failed uprising, Martínez was in all likelihood acting on three motivating factors:

first, the coffee oligarchy would not support his continued dictatorship unless he quelled the movement and restored a sense of security; second, the United States would surely intervene if he did not prove that the situation was well in hand; and last, Martínez himself was vehemently opposed to the ideology of the movement and was determined to eradicate it. The military response was decisive (see Anderson 1992:120–68).

In rural towns, campesinos were rounded up by the hundreds and thousands and shot after "trials" in which the characteristics and possessions of the individual in question were ascertained. People who had indigenous features, "dressed in a scruffy *campesino* costume," or carried a machete were immediately presumed guilty (Anderson 1992:170; Cockcroft 1989:123; Stanley 1996:41; Dunkerley 1982:28). Those whose guilt was not as easily determined were lured to their deaths. "Those who had not taken part in the uprising [were asked] . . . to present themselves at the *comandancia* (the military make-shift "court") to receive clearance papers" (Anderson 1992:170; Stanley 1996:42).

> In the plaza [at the Church of Asunción], from the wooden table in front of the military command post, a line of people dressed in white and indigo colors stretched as far as the eye could see. Each peasant stepped up to the table to receive "clearance" papers, thereby proving noninvolvement in the previous day's uprising against the landlords. If the peasant looked like an Indian or carried a machete, as was typically the case, then his thumbs were tied to those of his neighbor. In groups of 50, they were led to the massive stone wall behind the church. Every few minutes a volley of gunfire marked their final "clearance." The river of red [lava flowing from the recently erupted volcano] was soon a bubbling cauldron of human blood. (Cockcroft 1989:122)

Asunción was not unique; the military used similar tactics in rural communities throughout western El Salvador, slaughtering civilians and leaving mass graves or a trail of corpses in their wake. The urban roundup relied on a different tactic. The government had those handy voter registration lists and could easily identify the communists. The result was no less violent. "Every night trucks went full of victims from the *Dirección General de Policía* to the banks of the Rio Acelhuate where the victims were shot out of hand and buried in great ditches without even their names being taken" (Anderson 1992:173).

Victims, news reports, and even military accounts indicate that the police, Guardias, and civic patrols were jointly responsible for the massacres.

The civic patrols, or Guardias Cívicas, were part of Martínez's effort to reinforce the military response to the continuing, though weakened, rebellion. These civilian groups "proved to be the most active and unrestrained forces of the counter-revolution" (Dunkerley 1982:28). The total unpredictability of one's safety turned San Salvador "into a cemetery.... No one went out because of fear" (Anderson 1992:173; Stanley 1996:43). The mass killings became known as "La Matanza," the Massacre, and marked a pivotal moment in the history of El Salvador.

The total number of dead from Martínez's campaign of retribution and elimination is uncertain; estimates range from 8,000 to 10,000 (Anderson 1992:10) to 30,000 (Stanley 1996:2; Cockcroft 1989:123; Montgomery 1995:37). But Martínez's success was not so much in the number of "subversives" killed (Montgomery contends that of the estimated 30,000 killed, "less than 10 [percent] of those had participated in the uprising" [1995:37), as in the vast quiet instilled by the massacre. The left was not only broken up, it was decapitated and dismembered; what remained of civil society organizations disintegrated under the weight of fear that became part of the very political system in El Salvador. That immobilizing fear was prevalent not only among the poor and indigenous, who feared reproach, but also among the elite, who feared another uprising. LeoGrande describes this period as one during which the wealthy were convinced that "revolution could only be effectively met by bloody suppression" (LeoGrande 1998b:35).

Now with the full support of the elite, who viewed Martínez as their deliverer, the president expanded the internal security forces. Using anticommunist rhetoric, he expanded financial investment and instilled an acute sense of prestige in the domestic security forces. Favoring the National Guard and National Police over the army, Martínez expanded the budget and raised the already comparatively high salaries of the security forces, without giving equal benefit to the army (Stanley 1996:63; Dunkerley 1982:32–33). Meanwhile, the time-honored means of control continued. Just prior to the Matanza, the military had co-opted citizens to organize private militias to provide support should a rebellion occur, thus further legitimizing the arming of civilians in battle against fellow civilians. The civilian militias remained organized after the Matanza, as did the practice of military unit commanders "renting out soldiers as private security guards" (Stanley 1996:71). In addition, the Treasury Police (or the Policía de Hacienda) were created in 1936 and would later develop a reputation for intelligence gathering and vicious repression (Montgomery

1995:32), so much so that one U.S. diplomat compared the Treasury Police operation to the Nazi SS (Dickey 1983:18).

The president had a strong commitment to funding the security agencies, but perhaps more importantly he infused a sense of hierarchical loyalty, so that praise and promotion was dependent upon allegiance to the regime, rather than competence or professionalism. Martínez went so far as to create his own "secret police" force tasked with spying on military officials for the president (Stanley 1996:63). His emphasis on repression also created an environment in which "maintaining order" meant eliminating political organizations or activists who might pose a threat to the oligarchy's interests or to the military domination within the State. The indoctrination and promotion processes within these agencies produced a collective sense of purpose and duty around the ultimate objective of repressing and excluding the majority of El Salvadorans. By both broadening the types of agency exercising internal force and simultaneously strengthening the power and influence of the official forces, Martínez created a system where the government forces were operating parallel to an unofficial system of security forces, some of whom were armed and trained within the State military system.

Martínez further centralized power and influence around himself through his political party, Pro-Patria. Like the PRI in Mexico, Pro-Patria ("For the Fatherland") was used to co-opt and organize popular support and as the principal mechanism of patronage. The prohibition of all political parties other than Pro-Patria created a one-party system, eliminating all competition in elections and membership recruitment. In 1932, the National Assembly elections resulted in a legislative body populated entirely by Martínez supporters. Pro-Patria succeeded in supplanting not just political organizations, but nearly all overt collectivism within civil society (see Ching 2004:60).

Once Pro-Patria was established, Martínez began using it as a means of State control over local activities. For instance, in order to strengthen the ability of central authorities to prevent or altogether eliminate potential opposition, regional and local committees were required to spy on their neighbors. A 1934 circular informed local party leaders that they were to provide higher-ups with "lists of labor union supporters and communists so that they can be watched and prevented from posing as Martinistas." Foreshadowing what was to come during the 1970s (and resembling Colombian president Uribe's current strategy), local party leaders were further supplemented by an auxiliary "network of civilian informants and collaborators known as *orejas* (ears)." Some were employed specifically to gather information on others, while others were in a more informal position, providing "piecework" intelligence. Nearly every potential element of opposition was under surveillance by 1935 (Ching 2004:61, 69). In instances where graft and party operatives were not enough to ensure loyalty, the Martínez administration called upon the National Guard to "maintain order." Thus Martínez cemented the ties between the State, the oligarchy, and the security forces, so that the interests of the three became essentially a joint enterprise — one that would later give birth to the death squads of the civil war.

Martínez's disregard for the army spawned a failed military coup in 1944. Conspirators were met with heavy reprisal, and many of the leaders were executed. The regime's reaction to the coup seemed extreme to many of the elite, who consequently began to side with the growing anti-Martínez effort. A wide-scale strike crossing a variety of economic sectors eventually brought down the dictatorship. Martínez resigned his post to General Andrés I. Menéndez, who promptly announced that he would hold popular elections (Montgomery 1995:41; Stanley 1996:65). The prospect of a political opening again galvanized opposition organizations that had persisted underground. Members of the left promised a "complete economic and social overhaul" if elected (Stanley 1996:66).

But as had been the case during the previous attempt at free elections, the oligarchy found themselves with no real party organization and therefore no viable candidate. The military, meanwhile, took offense at the prospect of being subjugated to civilians — much less civilians who had opposed military rule under Martínez. The military, like the oligarchy, saw their status and even their role within the larger El Salvadoran political and social structure as dangerously exposed in a truly free and fair election. As O'Donnell and Schmitter so aptly described such situations, Salvadorans with vested interests in the system "refuse[d] to accept the uncertainties of the democratic process and recurrently appeal[ed] to the armed forces for 'solutions,' disguising their personal or group interests behind resounding invocations of the national interest" (O'Donnell and Schmitter 1986:31).

Menéndez never got to oversee the election he promised. In October 1944 he was ousted in a coup led by former police director and "one of the principal architects of the *Matanza*," Colonel Osmín Aguiere y Salinas (Stanley 1996:66; Dunkerley 1982:34; Montgomery 1995:42). Democratic activists were arrested and deported to Guatemala, and workers were threatened and suppressed. Once again, moderate and leftist voices were quieted, newspapers closed, activists rounded up, and elections rigged (Stanley 1996:66–67). The tradition of military rule continued with General Salvador Castañeda Castro, a former Martínez ally and leader of the elite's "aptly-named, highly financed, but remarkably anonymous *Partido Agrario*," who took office in 1945 (Dunkerley 1982:34; Stanley 1996:66–67).

Castañeda worked to establish a level of prestige for the army equal to that of the internal security forces. The general also tried to extend his stay in office beyond the allotted time but was instead ousted by a coup. In a move that would later be referred to as the Revolution of 1948, the coup leaders decided to create a "Revolutionary Governing Council" rather than appoint another president. The council, made up of three military officers and two civilians, was tasked with improving the economy and initiating reforms aimed at stabilizing the country politically (Stanley 1996:67). Dunkerley assesses this period as less revolutionary than establishmentarian, arguing that the only real change was the construction of a new facade that gave a democratic-looking face to the dictatorship. "This was certainly no full *aperatura* (opening) but rather a realignment of the forms of political control with a reduction in the reliance upon pure repression and an incorporation of democratic motifs within the dictatorial framework. The 'revolution' of 14 December 1948 . . . was, therefore, a belated readjustment and modernization of the *martinato*" (Dunkerley 1982:35).

The 1948 governing council paved a new path in El Salvadoran history, one that would ultimately be critical to the initial organization of death squads. The move away from a central political authority and toward a more committee-style rule was intended to implement pointedly moderate reforms that would at least give the appearance of compromise, in hopes of quelling some of the popular agitation. This move initiated what would become a forty-year tug-of-war between politicos who saw this strategy as one that would alleviate the stress on the system while also preserving the essence of the socioeconomic hierarchy, and more hard-liner leaders who saw this as the first step on a slippery slope leading to the devolution of the economic order. Twenty-five years hence, the factionalization that developed between the two points of view would prove to be one of the most important elements in the political opportunity structure of the PMGs.

In 1949, a revived official party organized, calling itself the Partido Revolucionario de Unificación Democrática (PRUD), or the Revolutionary Party of Democratic Unification. Rooted in the old Martínez "Pro-Patria," the party was intended to promote the official candidate and therefore successor to the incumbent, as well to incorporate the masses in a regulated way that allowed enough efficacy to minimize temptations to revolt (Stanley 1996:74; Dunkerley 1982:35). Despite the attempt at corporatism, the government continued also to rely on the right of repression protected by the Ley de Defensa del Orden Democrático y Constitucional, or the Defense of Democratic and Constitutional Order Law, which Dunkerley argues was used in the "suppression of all democratic guarantees" (Dunkerley 1982:36).

The PRUD and its advocates were never successful in creating a popular base of support; instead it operated primarily as a tool of self-regeneration, reaching out to the masses only during the preelection period to "get out the vote" (Stanley 1996:74; Wood 2000:230). Consequently, a large portion of the population continued to be disconnected from the political arena, keeping the system in a perpetual state of instability. State efforts to control civil society via government-sponsored organizations and institutions failed not only in terms of labor organizing, but also in terms of party organizing. Despite the State's continued proclivity for the use of force, students and other leftists continued to organize and formed the Partido Revolucionario de Abril y Mayo (PRAM), the Revolutionary Party of April and May. The PRAM and more moderate reform elements were soon cooperating under the auspices of the Frente Nacional de Orientación Civica (FNOC), or National Civic Orientation Front, uniting leftist organizations in the early 1960s and supporting candidates in local elections (Dunkerley 1982:42).

As elsewhere in the Western Hemisphere, the Cuban revolution spawned controversy in El Salvador. Some students rallied behind Castro in the streets, while those within the government debated how to prevent facing their own domestic uprising. Fidel Castro's shadow stretched far enough over El Salvador that even factions within the military advocated preventative reforms in hopes of avoiding a communist revolt (Dunkerley 1982:43). The growing cleavage between moderates and hard-liners contributed to weakening support for President José María Lemus, who had been appointed in 1956. Ousted by a coup, Lemus was replaced by another Revolutionary Governing Council of three military officials and three civilians, some of whom were quite promising to democratic activists but were too reform-minded for the country's oligarchy. Consequently, the council lasted only three months before a countercoup was orchestrated (Stanley 1996:76; Dunkerley 1982:43).

Thousands took to the streets protesting the countercoup, prompting the new leadership to call in the National Guard and National Police to regain order. A reported one hundred protestors were killed; the civilian members of the previous governing council were exiled, and a new council comprising two military officials and two civilians (all staunch conservatives) was installed (Stanley 1996:77; Dunkerley 1982:44). The politico-military establishment was forced to recognize that the corporatist plan had failed to galvanize a popular base.

Colonel Julio Adalberto Rivera was installed as president after a virtually uncontested election in 1962. The official party was renamed the Partido de Conciliación Nacional (PCN), the National Conciliation Party, and perhaps in an effort to prove the intention of conciliation, or perhaps in an effort to quell popular disquiet, steps were again taken toward establishing the appearance of legitimacy. The regime permitted some political organizing and opposition parties to run candidates (Stanley 1996:78–79; Skidmore and Smith 1992:334). By the 1967 elections, party competition had strengthened, though not enough to overcome the machinery or rhetoric of the PCN. The party's candidate, Colonel Fidel Sánchez Hernandez, claimed that voters "had a choice between communism and liberty" and became the next president (Montgomery 1995:60).

Among the country's political elite, debate focused not on ideological differences, but on how to accomplish an important shared objective: maintaining the system of socioeconomic stratification. Those willing to offer (usually meaningless or minor) reforms to pacify the poor had to contest those preferring to pacify via force. Because of the inability to reconcile their differences, the two factions of governing elite ended up with policies that vacillated between reward and punishment — first offering minor reforms that allowed a little access to the system and provided some minor economic relief while fostering a disproportionately great deal of hope among the popular activists, followed by severe repression, a tightly closed political system, and the arrest, exile, or assassination of activists.

## The Opportunity Structure Takes Shape

The constant shift back and forth was due partly to the fact that neither the oligarchy nor the military was a monolithic entity, and both had factions advocating moderate reform while others were committed to severe repression. Presidents Rivera and Sánchez both initiated land redistribution programs, arguing that they were necessary reforms (Stanley 1996:73–80), and both faced opposition from within the oligarchy and their own ranks (Wood 2000:231). Likewise, the civilians appointed to the governing council in 1960 were considered unfit by their fellow elites and overthrown because of their reformist ideas (Stanley 1996:76, 78; Montgomery 1995:52). Within the military, the divide ran deep and is evidenced in the number of times reform opponents overthrew reform advocates and vice versa. Administrations like Araujo's, which started out talking about reform and enjoying some military support, often ended up as Araujo did, ousted by a military faction led by antireformists; others were pressed into embracing strong repression tactics. The divisions within the elite and the military led to realignment and entrenchment of factions along reform/antireform lines. A coalition of the very conservative within the oligarchy and another from within the upper echelons of the armed forces provided the strong arm behind a counter reform agenda; it was this coalition that would eventually prove to be the backbone of the paramilitary campaign.

The 1960s were watershed years for hard-liners on the right, and the 1970s were equally important for reform advocates on the left, in terms of mobilizing broad-based support and militarizing elements of their respective camps. Both sides also found a network of allies overseas — "the weapons for the right came from the U.S. government, and for the left from the churches and universities"[§4] — which had an effect equivalent to throwing gasoline on an already flaming inferno. By the end of the 1970s, both sides were well organized, had mobilized swaths of support, and had established reliable allies who could provide the necessary resources to wage a military campaign against the other. El Salvador was soon to become a bloody and indiscriminate war zone.

### The Right

For the right, reform seemed the equivalent of acquiescing to the enemy and was not an option. Instead, hard-liners focused on strengthening the security forces. The Partido de Conciliación Nacional (PCN) was organized to pursue this agenda. It did not play the typical roles of a political party — recruiting party loyals, mobilizing voters, competing with opposition parties. Instead, it was used primarily to run candidates chosen by incumbents who would continue to work for the party's constituency, the oligarchy and military (Montgomery 1995:277n5, 53; Dunkerley 1982:72; Diskin and Sharpe 1986:52). The election of the first PCN president, Julio Adalberto Rivera in 1962, exemplifies the superficiality of the "party" role. Rivera ran in an "election" that excluded all other political parties, though university students managed to make a statement by offering a donkey as a candidate; it was Rivera's only competition (Montgomery 1995:53; Dunkerley 1982:72). The right relied instead on its much more sophisticated security apparatus to ensure its continued dominance.

Nonetheless, after his "election" Rivera did come to terms with the fact that certain reforms would have to be made if he wanted to avoid revolution, and he shifted toward the moderates. He redesigned the National Assembly so that it would be based on proportional representation, and he opened up the next elections to party competition (Montgomery 1995:53). In 1967, Rivera chose General Fidel Sánchez-Hernández as his successor, and the efforts at moderation continued to an extent, much to the consternation of the oligarchy and private sector. But when popular opposition to the regime began rising, Sánchez-Hernández coupled his reform rhetoric with repression. Like his predecessors and successors, when push came to shove, Sánchez-Hernández turned to the one tool the right could rely upon, and that was the strong-arm tactics of repression. In addition to the army, the three official agencies central to the most ruthless repression were the National Police, the National Guard, and the Treasury Police.

The extensive capabilities of the right's security forces came with some outside assistance. During the 1960s, the United States acted to bolster El Salvador's internal forces against what was framed as communist organizing. Particularly after Cuba's revolution and given the guerrilla activity in Guatemala and Nicaragua, evidence of a black market arms trade and "subversive materials" inside El Salvador were unsettling (Stanley 1996:80).[5] In an effort to address concerns about the spread of communism, the United States established the Central American Defense Council (CONDECA) in 1964, an organization intended to improve the flow of information between governments and to foster "joint maneuvers" in the region. El Salvador was among the initial members.[6] The United States also began training troops (particularly in the National Guard), providing arms, and increasing military aid to the country (Dunkerley 1982:74). Again it was the National Guard and National Police who benefited from the assistance, rather than the army. In fact, a U.S. official is quoted as recognizing the El Salvadoran "National Guard as the linchpin of the security system, and is probably one of the most efficient police forces in Latin America," but the same official determined it "deficient" nonetheless, given the potentially sizeable communist threat (Stanley 1996:81).

With help from the United States, the internal security agencies would experience a decade of impressive growth as they expanded and improved. The primary focus was on improving intelligence-gathering abilities, and it was José Alberto Medrano who served as one of the important links between the U.S. training and the El Salvadoran implementation. A recipient of the silver Presidential Medal from the Johnson administration, Medrano worked closely with U.S. special operations forces and was on the CIA payroll. He established some of the first professional agencies focused strictly on intelligence, beginning with the "Security Service," an "elite intelligence-coordinating agency" that blossomed into the Agencia Nacional de Servicios Especiales de El Salvador, or the Salvadoran National Special Services Agency, commonly known as ANSESAL (Stanley 1996:81; Nairn 1984; Dickey 1983:18). ANSESAL was based on the same principle as the intelligence-gathering squadron Martínez wove within his Pro-Patria party decades prior. The objective was to create a nationwide network of informants who would provide the regime with information on individuals or activities that might be considered threatening or unfavorable to the State.[7]

Throughout this period of maturation, the security apparatus "tended to maintain close mercenary relationships with land owners and business elites" (Stanley 1996:72). As had been the case since before the Matanza, conservative military officers and conservative landowners were closely allied and consequently had contacts and even access to one another's political sphere of influence. On the local level, security forces established strong relationships with the local landowners, "enjoy[ing] supplemental pay and other perquisites as a reward for defending upper-class interests from union organizers and other menaces" (Stanley 1996:72). Many times, National Guard posts were actually situated right on the private haciendas, making the ties between the landowner and the Guardias inevitably close (Stanley 1996:81–82; Dickey 1983:18). The relationship Mario Zapata had witnessed more than thirty years prior had grown only stronger.

The fact that the new, modernized armed forces were built within the traditional hierarchical and security norms kept them tied directly to El Salvador's elite. The armed forces were not designed nor institutionalized as a national force to protect the country, but as localized forces to protect the wealthy. Thus while the scope, resources, networking, and preparedness of the country's armed forces did mature and modernize, and continued to provide staunch conservatives with the force needed to dole out heavy-handed repression, neither the localized focus nor the primacy of loyalty to the elite of the security forces changed dramatically over time. The messianic self-image prevailed.

The nature of the new intelligence organization, ANSESAL, reflected this bimodal military emphasis on maintaining the traditional power structure while modernizing the capabilities of the armed forces. Members of ANSESAL benefited from the expertise and training of the United States and used that training at the behest of their wealthy patrons. The organization's offspring, ORDEN, the Organización Democrática Nacionalista, or the Democratic Nationalist Organization,[8] started during the early 1960s, and the two became an expansive counterinsurgency intelligence gathering network. Medrano, who worked with the United States to establish ORDEN a few years before his term as head of the National Guard came to a close, explained that the organization "grew out of the State Department, the CIA, and the Green Berets" as part of a broader plan known as the Public Safety Program to control the spread of communism. Medrano said that "these specialized agencies [were created] to fight the plans and actions of international communism" (Nairn 1984:21).

ORDEN's founders shared common fields of expertise and were committed to a single ultimate goal. Medrano's chief assistance in organizing and training ORDEN came from the U.S. Green Berets, whose commander of the "Eighth Special Forces Group in Panama sent Medrano a team of ten counterinsurgency trainers" (Montgomery 1995:56; Nairn 1984:23). Medrano claims that in brainstorming about the type of operation they would run, the group discussed the fact that "he who has the population wins the war." Despite the alleged talk of "catechisms," it soon was clear that the ultimate objective of each member of the team was to snuff out subversives rather than to "win the hearts and minds" of rural Salvadorans (Montgomery 1995:56; Stanley 1996:69–71, 88). In the same interview in which he talked about winning the support of the people, Medrano said, "In this revolutionary war, the enemy comes from our people. . . . They don't have the rights of Geneva. They are traitors to our country. What can the troops do? When they find them, they kill them" (Nairn 1984:23). His efforts more closely resembled an exorcism, where Medrano was trying to remove the evil communists from the pure (elite) soul of El Salvador.

The plan developed by Medrano and his advisory team was to create a hierarchical network of loyalists that harked back to Martínez's civilian spies. Low-level recruits, the *orejas*, would inform on their neighbors, on local activities, on whatever seemed suspicious or might be useful information for their superiors. Medrano described the process by which "subversives" were identified, identifying their telltale characteristics as anti–"Yankee imperialism," and outspoken opposition to the oligarchy and military (Nairn 1984:23). Coordinating with the three domestic security forces, ORDEN quickly became a "nation-wide, grass-roots network of informants" (Stanley 1996:81). The lower rungs created a sort of spiderweb intended to trap subversives and probably also intended to make potential guerrilla supporters too afraid to act on their conviction. The higher-ups were primarily well-trained military men, and they sifted though the information and passed along whatever was deemed important to their ANSESAL superiors. ANSESAL agents then determined which information should be acted upon, and the elite within ORDEN were called in to deal with the threat, which usually entailed the elimination of an alleged subversive (Montgomery 1995:56; LeoGrande 1998b:48). In addition to intelligence gathering, ANSESAL also worked directly with the country's wealthy landowners to provide them with personnel who could protect their property and interests from troublemakers (Stanley 1996:99).

As president, Sánchez-Hernández relied heavily on the system to repress growing labor activism and strikes (Stanley 1996:82), a role that was secured for ORDEN after a major labor demonstration in 1968. The teachers' union, ANDES, went on strike (opposing restrictions implemented by the official, legal union) and soon won the support of the Unitary Union Federation of El Salvador (FUSS). The strike, demonstrations, and rallies convinced the regime to call in the security forces, this time with ORDEN accompanying the National Guard. In addition to the arrests and physical beatings, two teachers were "disappeared" (Dunkerley 1982:69; Stanley 1996:82).[9] This perhaps marked the initiation of ORDEN as a tool of state-sponsored repression in El Salvador; its countersubversive capabilities continued to be heavily employed during the Molina administration.

### The Left

Perhaps the irony in the dogmatic and violent development of the right was that the "left" it was built to respond to was, at the time, actually dominated by moderates. Indeed, researchers encountered difficulties trying to determine the exact year of ORDEN's inception due to the inactivity of the group during the mid-1960s, when "there was only intermittent need for a militia 'to counteract communist subversion'" (Dunkerley 1982:77). The small militant groups that did exist were only in their infancy and were neither well organized nor broadly supported. There simply was not a lot of work for people trained specifically to respond to militant left-wing activities. For the left, the 1960s belonged to the moderates.

The Partido Demócrata Cristiano (PDC), or Christian Democrat Party, was trying to negotiate a "third way" between communism and military dictatorship, demanding democracy and capitalism (Montgomery 1995:54; Dunkerley 1982:78). Led by José Napoleón Duarte, the PDC ran competitive candidates in the 1964 elections, challenging the military rule with a reform platform targeting economic disparity. Duarte was among those who campaigned and won in 1964, becoming mayor of San Salvador, an office he would occupy until 1970. The fact that the military allowed the PDC to run and genuinely compete electorally provided a significant boost to the party's support. They were able to challenge more militant leftist claims that insurgence was the only route to change, and thus became the primary antiestablishment voice (Dunkerley 1982:79; Stanley 1996:78–79; LeoGrande 1998b:35–36, 42).

Though land reform proper was not the most emphasized point on the party's agenda, the PDC did advocate for workers and "a classless society." Despite this, the party was clearly distinct from more socialist tendencies in that it did espouse capitalism and the principle of "private property [as] a natural right" (Dunkerley 1982:78). The new generation of the Partido de Acción Renovadora, or the Renovating Action Party (better known as the PAR–Nueva Linea), represented a faction of the social democrats and was wholeheartedly focused on "immediate agrarian reform" (Dunkerley 1982:79). Likewise the Movimiento Nacional Revolucionario (MNR), or National Revolutionary Movement, was organized around a socialist democratic ideology and was resolute on the issue of land reform. The MNR's central figure, Guillermo Ungo, would later partner with Duarte in leading the efforts for an electoral solution to the conflict. Less moderate was the Unión Democrática Nacionalista (UDN), or National Democratic Union (Dunkerley 1982:80–84; Diskin and Sharpe 1986:52).

The moderate election success of the PDC during the 1960s looked like a real political opening for the opposition and energized their cause for a peaceful, institutionalized path to peace and stability. But just as in the past, testing the democratic waters proved dangerous as the government acted quickly to shut the door. The PAR was outlawed in 1967, and elections continued to be marred by the traditional fraud that had seemed to ebb a few years earlier (Dunkerley 1982:80). Despite the modest success of the Christian Democrats, the left remained relatively weak in that there was still no consensus around the best tactical route to democratic change. Most of the moderates and a significant portion of the Salvadoran Communist Party, Partido Communista de El Salvador (PCS), remained committed to the electoral, democratic path and opposed militant action. But there were many (particularly younger) activists who had little faith in the regime's willingness to change of its own accord, and they continued to see armed revolt as the only possible means of access to the political system.

Most of the militant leftist groups in El Salvador rejected the idea that a tight-knit group of guerrillas could rise up and spark an unorganized and spontaneous peasant uprising (known as *"foquismo"*). Instead, they believed that the peasants and workers and popular support base had to be organized, committed, and expect a long effort that would face full-throttle repression. The Fuerzas Populares de Liberación–Farabundo Martí (FPL), or Popular Liberation Forces–Farabundo Martí, was formed in 1970 by members of the PCS who lost confidence in the democratic path (Dunkerley 1982:91–97). The Bloque Popular Revolucionario (BPR) also fell within the fold of guerrilla organizations and brought with it the support of a wide range of organizations, including the Union of Slum Dwellers, the National Association of Salvadoran Educators (ANDES), the Christian Federation of Salvadoran Rural Workers (FECCAS,) and the Revolutionary Movement of Secondary Students (Dunkerley 1982:89, 99–101). The Ejército Revolucionario del Pueblo (ERP), or Revolutionary People's Army, was formed in 1972 by a PDC splinter group and suffered through its early years squabbling over the strategic benefits and shortcomings of *foquismo*, which it pursued for a period of time (Dunkerley 1982:92; Montgomery 1995:104–11).

The Resistencia Nacional (RN), or National Resistance, also known as the Fuerzas Armadas Resistencia Nacional (FARN), or Armed Forces of the National Resistance, was formed in the middle 1970s. Despite being an armed organization, the RN was opposed to an armed uprising. Instead, the group saw itself as more of a stopgap mechanism that could be used to defensively respond to the State security apparatus and give the left the time it needed to mobilize a broad base of popular support. In addition to the political parties and the RN, the Frente de Acción Popular Unificada (FAPU), the Unified Popular Action Front, served as an umbrella organization for a series of unions, including the FUSS and FENASTRAS, a union that had united workers from a variety of fields a decade or more prior (Dunkerley 1982:59).

Undercurrents of resistance were present before the 1972 elections (the FPL, for instance, was organized two years before the election), but resistance was severely marginalized by popular support for the elections. Preelection activities seemed to indicate that party competition and widespread political participation might become realities. The Christian Democrats had been collaborating with fellow opposition parties who united to form the Unión Nacional Opositora (UNO), or the National Opposition Union. Duarte was on the UNO ticket running for president with Ungo running as his vice president. "Popular imagination was fired and expectations were high" (Dunkerley 1982:85, 84).

As optimistic and enthusiastic as the moderates were, 1972 would prove to be the real testing ground of the electoral option. Indeed, even the far right had divided with a breakaway faction adding itself to the list of parties competing in the election. General José Alberto Medrano collaborated with an "important faction of the oligarchy base" in organizing the Frente Unido Democrático Independiente (FUDI), or the Independent United Democratic Front, and they launched a campaign of their own.

Squeezed between UNO demanding reforms and FUDI threatening the traditional system of appointed succession, Sánchez-Hernández took the usual steps of political repression and election fraud to ensure the success of his "candidate," Colonel Arturo Armando Molina (Montgomery 1995:63–64). "Duarte's increasingly exuberant campaign tour was attacked and an aide shot dead, UNO broadcasts were sabotaged and control of the voting booths secured by government supporters" (Dunkerley 1982:85). The night of the election, UNO had a promising lead of 62,000 votes with more than half of the ballots tallied, when all electoral broadcasts were shut down by the government. The next election report was issued the following day, announcing Molina's win by less than 10,000 votes. Molina did offer a recount (some suggest in an effort to rebut the expected allegations of fraud), but UNO was not satisfied with a recount of the existing ballots, and futilely demanded an entirely new election (Dunkerley 1982:85; Wood 2000:230).

The hope of achieving political reforms through elections dwindled quickly. The National Assembly confirmed Molina's election, and he was sworn into office early. UNO tried to rally voters from all political leanings against the election fraud. Under El Salvador's election laws, an election in which there are more "spoiled" ballots than votes cast has to be ruled null and void. So instead of simply boycotting the National Assembly and local elections, UNO campaigned for voters to "spoil" their ballots. The effort was unsuccessful everywhere but San Salvador. With this last-ditch effort to overturn the elections lost, the left fell into near disarray. The National Guard attacked and assassinated members of UNO. Guerrillas managed a few offenses against State security forces. Junior officers in the San Salvador barracks attempted a coup, but their uncoordinated effort collapsed

(Dunkerley 1982:85–86; Montgomery 1995:64). In the election fallout the military regained control, a state of martial law was imposed, and Duarte was beaten and exiled (Dunkerley 1982:86; Southerland 1981b:2; Sharpe 1981).

The "popular imagination" and "high expectations" that had filled the air prior to the 1972 election were quickly doused. The government's management of the election results spawned a wave of leftist activism and militancy as civil society organizations, political parties, and nascent guerrilla groups became increasingly agitated and determined (Dunkerley 1982:84–102). Over the next five years, civil society organizations and guerrilla fractions began to strengthen and mature, joining the more established voices of the left.

Molina's "election" ushered in a period of uncertainty, as moderate claims of a peaceful path to change lost credibility. Increasing numbers of the moderate left were losing faith in elections and institutional reform and looking to a military uprising as the only alternative. The ERP began a campaign of urban bombings, looking to *foquismo* tactics during the early 1970s, while other guerrilla groups worked to mobilize masses of support. Early attempts at unifying the left failed, though Dunkerley argues that an important early success of the guerrilla groups was their "fusion" to, or within, the party and union structures of civil society. Dunkerley suggests that the guerrilla groups followed the PCS model of participating politically despite its illegality by using the UDN. Thus it was through these civil organizations that "the Salvadorean guerrillas were able to make a qualitative breakthrough and take a leading role in the mass movement" (Dunkerley 1982:104, 95, 96, 98).

### ORDEN: A Paramilitary Central Nerve System

As the moderate left gave way to more militant groups after the "election," the security apparatus that had been established during the 1960s was increasingly relied upon by the right. The intelligence agencies and armed security forces complemented each others' roles well in achieving the ultimate objective of completely demobilizing and eliminating dissent. Enabling this show of force were the country's most elite families and the military government. Thanks to this early convergence of triad elements, ORDEN quickly became one of the most dangerous and powerful organizations in El Salvador and would evolve into the central nerve system of the country's death squads.

Because ORDEN was organized under the auspices of ANSESAL, it was directly tied to the State security apparatus from the start, though it operated and evolved in more of a quasi-State fashion. ORDEN apparently was not included in the federal budget, nor were there any laws, regulations, hearings, or official meetings leaving a paper trail detailing the creation of ORDEN. However, the official chain of command clearly links the organization to the State. Dunkerley asserts that "no secret was made of the fact that" for all intents and purposes, the president of the country was also head of ORDEN, "and that daily control rested with the Ministry of Defense" (Dunkerley 1982:75–66). This assertion is supported by Medrano himself, who claimed that the intelligence gathered by the organization was then forwarded "to the president, who would take appropriate action" (Nairn 1984:23).

Because of the role played by ORDEN in intelligence gathering and counterinsurgency, the organization was closely tied to the armed forces and security apparatus. General Medrano founded ORDEN while head of the National Guard, and the organization was later led by Colonel Roberto Eulalio Santiváñez. Major Roberto D'Aubuisson was the colonel's deputy director (LeoGrande 1998b:49). Many who served in the network were recruited from the military, as former soldiers or officers were believed to be more likely to be loyal to the State and had presumably received some degree of relevant training. The hub of ORDEN's military connections, what Dunkerley refers to as the "real military kernel of ORDEN," was estimated to be 10 to 20 percent of the organization's total membership. This core comprised an estimated ten thousand troops who were overt security agents, known as *patrullas cantanales*, or regional police, "the part-time police force of the villages" (Dunkerley 1982:76). The balance of ORDEN's membership, estimated to be between forty thousand and ninety thousand, were primarily "auxiliary" forces responsible for being the eyes and ears of the State in their own communities and reporting what they saw to ORDEN higher-ups (Dunkerley 1982:76).

The recruitment of the thousands of ORDEN foot soldiers was also successful thanks in part to the extraordinary level of fear instilled in civilians by its security apparatus. Flashing an ORDEN membership card could mean the difference between life and death were one to be stopped by a National Guard or Treasury Police patrol. In accordance with the old "if you can't beat 'em, join 'em" adage, to be a member of ORDEN was to be protected from the military because you were seen as one of them (Dunkerley 1982:76).

ORDEN came by its elite allies with relative ease. ANSESAL had already established a trusted relationship with many of the country's elite, serving as a sort of go-between or "employment agency" that matched "landlords and industrialists looking" to hire private security forces with National Guard or other security troops willing to work in this capacity (Stanley 1996:99). These *supernumerarios*, or troops who worked both in an official capacity with the State's armed forces and as privatized security agents for the wealthy, were not a new phenomenon; the line between "public" and "private" armed forces had been historically fuzzy to say the least, as has been discussed. But what is notable here is the role played by ANSESAL and the way in which that role allowed the organization and its personnel to ingratiate themselves with the country's wealthiest families.

The recruitment and retention of ORDEN's troops was in large part due to the country's elite, who provided the financial incentives to make service nearly impossible for destitute peasants to pass up. Some of the funding was redistributed from the wealthy to ORDEN via the government. For instance, President Sánchez-Hernández secured increased funding from the country's elite families to finance the expansion of ORDEN during his administration (Stanley 1996:82; 99). But it seems that most of the incentive was provided via more direct patron-client type relationships. ORDEN recruits were promised "land, cheap credit and supplies, permanent work and medical facilities," and then served at the behest of the landowners, protecting their interests from dissenting organizations or activities (Dunkerley 1982:76; Stanley 1996:70).[10]

The confluence of state, military, and elite resources in the construction of what would become a paramilitary organization was long in the making in El Salvador. The military and elite had been building a sort of dysfunctional codependent relationship for decades, and out of that grew the "official" political party focused on preserving and furthering that relationship. Once each sector divided into hard-liners and moderates, the former factions united to marshal what was necessary to organize, mobilize, and provide impunity for what would develop into the most efficient killing machine in the country.

The right in El Salvador had been slowly dividing over the past few decades, with the division increasingly difficult to paper over. The fact that the localized networks between military units and landowners remained intact and strong during the period of military augmentation became an increasingly important factor, not only in terms of the roles played by

ORDEN and ANSESAL, but also politically in terms of the division within the right deepened over Molina's presidency. The realignment that had begun years earlier now had real political implications. The ties between the military and elite hard-liners created a potent combination of forces with nearly unparalleled resource mobilization capabilities.

By the time Molina became president, the internal struggle between right-wing moderates and hard-liners was nearing its breaking point. Still, Molina followed the path laid by his predecessors, he employed harsh repression against the opposition while initiating some reform measures. ORDEN's counterinsurgency efforts were stepped up. The scope of the strategy was broadened, taking specific aim at the Catholic Church, human rights workers, and democracy advocates (Dunkerley 1982:103, 107–8). This approach won support from some of the highest Catholic officials in the country, who refused to admonish the attacks against priests and other church personnel and enabled the military to continue their campaign without repercussion.

Where Molina broke with previous administrations was in the Agricultural Development Plan for 1973–77 (Stanley 1996:93), which provided for the "nationaliz[ation] of almost 61,000 hectares" of land in 1976 for redistribution "among 12,000 *campesino* families" (Montgomery 1995:67). His land reform package won support from the United States and drew the involvement of U.S. advisors within El Salvador. Despite the fact that Molina began this reform while continuing the violent suppression of the left, the country's elite were increasingly discontent with the efforts of "the official repressive apparatus" and were downright incensed with the land reform (Dunkerley 1982:103).

### Escuadrónes de la Muerte: El Salvador's PMGs

Many of the country's staunchest right-wingers began taking action to fight the reform efforts and to supplement what they considered to be Molina's lackluster counterinsurgency efforts. Beginning a two-pronged approach, organizations like the Asociación Nacional de Empresas Privadas (ANEP), the National Association of Private Enterprise, worked first to undermine support for Molina's reform packages with "*campos pagados* (paid political advertisements)" that served as a smear campaign against Molina's initiatives (Montgomery 1995:68; Dunkerley 1982:65).[11]

Second, ANEP worked with the Frente de Agricultores de la Región Oriental (FARO), or the Agricultural Front of the Eastern Region, to look beyond the official limitations of the State to organize militant groups that could not only combat the left, but also eliminate it altogether. FARO was a relatively new organization, "formed by landlords from the east of the country to fight the reform law." Showing more militancy than the ad campaign of ANEP, FARO first undertook a mobilization project "within the officer corps" trying to rally support against Molina's project. FARO also organized security forces who served as private militias for the landlords. These early antireform squads would later be organized into the paramilitary groups that would cooperate with allies within the armed forces to eliminate the regime's opposition (Dunkerley 1982:65, 103).

In the early-to-middle 1970s, ANEP and FARO established and financed paramilitary groups intended to supplement ORDEN and skirt the perceived limitations of the quasi-State organization. One such organization, the Fuerzas Armadas de Liberación Nacional — Guerra de Exterminación (FALANGE), was established in 1975 and had connections to D'Aubuisson himself. The Mano Blanco, or "White Hand" paramilitary group, noted by LeoGrande as the country's "first death squad," was organized out of the *especiales* — the ANSESAL squadrons used to carry out hits against alleged subversives (LeoGrande 1998b:49, 48). Raul Castro, who was the U.S. ambassador to El Salvador during the late 1960s, called Mano Blanco an "offshoot of ORDEN, and the same people in ORDEN were to some extent the same people in the Mano Blanco. Even today [in 1984], some of the same people are in the death squads. That was the origin" (Nairn 1984:23).

Unlike ORDEN, these organizations operated without the official endorsement of the State. Nonetheless, Mano Blanco, FALANGE, and their fellow paramilitary organizations followed the model of ORDEN in that they relied upon the financial support of the oligarchy; the personnel, expertise, and arms of the military; and the political ideology and support of the far right. Interviewees in El Salvador confirmed that the resource mobilization necessary to finance, arm, and supply the paramilitaries was in large part done by the country's landed oligarchy. One said that while the military was the primary resource, the oligarchy was also critical to the support system:[12] "Not all of the rich, but a small group of the wealthy funded these groups."[§] Colonel Adolfo Majano, member of the 1979 junta, explained that members of the far right were determined to "put up an organized battle. . . . They began to create clandestine groups like the White Warriors Union. . . . They began to create a network of their people inside the armed forces. But they were outside the armed forces, too, and that was very important" (Montgomery 1995:76). A high-ranking member of the Salvadoran military told a U.S. journalist,

> Naturally the minute the conflict intensified and the left began to put on pressure, murdering anyone in a uniform and that sort of thing, then all the vendettas began, and naturally they [the *guardias*] identified more with the *patron* than with the policy of the armed forces. That's where the complicity is, precisely, of the security forces. (Dickey 1983:18)

Politically, paramilitary activities had to be autonomous of the armed forces, because "plausible deniability" was critical to the military if it wanted to preserve the image of legitimacy necessary to secure foreign aid. But it was also strategically and tactically important for the PMGs to maintain connections with the military, however unofficial and underground. Therefore, the unofficial and official campaigns were not waged independent of one another. Cooperation between personnel of both efforts was a critical component of the overall objective of eliminating opposition; therefore, the membership overlap with the legal armed forces was among the most important shared features of the various PMGs. This connection served as a supply chain in terms of recruits and resources that ran from elements within the military to the paramilitaries, often through D'Aubuisson. One interviewee explained the role played by D'Aubuisson with a robust, open-mouthed laugh. "Well! He was an assassin! He was the nexus of the whole thing. He was in the military, you know, and then he led the death squads . . ." "All of them?" I asked. "No, not directly," he explained. "But they were all connected."§

Information collected in my own interviews and by various other agencies confirms that D'Aubuisson did indeed play a central role in the development and operation of the PMGs. The U.S. Select Committee on Intelligence commissioned some research on the violence in El Salvador in the early 1980s and reportedly collected substantial evidence that D'Aubuisson "directed and controlled" the PMGs (Pyes 1984:350). Nelson Funes, an ARENA representative in the House of Deputies in 2000, indirectly confirmed the centrality of D'Aubuisson's role in the death squad organization, arguing that when D'Aubuisson agreed to the negotiated peace, the death squads "just ended — stopped operating" (Funes 2003). All of this is corroborated by D'Aubuisson's own words; he "describe[ed] to a reporter the military's frustration with normal judicial processes during the late 1970s. 'We began to act incorrectly, and not take them [suspected subversives] to the judge, but make them "disappear" instead,' he explained" (LeoGrande 1998b:49).

A military official who was high ranking and active at the decision-making level during the civil war, and who played a significant role in negotiating the peace, described the supply chain to me as involving "a small group of individuals within the army . . . the police, the National Guard, and the *patrullas*," who gave information, arms, and ammunition to D'Aubuisson.[§] But the evidence suggests that the overlap was indeed significant, so much so that the PMGs may have been primarily military personnel working off duty or simply illegally, organized (or at least populated by) high-ranking military superiors, using the pretext of a paramilitary group to mask their activities. Military informants who provided information to a reporter for the *Christian Science Monitor* during the 1980s provided information that Colonel Carlos Reynaldo Lopez Nuila, head of the National Police, worked with Roberto D'Aubuisson to man death squad operations, and "organized such death squad actions himself" (Volman 1984:5). Lopez Nuila later called for an investigation against his own agency, given the published charges of complicity with death squads. Despite the colonel's established and amicable relationship with the U.S. Embassy in San Salvador, one embassy official evaluated the investigation as nothing but a "farce" (Volman 1984:5).

Indeed, evidence connecting high-ranking military officials to death squads and military human rights atrocities was so strong by 1984 that after being elected president, José Napoleón Duarte called for the resignation of several senior officers, citing their complicity. Colonel Nicolás Carranza, longtime associate of Roberto D'Aubuisson and head of the Treasury Police, former Treasury Police head Colonel Francisco Antonio Moran, Lieutenant Colonel Mario Denis Moran, and Lieutenant Colonel Roberto Mauricio Staben (who was in charge of one of the rapid-response battalions, also known as BIRI), Lieutenant Colonel Jorge Adalberto Cruz, and Colonel Juan Rafael Bustillo, commander of the air force, were all among those strongly suspected of cooperating (at least) with PMGs or of committing gross human rights violations (Hedges 1984).

U.S. officials who worked in El Salvador at the time confirm reports given by El Salvadoran defectors and officers who testified about their own involvement in the PMGs. Information from all these sources taken together indicates that the death squads were probably more military personnel than nonmilitary, though we cannot rule out the possibility that there were groups operating with more civilians than military personnel. The very nature of PMGs and the ways in which they operate of course makes the actual ratio of military to civilian personnel difficult to determine; but in the case of El Salvador, it is clear that the military was intimately tied to the death squads.

A U.S. official in San Salvador during the early 1980s reported that "every garrison of any size had death squads. It's that simple" (Nairn 1984:25). In addition, testimony given by a number of credible individuals indicates not only that death squad personnel overlapped with military personnel, but also that such overlap occurred across the various security branches, including the National Police, the Treasury Police, the army, the civilian patrols, and the National Guard (see AI 1988:3). Members of the National Guard who did double-duty in the death squads were known as *golindrinas* (Pyes 1984:353). One example comes from a Salvadoran who had served in the National Guard for fifteen years and acknowledged that he had gone "on death squad missions while stationed in La Libertad. 'We got names and addresses and were told to pick them up, get information, and kill them later'" (Nairn 1984:24). The informant said that they were given "written orders," and in some cases "lists" of those they were to pick up.

Based on numerous testimonies such as this one, Amnesty International "conclude[d] that [El Salvador's paramilitary organizations] were made up of regular police and military personnel, often operating in plain clothes but under the orders of superior officers." Amnesty also determined that at least during 1988, "detaining forces . . . reportedly dumped the bodies of unacknowledged detainees who die[d] in custody as if they had been 'death squad' victims" (AI 1988:18, 1, 5). Such findings are consistent with information given by Roberto D'Aubuisson in a 1981 interview: "Security force members utilize the guise of the death squads when a potentially embarrassing or odious task needs to be performed" (AI 1988:18). A former officer in the Salvadoran army who participated in the assassination of Archbishop Romero in 1980 served as an informant to the U.S. embassy in San Salvador; he was found to be reliable by the staff there and was used repeatedly in gathering information on the PMGs. The informant explained that "death squads were necessary because government restraints on the security forces compelled soldiers to take illegal action" (Pyes 1984:351). Thus in some cases, the PMGs were off-duty military officers acting outside the official confines of the State.

Despite these testimonies, there are also indications that the PMGs, or some of them, were autonomous of the formal structures of the armed forces. For instance, in 1988, the Gremio Anti-Comunista Salvadoreño (GAS), the Salvadoran Anti-Communist Guild, released a statement promising that their organization would "act alongside the armed forces" against those who "interfered" in the elections—especially "unionists and politicians" (AI 1988:10). The phrasing of the note indicates that the GAS was separate from the official military, but there is no way to verify that the wording was not crafted in order to disguise the group's true affiliations or nature.

Monetary funding, arms, and personnel were only some of the resources necessary for paramilitary organizations to survive. Like the Guardias Blancas in Chiapas and the civic patrols in Colombia, ORDEN served as the structural and conceptual precursor for El Salvador's paramilitary groups. Interviewees confirmed previous research that found that most if not all of the PMGs were indeed connected to ORDEN to one degree or another, linked by their determination to stop whatever potential success the left might have. Thus ORDEN served as sort of an ideological "hub" of the political right's soldiers, providing legitimacy and purpose. And it is critical to note here that in El Salvador, even more so than in Mexico or Colombia, the oligarchy and the military were indeed the political elite, the "State." So to say that the PMGs had ties to the oligarchy and the military is to inherently say that they had ties to the State.

Anticommunism provided the PMGs with a purpose. Most of my interviewees concurred that the paramilitaries were created and operated in order to protect the system of spoils in El Salvador, to protect the wealthy from reforms that might redistribute wealth. The overwhelming fear was that the leftists would win (be it through elections or arms) and would destroy the oligarchy. The interviewee who had heartily identified D'Aubuisson as the "nexus" of the death squad network explained that their objective was to protect the concentration of wealth, that their very purpose was to do what the wealthy asked, and that they were willing to do it for monetary compensation. "The rich would say, here, here is some money, and [give them a name], and then . . . *muerte*. . . . They wanted to preserve the system. They wanted to stop any reform, protect their control over the land, money."§ Salvador Samayoa, who had served in Romero's cabinet, later joined the FPL and eventually served as a representative of the FMLN in the peace process (Samayoa 2002), reinforced this emphasis on money in an interview in 2003. I asked him what the right wanted, and what were the motives behind their campaign against the left. "To protect the money, the system," he said. "To stop communism and change. Nicaragua and Panama caused fear" (Samayoa 2003).

One of the country's leading Christian Democrats told me that the paramilitaries were "most definitely political" and noted that the assassinations were intensified "around the time of land reform." He noted that "they hated the Christian Democrats for being proponents of democracy, and land reform."§ A Salvadoran academic said that 1972 sparked a sort of "political crisis" for the right when it appeared that a leftist might win a presidential election, and that the crisis only got worse in 1976. He said that what the left "wanted, ultimately, was land. But the right wanted to protect the concentration of land."§ One of my interviewees was a high-ranking military spokesperson who denied any connection between the military and the PMGs, arguing that they were created by people who were afraid for their land and their security. He did, however, agree that the death squads were created to achieve essentially the same objectives as the military, "to fight against communism, to protect" the system and democracy.§

And indeed the threats and declarations made by the death squads themselves indicate their very political intentions. The FALANGE, which renamed itself the Unión Guerra Blanca (UGB), or White Warriors Union one year after its formation, "promised the extermination of 'all communists and their collaborators'" (Dunkerley 1982:103). The organization busied itself with living up to its promise, killing thirty-eight people in one week of October 1975 alone. This group, though operating underground, was quite forthcoming with its objectives. In 1976, it issued a blanket conviction of all priests in El Salvador with its infamous slogan, "Be a patriot — kill a priest!" The group also released a proclamation entitled "War Bulletin No. 6," which "accused 46 Jesuits of 'terrorism' and gave them until 20 July to leave the country; after that date their executions would be 'immediate and systematic'" (Dunkerley 1982:109; AI 1988:8). D'Aubuisson himself identified Jesuits as "the worst scum of all" (Diskin and Sharpe 1986:63).

The dissent within the right that culminated with ANEP and FARO forming their own security apparatus might have been fatal and weakened the right altogether, but it instead proved to be a source of great momentum. As the hard-liners pulled support from the State and poured it into private armies, they simultaneously forced the government to shift right in order to prevent becoming obsolete altogether. That is not to say the country's conservatives moved wholesale to the hard-liner position; some moderates remained willing to give up small pieces of their fiefdom in order to preserve the entire system. But these moderates were rendered ineffectual in practice. Working outside the official structures of the State, ANEP, FARO, and the PMGs had made the critical move that would enable a facade of reform and even elections to continue without giving any real ground or posing genuine obstacles to the strong-arm tactics of repression and elimination.

# EL SALVADOR'S
# PMGS PEAK AND
# RECEDE

President Molina's heavy-handed repression, particularly against the university, and his choice of hard-liner Carlos Humberto Romero as candidate for his successor, drove many younger, more moderate officers within the military to organize outside the parameters of the armed forces. The Movimiento de la Juventud Militar (MJM), the Military Youth Movement, found its members among PCN loyalists who viewed the original corporatist plan as promising more stability than the Molina/Romero hard-line approach. Formed in 1976, the MJM openly criticized what it referred to as Molina's "police-terrorist clique," the political alliance of the State leadership and the security forces, at the expense of the armed forces, against the people, the "police-oligarchic cliques," and those misguided officers who viewed themselves as "in the service of a closed elitist minority that controls and appropriates the benefits of almost the entire wealth of the nation'" (Stanley 1996:92–95, 99; Dunkerley 1982:103). The oligarchy/security force "clique" so maligned by the MJM was indeed a tight group, and it would prove a fruitful alliance for the far right as the Romero administration dealt with heightened militancy from the left. Like the moderate political elite, the MJM was a voice of opposition, but it was also a minority faction.

Deflated by the blatant fraud that had brought Molina's presidency, factions of the left boycotted the 1976 election. Despite this, and in spite of increasing repression, UNO tried again to compete in national elections. Candidate Ernesto Claramount (who was a former military man himself) ran against the PCN candidate, Carlos Humberto Romero, who, after a day of ballot stuffing and attacks against UNO voters, was declared the winner. The UNO observation teams who had managed to oversee their polling stations unharassed had reported a lead by Claramount, which raised suspicion of the announced outcome. The fact that they had been permitted to observe the elections in the first place may indicate that these particular polling areas were unusually staunch UNO strongholds, and not at all representative of voting in the rest of the nation. Nonetheless, UNO supporters protested the fraud and occupied the Plaza Libertad in San Salvador. An initial crowd of fifteen thousand swelled to over fifty thousand in three days and was violently broken up by the National Police after midnight on 27 February (Montgomery 1995:72; Dunkerley 1982:104–6).

Though there are various accounts of precisely what happened that night, most converge around this sequence of events: The National Guard instructed everyone to leave the plaza and shortly thereafter opened fire (IACHR 1978:II.8, 10; Dunkerley 1982:106). Military authorities reported only one death; other sources reported hundreds. Other estimates fall in the middle, Montgomery arguing that "at least four dozen people were killed as Claramount and 1,500 supporters fled into El Rosario Church" (1995:72). Tallying the number of dead was complicated by government efforts to "clean-up," "gather[ing] the bodies of the dead and wounded following the confrontations with the security forces and bury[ing] them in secret places" (IACHR 1978:II.8). Like Duarte before him, Claramount and other UNO leaders went into hiding; others were apparently disappeared before they could escape (IACHR 1978:II.10; Dunkerley 1982:107). Attacks against the protestors did not end with the breakup of the demonstration. One of the priests who spoke out at the protest, Father Alfonso Navarro Oviedo, received a number of threats after the February protest, and his residence came under fire in April. He was murdered on 11 May 1977, by the White Warriors Union (IACHR 1978:II.4–5).

The Molina administration declared a state of siege the day after the Plaza Libertad demonstrations (29 February 1977) and did not lift it until late June. The Law for the Defense and Guarantee of the Public Order, Decree 407, was then adopted in November of the same year and would for years give "the military virtual carte blanche to pick up anyone it remotely suspected of being subversive in word or deed" (Montgomery 1995:73; LeoGrande 1998b:39). The law established a state of emergency under which any number of exceedingly broadly and generally defined activities could easily be construed as dangerous and even subversive (Dunkerley 1982:115). "The number of disappeared doubled, and political assassinations increased ten times" after the implementation of Decree 407 (Montgomery 1995:73; Diskin and Sharpe 1986:54).

President-elect General Humberto Romero had been president of CONDECA in the early 1970s (Dunkerley 1982:105) and had served as defense minister prior to being "elected" president. While serving as minister, Romero had worked diligently to block all attempts by moderates at land reform (LeoGrande 1998b:37–38). He had also earned a reputation for supporting (and perhaps overseeing) some of the worst and most uncontrolled violence unleashed upon the El Salvadoran public to that point. The presumption that he was clearly connected to or in control of the massive increase in violence was evident even at the international level. In 1977, when the White Warriors Union publicized their intent to eliminate the country's Jesuit priests, General Romero was contacted by U.S. officials trying to prevent the murders. The warning was heeded, as "the wholesale slaughter of the Jesuits never materialized," and indeed "the activities of the death squads subsided temporarily" (LeoGrande 1998b:38; Montgomery 1995:73).

General Romero spent his brief administration as Molina had, faced with the demands of the moderates and the diametrically opposed demands of the hard-liners. As a result, policy decisions often meant little in terms of meaningful changes. For instance, in 1979 Romero was pressured into removing the National Guard's head, General Ramón Alvarenga, who was "widely identified as the leading figure in the right's terror campaign" (Dunkerley 1982:127). But this move had little if any effect on the ground, since Alvarenga "still had considerable influence" and was working closely with Medrano and D'Aubuisson, who was, at the time, assistant chief of intelligence. Whether in official or unofficial positions, the right managed to continue their efforts unabated. In March and April 1979 alone, at least 130 people were "disappeared" by paramilitary forces, "and at least fifty members of the *Bloque* (BPR) were killed by ORDEN" (Dunkerley 1982:127).

More than seven hundred people were killed by the government and/or death squads between 1978 and 1979. Indeed it is clear that while Romero had to deal with contradictory demands by moderates and hard-liners, he himself favored the latter. The administration was finally "condemned ... for its systematic torture, murder and persecution of political dissidents" by the international NGO Amnesty International, by the Organization of American States, and by the U.S. Department of State (LeoGrande 1998b:39). But criticism could not undo the legacy of Romero's brief tenure; the administration had initiated an intense and unmitigated counter-insurgency push based on legislation that would continue to buttress the government's hard-liner approach for more than a decade to come.

Romero was ousted in a coup in 1979 by reformers within the military working in conjunction with like-minded civilians, most of whom were intending to end the political repression and address the rampant economic oppression. However, the original coup organizers were undermined by hard-liners within the military who got wind of the coup plan and played their cards perfectly to seat themselves in the highest positions of the new junta. This "JRG," or Junta Revolucionaria de Gobierno (Revolutionary Government Junta), came under the leadership of right-winger Colonel Jaime Abdul Gutiérrez, who then brought on Colonel José Guillermo García (minister of defense) and Colonel Nicolás Carranza, "who was on the CIA payroll at $90,000 per year" and who would play a significant role in ratcheting up the level of violence throughout the civil war. The more moderate Colonel Adolfo Majano also became a member of the governing junta, but he did not align himself with the extreme right-wing positions taken by his peers on many issues (Montgomery 1995:75–76). The junta's membership was rounded out by Universidad Centroamericana (UCA) rector Román Mayorga Quiros and Guillermo Ungo, who would represent the Foro Popular and social democrats (Stanley 1996:148–49). Despite the fact that the coup was originated by more moderate individuals, they were quickly sidelined by members like García and Carranza and were soon to have little if any impact on the direction of the country (LeoGrande 1998b:47).

The JRG promised to deal with human rights abuses, enact reforms to address the problems of political corruption and economic disparity, and hold the elections scheduled for 1982 (UN Security Council 1993:III:2). The junta also enacted some limited land reform under Decree 43, which "restrict[ed] landholdings to a maximum of 100 hectares." Some seemingly radical reforms dismantled ANSESAL and ORDEN and opened an investigation into the "disappeared." Within a month,

> a civilian court convicted an ORDEN leader for killing a teacher. . . . National Guardsmen (not officers) were dismissed from the service for "various violations," . . . [and] the junta appointed an additional commission to investigate secret burial sites. . . . On 28 November, the special investigative commission called for the trial of ex-presidents Molina and Romero and the former directors of the National Police, the National Guard, and the Treasury Police under the past two administrations. The commission claimed to have concrete evidence linking these commanders to 50 deaths. (Stanley 1996:150)

Despite the efforts, political tensions remained on the rise. Indeed, while the moderates were talking about reform and accountability, the right-wing members were doing everything they could to stop them. One example lies in the moderates' promise to investigate the disappearances of "300 missing political activists." A mere "two weeks after coming to power, the junta claimed it could not account for any of them." Of course, such an investigation would have required a serious inquiry into the military and Romero himself, something that was certain to "shatter the fragile unity of the armed forces, something the progressive officers refused to risk" (LeoGrande 1998b:41). Thus the junta was a combination of opposing forces with incompatible objectives, incapable of working in tandem.

Another prime example of the inconsistencies of the junta was that amid the talk of human rights and reform, García's first act was an all-out affront against the ERP guerrilla holds around San Salvador, arguing that counterinsurgency efforts trumped any talk of reform (Montgomery 1995:76). Indeed, while the governing council was making reforms that were to end military impunity and hold some of the most severe violators accountable, "either García or Carranza" instructed Roberto D'Aubuisson "to salvage [ANSESAL] files" from the commission investigating former regimes in order to continue their counterinsurgency outside the parameters of the State. D'Aubuisson in fact "spent three to four days at ANSESAL headquarters after the coup, then went into hiding" (Stanley 1996:150), strategically taking files that "contained photos and personal histories of suspected 'subversives'" (Montgomery 1995:76). He

> slipped into Guatemala under an assumed identity "so that if anything came up about human rights violations, he would be out of the country and they wouldn't try to pursue anything legal with him." He resigned from the military and returned secretly to El Salvador, where he worked on intelligence files, "on assignment" from someone in the Ministry of Defense, most likely Carranza. (Stanley 1996:150)

> D'Aubuisson made copies for himself, then . . . reorganized ANSESAL under the army chief of staff's office; it acquired a new name, the National Intelligence Agency (ANI)[,] and expanded responsibilities, and, like its predecessor, had close links with the CIA. (Montgomery 1995:76)

Promises to shut down ANSESAL and ORDEN operations therefore came to naught. While both organizations were officially disbanded by the Junta in 1979, Gutiérrez, D'Aubuisson, and probably Carranza worked to preserve the structure and objective of the organizations. D'Aubuisson made no bones about the intentions of himself and his comrades when he claimed in a speech that ORDEN had been "born in the bosom of the armed forces," and that though "ORDEN ha[d] ceased to exist to function with that name . . . its principles live and are newly serving the fatherland with the *Frente Democratica Nacionalista*" (FDN), the Democratic National Front, the new group D'Aubuisson started to continue the countersubversive work (Nairn 1984:28). Thus again we see the inability of the moderates to shut down hard-liner operations, in this case thanks to the fact that the reconfiguration of political allies (resulting in the triad necessary for paramilitary formation) was already in place and ready to take the operation underground.

By the 1980s, D'Aubuisson had positioned himself so that he no longer needed the official military structure to operate the network that had been mobilized under ANSESAL and ORDEN. D'Aubuisson had the experience and materials necessary to continue the operation, which he did first under the army chief of staff's office, and later underground. D'Aubuisson's allies within the governing junta gave him the opportunity to work directly under the nose of the reformers who were trying to reign in the exact operations he was reestablishing. García was particularly useful in that he was "repeatedly lying to civilian junta members about the location and actions of military units." This of course permitted those very same units to carry out the "repressive actions" that the civilian officials were working to stop (Stanley 1996:167). D'Aubuisson had successfully shifted the former ANSESAL responsibilities of the so-called intelligence gathering, and then used "a special 'investigations' section of the National Police" to resume the "operational aspects of ANSESAL (the actual killing)" (Stanley 1996:167).

## Moderation and Escalation

In 1979, the civilian members of the junta resigned after giving their military counterparts an ultimatum: replace García as minister of defense or the moderates would walk. García stayed, and the civilians kept their word, claiming that "the false notion of the neutrality of the military as an institution . . . has generated a rightward turn in the process of democratization and social change" (Diskin and Sharpe 1986:56; Sharpe 1981:2). This process has since been referred to as "*derechización*," or a shift to the right. The former junta members no longer saw any prospect for change in working through the institutions of government and organized the Frente Democrática Revolucionario (FDR), or the Revolutionary Democratic Front. The new organization brought together "Social Democrats, liberal Christian Democrats, and members of labor, student, professional and popular organizations" (Sharpe 1981:2), and it eventually served as a political arm to the FMLN to form the FDR-FMLN. Prospects for averting all-out war were dimming.

Determined to prevent further spiral into civil conflict, U.S. officials convinced some Christian Democratic leaders to give the institutions of government another try. This second junta included PDC members José Napoleon Duarte and Antonio Morales Ehrlich, both of whom had been exiled after the 1972 election (IACHR 1978:VI.1). Duarte and Ehrlich agreed to join the second junta on the condition that the military would begin respecting human rights. A year after taking office, Ehrlich conceded the tautological challenge preventing such objectives. "We have to change the way of thinking of the military; . . . It's better to have peace for that" (Southerland 1981b:3).

Meanwhile, the United States also became a central actor in pushing a land reform program. A team of U.S. advisors worked with (or through) the El Salvadoran legislature to devise a plan similar to that used in Vietnam and based on the thinking that giving some land to the peasants would defuse their potential or active support for the extreme left. The plan had three "phases," each intended to break down the oligarchy's concentration of landownership. The "Basic Agrarian Reform Law" (Phase I) was enacted in 1980 under Decree 153. The program raised hopes that the disparity underlying the intensifying civil conflict would be mitigated, undermining peasant support for the guerillas. Some estimates were that 80 percent of rural El Salvadorans would receive some land parcel, so that "the program w[ould] bring the first significant reshuffling of land holding patterns in El Salvador since colonial times" (Nelson 1980).

U.S. officials predicted that implementation of Phase I would require a strong security presence on the ground, and rightly so given that Decree 153 provided for the nationalization of all landholdings that exceeded five hundred hectares in size (Dunkerley 1982:154). By March 1980, the army had "seized fifty of the nation's largest plantations to begin the land take over" (Nelson 1980). But the decision to position the El Salvadoran military to help enforce the reform plan backfired when the troops instead punished those who were trying to implement the law.

One ISTA [Instituto Salvadoreño de Fomento Industrial, or Salvadoran Institute for Agrarian Transformation] technician assigned to oversee the reform related that, "the troops came and told the workers the land was theirs now. They could elect their own leaders and run the co-ops.

The peasants couldn't believe their ears, but held elections that very night. The next morning the troops came back and I watched as they shot every one of the elected leaders." (Dunkerley 1982:154)

The minister of agriculture provided further evidence of the extent to which such incidents took place. In his letter of resignation from the ministry (given shortly after Decree 153 was enacted and in "protest at the violence"), Jorge Alberto Villacorta wrote,

> During the first days of the reform . . . five directors and two presidents of the new *campesino* organizations were assassinated and I am informed that this repressive practice continues to increase. Recently, on one of the *haciendas* of the agrarian reform, uniformed members of the security forces accompanied by someone with a mask over his face, brought the workers together, the masked man was giving orders to the person in charge of the troops and these *campesinos* were gunned down in front of their co-workers. (Dunkerley 1982:155; Diskin and Sharpe 1986:62)

It was not only the campesinos and reform workers who were targeted. Elected officials who took the "wrong" stand on land reform were just as vulnerable. During a "heated debate on land reform" in October 1983, one assemblyman received a phone call while making a speech. Someone proving the near omnipresence of the operatives of the far right warned him to "shut up . . . [or] something serious would happen to [your] family" (Dickey 1983:17).

Phase I was implemented for only two months, and Phase II never made it out of the planning process (Dunkerley 1982:159). Despite the pullback, land reform workers and advocates continued to be harassed and assassinated. In 1981, the AIFLD (American Institute for Free Labor Development, an agency connected to the AFL-CIO in the United States) reported "evidence that most of the killings of land reform workers and beneficiaries have been carried out by the government security forces or rightist groups allied with some elements of those forces" (Southerland 1981a:3).

If it had been put into operation, Phase II was the element of the agrarian package that had the potential to do the most damage to the oligarchy's concentration of land ownership. Phase II would have nationalized all properties between 150 and 500 hectares in size and would have provided for the compensation of previous owners according to the "tax evaluations" of property values.[1] According to Dunkerley, "60 [percent] of all coffee production took place on farms of this size," so this part of the agrarian reform "posed the real threat to the power of the oligarchy" (Dunkerley 1982:159). An even bigger threat to the oligarchy was the basis of the compensation plan — those "tax evaluations" had been conducted by the landowners themselves, who had frequently undervalued their own property so as to pay fewer taxes. Many landowners found loopholes and avoided the nationalization and appropriation of their land by parceling and selling it off themselves. Such was the case of San Carlos de Guirola, a farm outside Santa Tecla, formerly owned by Elena Guirola.

> To avoid expropriation, [Elena] had sold it right before the land reform to a group of two hundred of her friends. . . . The owners were still the rich; the coffee harvesters were still landless. . . . The first people I saw were a family of workers cooking coffee, tortillas, and rice with carrots over an outdoor fire in back of the shed they slept in. They were migrant farm workers and earned 140 *colones* ($28) for fifteen days' work. . . . Other landowners heavily mortgaged their land, killed their cattle, and sold off the machinery right before the reform. (Rosenberg 1991:246)

The third phase of the agrarian reform was intended to give renting peasants the land they worked "once they had met the market price through aggregate payments of rent" (Dunkerley 1982:158). However, the program was ill designed for El Salvador and the topography of its rural areas. Most landless peasants who rented plots cooperated informally with each other to rotate crops while allowing others to lie fallow, a system that was crucial to productivity given the quality and type of land they were farming. Phase III of the land reform project did not allow this informal rotation to continue, locking peasants into problems with erosion and declining yield. In addition, the shift to coffee decades earlier had changed the labor force and left many peasants without even a plot to rent, making Phase III worthless for the majority of the country's poorest (Dunkerley 1982:158–60; Southerland 1983d).

While the junta was proving its inability to enact meaningful reform, the guerrillas were, allegedly on the advice of Fidel Castro, working to overlook their differences and exploit their potential strength in numbers. The FMLN was organized in 1980, joining the ERP, the RN (FARN), and FPL, along with the Partido Revolucionario de Trabajadores Centroamericanos (PRTC), or Revolutionary Party of Central American Workers, and the Fuerzas Armadas de Liberación (FAL), the Armed Forces of Liberation (see UN Security Council 1993:III:3; Montgomery 1995:110; and Dunkerley 1982:169). The FDR later joined the organization, and it came to be known as the FDR-FMLN. Shortly thereafter, the group was "recognized as a 'representative political force' by the Mexican, French, Dutch and Spanish governments" (Diskin and Sharpe 1986:58). The FMLN employed a diverse range of tactics in its effort against the government and the military, attacking the variety of individuals and offices the government was trying to use to co-opt moderates, collect information on guerrilla activity, and repress political activism.

In response to the strengthening guerrilla movement, El Salvador's military heightened its counterinsurgency campaign, largely with the help of U.S. military aid. The U.S. efforts to pursue democratization in the reconstitution of the junta was directly contradicted by a simultaneous increase in military aid. As the United States was pushing for a moderate power-sharing arrangement, it was also sending counterinsurgency advisors and six military helicopters (LeoGrande 1998b:45–46). This was while the very civilians the United States had convinced the join the junta argued that the military was "where the problem begins" and openly acknowledged links between the military and the death squads (Southerland 1981b:2, 3).

Nonetheless, the outgoing Carter administration, which had made human rights standards part of its overall foreign policy agenda, stood in stark contrast to the incoming republican Ronald Reagan. More conservative and hawkish, Reagan and his cabinet weighed the balance between holding the El Salvadoran army to certain standards and holding the communists at bay differently than the Carter administration had; for Reagan, Central America was the new battleground against communism. In El Salvador as elsewhere, the Reagan administration saw an immediate threat of a Soviet proxy in the Western Hemisphere, and that threat called for a return to a style of international intervention predating the Carter administration. Foreign leaders who were loyal allies of the United States in the stand against communism received full U.S. support, regardless of their domestic popular support or human rights record (see LeoGrande 1998b:5–6).[2]

Archbishop Oscar Romero, a significant religious and political figure in El Salvador, advised the United States against increasing the military aid in 1979, predicting it would only enable the right to "sharpen the 'regime's injustices and repression'" (LeoGrande 1998b:44; Pyes 1984:353). The archbishop's prediction came to pass. The military aid continued, and Christian Democrats were among those increasingly targeted by

D'Aubuisson and his death squads. In the first three months of 1981 alone, there were an estimated 689 political assassinations (Diskin and Sharpe 1986:56). Over the course of the year, 60 PDC "mayors and other officials [were] assassinated by death squads" (Montgomery 1995:158). Instead of peace and stabilization, "the process of political polarization triggered an unprecedented increase in death squad activities" (UN Security Council 1993:III.2).

The 1980 implementation of land reform, the increasing organization and mobilization of the guerrilla organizations, and an increasingly restless and outspoken civil society was agitating El Salvador's nervous and disconcerted right. A state of siege was declared in March 1980, which effectually limited or ended most civil liberties, including "freedom of movement . . . and freedom of assembly . . . [and permitted] detention for six months without charge or access to counsel, . . . extrajudicial confessions — for example those coerced through torture — to be used as evidence" (Diskin and Sharpe 1986:57). Amnesty International later recognized this policy as "facilitat[ing] 'death squad' 'disappearances' and killings" in that it allowed the military to take individuals into custody without acknowledging that they had done so. This created a situation in which individuals could be taken, tortured, and murdered by security agents who could blame the "unacknowledged arrest" on the invisible "death squads" (AI 1988:12). Perhaps as a result of the state of siege or frustration with the limited military activity, death squad violence was about to increase exponentially.

Indeed 1980 was a year of unprecedented violence in which El Salvadorans learned that absolutely no one was safe from the far right's campaign. The FPL and ERP stepped up their operations. Death squads did the same. Mario Zamora, then leader of the Christian Democrat Party, was assassinated in his home in February; Archbishop Romero was assassinated while giving mass in a hospital chapel in March; dozens of attendees were then gunned down at the archbishop's funeral. More than one hundred strikers were killed during an FDR demonstration, and three months later six of the group's leaders were disappeared by the Anti-Communist Brigade–Maximiliano Hernández Martínez death squad, "their bodies . . . found later, bearing signs of torture" (UN Security Council 1993:II.3; LeoGrande 1998b:59). The Christian Democrats again began to withdraw from the government, seeing the impotence — and downright danger — of their work (LeoGrande 1998b:46). The situation only highlighted the total and complete separation between the civilian government, within which the Christian Democrats were working, and the military, who were supporting the death squads and eliminating the Christian Democrats. Estimates are that by the end of the year, there were an average of two hundred "civilian noncombatants" killed every week (Diskin and Sharpe 1986:58), with death squads alone being responsible for thirty to forty every day in November 1980 (Southerland 1981a:1).

The Rapid Deployment Infantry Battalions were organized as part of the expanded counterinsurgency campaign in the early 1980s and were designed to be "specialized in anti-guerrilla warfare" (UN Security Council 1993:III.4). These battalions, known as BIRI (Batallón de Infantería de Reacción Inmediata), and the Atlacatl Battalion in particular (which was created in 1981 and trained by advisors from the United States), earned a reputation for some of the war's worst violence against civilians, including the El Mozote massacre (UN Security Council 1993:III:4, III.B:1).[3] El Mozote is a small town in Morazán and was one of three such towns attacked on 11 December 1981, by the Atlacatl Battalion. Using a strategy reminiscent of the "slash and burn" deforestation technique, the battalion moved through the three towns, killing more than 900 civilians (LeoGrande 1998b:155). Of those murdered, 482 were in El Mozote, and "280 [of those] were under fourteen years of age" (Montgomery 1995:152). More than ten years later, UN officials working at a mass grave at El Mozote "found 143 skeletons, of which 85 [percent] belonged to children less than twelve years of age" (Stanley 1996:225). The FMLN had received intelligence regarding the impending attack and was evacuating thousands from the area before the BIRI arrived. However, hundreds who were not affiliated with the guerrillas and had never been attacked by the military before chose to stay behind, believing they would not be targeted (Montgomery 1995:153; Stanley 1996:225; UN Security Council 1993:IV.C.1.).

El Salvadoran officials justified the attack at El Mozote—despite the lack of evidence connecting the victims to the FMLN—and the continued use of this "slash and burn" technique, arguing that "Civilians who don't want to cooperate [with the guerrillas] leave the area and those who remain are collaborating" (Montgomery 1995:152). This sort of generalization was repeatedly used by the military in place of genuine intelligence, despite the hyperdeveloped intelligence capabilities of the State. The Atlacatl Battalion was later involved in a massacre at Las Llanitos that took the lives of forty-two peasants, after which a major explained that his troops were justified because "There are no people living in those hamlets—only terrorists" (Diskin and Sharpe 1986:76). Another commander likewise asserted that "I can massively bomb the red zones because only subversives live in them" (Montgomery 1995:152), further indicating that the countersubversive strategy did not differentiate innocent civilians from enemy combatants. This conceptualization of the enemy would soon prove to be a divisive issue for the far right, and one that would only fan the paramilitary fire.

Overall, efforts to augment the military and improve its counterinsurgency performance paid off. Between 1980 and 1984, the El Salvadoran military more than tripled in size (from 12,000 troops to 42,000). Of the 5,639 people who were killed in El Salvador in 1982, only 762 were military, while 2,547 were guerrillas and the balance — 2,330 people — were civilians (UN Security Council 1993:III:5). Despite the apparent strength of the forces, there were contentious issues that divided the leadership. Majano led a faction that supported and actively tried to implement restraints against human rights violations (Stanley 1996:167), and he was described as "politically close to UNO" (Dunkerley 1982:135). The García faction preferred the traditional hard-liner strategies. Majano had played a critical role in working with U.S. officials to arrange the power-sharing junta. Indeed, he was viewed by the United States as moderate enough to serve as a negotiator with the leftist opposition forces (LeoGrande 1998b:46–47). All hopes of Majano and his allies taking a conciliatory leadership role were dashed, however, as the group was eventually "marginalized," and the García faction continued to gain traction, though notably not without some help from allies in Washington (Dunkerley 1982:136). Majano was eventually pushed out of the junta, "arrested by his military colleagues and sent into exile" (Southerland 1981c:1; Sharpe 1981:2).

But Majano's removal did not resolve the problems for the right. As the campaign against the guerrillas intensified, it became increasingly evident that El Salvador was engaged in an unsustainable strategy. Although the military was determined to use brutal and definitive tactics against the subversives and their suspected sympathizers, they were also an eager recipient of U.S. aid. As U.S. support more than quadrupled from 1980 to 1981, and then again by 1983 (Montgomery 1995:131, 151; Alonso 1984:177), the monies were accompanied with pressure to stop the more heinous military activities and support U.S. reform initiatives. Where the far-right politicians and military had once been indivisible due to perceived shared interests, the foreign money and support coming into the military began to undermine this solidarity. The far right, consistently against land reform and in support of the strong-arm military tactics, found that the United States was increasingly able to manipulate the military using the aid monies like puppeteer strings. The pending division between them and the military, lured by the U.S. incentives, became painfully evident to the right's hard-liners in 1982.

It soon became apparent that if the military were on the wrong side of the land reform issues, then military aid would be in jeopardy. Much to the consternation of the right, this was enough to get the armed forces to change their tune, and the military began intervening on behalf of the peasants, returning them to their plots and preventing further displacement (LeoGrande 1998b:166–70). Fortunately for the far right, the death squads were not beholden to any such foreign entity and provided a means by which two seemingly incompatible goals could be pursued: the extermination of insurgents and the financial support of the United States.

## Bullets and Ballots

Protected under the shroud of cold war anticommunist rhetoric, the country's paramilitary groups kept up the campaign against the left after pressure from the United States prohibited the official State security apparatus from doing so. Groups that had long been targeted by the State, including unions, peasant organizations, and leftist political parties, were prime targets, along with Catholic priests, nuns, and social organizations; teachers and students; and human rights and aid workers. While the military may have publicly adopted a policy for land reform, the collusion with PMGs was apparent. Indeed, even a "death list" published by the army's official press office in 1981 was a replica of one put out previously by a "death squad." There were 138 people on the list, many of whom were subsequently disappeared, held in prison, or exiled (AI 1988:10). The army press copy closed with the following: "The Armed Forces, complying with their constitutional mission to defend the Salvadorean people, incessantly tracks down all those traitors to the country, to pay for all the great harm they have done" (AI 1988:11).

Among the plethora of examples illustrating the relationship between PMGs and the military in their campaign against moderates is the assault on and murder of six FDR leaders in 1980. In November of that year, Enrique Alvarez Córdoba, Juan Chacón, Enrique Escobar Barrera, Manuel de Jesús Franco Ramírez, Humberto Mendoza, and Doroteo Hernández were kidnapped from the Colegio San José by "a large number of heavily armed men." The FDR leaders were taken the morning of the 27th from a campus that was in close proximity to the heavily protected U.S. Embassy and were subsequently "tortured and, after a short period in captivity, executed in

San Salvador."[4] The "number of vehicles" that were used to enter the campus and carry out the abduction apparently did not draw the attention of those guarding the embassy. Security forces and justice officials were similarly ineffective after the incident, when only four of the reported "considerable number" of witnesses of the incident were interviewed by police officials. Those same officials subsequently refused to hand their report over to the Truth Commission (UN Security Council 1993:IV.B.2:5).

Despite having to deal with an uncooperative National Police force, the Truth Commission did reach a series of important findings on the case of the six assassinated FDR leaders. The commission found that "the operation was carried out by paramilitary groups, by security forces or by a combination of the two; it may also have been an independent operation by members of those State organs." They report that credit for the attack was claimed by the Brigada Anticomunista General Maximiliano Hernández Martínez,[5] but that

> Indeed, the time, the place, the number of personnel, the radio equipment, vehicles, weapons and uniforms used, the slang and the chain of command, the fact that the participants withdrew without any problem and the absence of a proper investigation by the security forces indicate the extent to which those forces were involved.... The Commission has substantial evidence that the Treasury Police carried out the external security operation which aided and abetted those who committed the murders. (UN Security Council 1993:IV.B.2:5–6).

In addition to concluding that the attack could not have been carried out without some significant support from within the official military structure, the commission also reported that the Anti-Communist Brigade, the PMG that claimed responsibility for the murders, was one that had been "identified as one of several which the extreme right-wing used to claim responsibility for such actions." In other words, the PMGs were being used by the far right to carry out those activities, to take care of those members of the opposition, which the official military could not do without facing serious repercussions. In addition, the commission received witness testimony that "at the time the incident occurred, some soldiers in active service were members of the [Anti-Communist] Brigade" (UN Security Council 1993:IV.B.2:5).

One interviewee, a Christian Democrat who had been very outspoken and active politically during the civil war, said that the hard-liners within the military and the death squads were trying to eliminate the entire Christian Democratic party, and that without intervention from the United States on the side of the moderates, there would have been many more killed. In 1980 when Duarte and other PDC officials agreed to cooperate and even serve in the second junta, there was significant dissent within the party due to the fact that this required cooperating with individuals suspected of having ties to the death squads. And even as early as 1980, the "losses in the party [had] been high, and most of them . . . attributed to right-wing death squads" (Southerland 1981b:2). High-ranking party leaders like Zamora as well as general members of the party were targets throughout the 1980s, some of whom were disappeared and later found killed.

The violent campaign against the Catholic Church and its leadership is probably among the most well-known and historically studied of those carried out by El Salvador's security forces in cooperation with PMGs. Oscar Arnulfo Romero had been trusted by the right prior to his appointment as archbishop. But after his appointment, Romero strongly advocated for the country's poor and spoke in defense of human rights and democratic principles. Romero's strong voice, position of leadership, and growing popularity quickly made him an enemy of the far right. The archbishop was giving mass on 24 March 1980, when a man later identified as Héctor Antonio Regalado entered the chapel and assassinated him, shooting him in the back in full view of parishioners. Regalado was (and continued to be for several years afterward) the personal bodyguard to Roberto D'Aubuisson. He arrived at the chapel in a car that was driven by the personal driver for the military's Captain Alvaro Sarávia (UN Security Council 1993:III:3; Stanley 1996:196; IACHR 1989:5).

Official investigations by a number of unrelated but reliable sources into the assassination found that neither the driver nor the bodyguard were acting independently of their employers. Sarávia was found to have taken a lead in planning Romero's murder, with assistance from Captain Eduardo Avila, and to have paid the assassin.[6] The Commission for the Investigation of Crimes by the Salvadoran government also found credible evidence that directly connected D'Aubuisson to the plot (UN Security Council 1993:III:3; Stanley 1996:196; Montgomery 1995:97; IACHR 1989:5). Indeed, the commission found that the first stop made by the assassin and driver after shooting Romero was at D'Aubuisson's house, allegedly "to report accomplishment of the mission of finishing off the prelate" (IACHR 1989:5). None of these faced prosecutorial justice in El Salvador. This single assassination and the utter absence of any investigation, arrests, or prosecution in the months and years that followed left no doubt about the unmitigated power and influence of the PMGs or about their connections within the military and State institutions.

Civil society organizations mobilized around victims' rights, human rights, and indigenous people's issues were targeted by the right, as well. The Marianella García Villas organization and the Monsignor Oscar Arnulfo Romero organization, both "Mothers' Groups" formed by mothers of war victims, were targeted by the armed forces, the police, and PMGs. Offices were searched and individual women were questioned, arrested (some of them repeatedly), and accused of being guerrilla sympathizers (IACHR 1986:4). The quarters of Las Comadres, the Mother's Committee, were attacked by "heavily armed men dressed in civilian clothes" in May 1987 who detonated a bomb outside the offices (IACHR 1987:4). The head of the Human Rights Commission, an NGO operating in El Salvador, was assassinated in October 1987 outside his home (IACHR 1988:2).

The historical harassment of unions and trade organizations likewise intensified during the civil war. Cooperatives in particular suffered at the hands of the far right, even during periods when human rights violations were less severe, as during the mid-1980s. Activists were "arrested, mistreated, wounded and, according to the reports, some have even disappeared" (5). One cooperative suffered a particularly brutal attack by "two hundred soldiers . . . with M-16 rifles" in February 1983. The Indian tribe residing on the cooperative had refused the owners of the adjacent property permission to construct a road through the cooperative. Shortly thereafter, the soldiers came and took eighteen of the tribal men, thumbs tied behind their backs, a practice frequently used by El Salvadoran security forces. The men were among the country's many "unacknowledged detainees," as the local authorities denied that any members of the cooperative had been detained. "Later that day, the Indians found the corpses of eighteen of their men in the bushes, shot dead, their thumbs tied behind their backs" (Zuckerman 1983:11). Over the course of September 1983, at least one hundred union activists were disappeared (Hedges 1983:1).

As in Mexico and Colombia, teachers and students were also targets in El Salvador. The University of El Salvador (UES) and the University of Central America (UCA) both were targeted by State and PMG operations at various times throughout the course of the civil war. Teachers were increasingly targeted in 1980 and 1981, even when urban assassinations seemed to be decreasing (Southerland 1981a:1). Works published by UCA were collected by intelligence officials and stored at the "National police political intelligence archive" (Nairn 1984:24). In 1989, the military's "Operation Tornado" isolated UES from the surrounding areas, claiming that guerrilla supporters were using the campus to store weapons and provide cover for insurgents (IACHR 1989:5).

Enabling this systematic elimination of opposition was the terror campaign waged against the justice system. Attacks against and manipulation of judges and other officers of the court resulted in the "collapse of an entire judicial system" (Southerland 1983b:2). The PMGs operated in an environment in which they enjoyed full and total immunity; the armed forces of course did not seek justice for any of the crimes committed by the paramilitaries, as most of their members and operations originated from within their ranks, and the civilian system of justice was effectively disabled (see Southerland 1983b). Thus impunity was assured.

The Truth Commission took up the question of why and how this vast array of civil society actors became legitimate military targets to the country's far right. Consumed by what the commission referred to as a "warped psychology engendered by the conflict," the right allegedly became victim to tunnel vision characterized by "the doctrine of national salvation and the principle of 'he who is not for me is against me,'" which then enabled them to "ignore the neutrality, passivity and defenselessness of journalists and church workers" (UN Security Council 1993:I.3). However, the fact that the right had been targeting this same range of groups for decades cannot be ignored. Priests were being murdered for advocating democracy in the early 1970s, and opposition parties and labor unions had been violently torn down for decades prior to that. History tells us that these groups did not become targets after the conflict had begun, and even less so after it had raged long enough to "engender . . . a warped psychology." Rather, the targeting of these groups became *intensified* during the civil conflict, as the possibility of losing control over the system of spoils became increasingly real in the military's failure to quickly and decisively defeat the guerrillas. The historically consistent pattern of repression indicates that El Salvador's oligarchs and military officials had long viewed a lack of submission to their supremacy as dangerous subversion. The period immediately preceding the civil war and the civil war itself are distinguished in the extent and intensity of violent repression used against the "opposition," an answer to the unprecedented level of organization and resource mobilization on the part of the left.

Taken together, the relationship and overlap between the armed forces and the death squads and the nearly identical list of targets raises an obvious question: If the security forces, the military, and the death squads had a shared objective, shared resources, and even overlapping personnel, why was it necessary to have all of them? Why didn't the military just take care of everything itself? Why create additional or external organizations, a process that would seemingly decrease efficiency and perhaps even create the potential for autonomy from one another, diluting centralized power?

An established Salvadoran academic explained in an interview that the security forces, the armed forces, and the death squads were "not distinct at all, [in that they were] part of the same. They all fell under the military." They did not have one central leader or commander, he said, but they were "all directed or connected by their connection to the military."[§] Salvador Samayoa concurred, observing that "the death squads and patrols and police and army, the government, were all one — they were the same" (Samayoa 2003). When I asked the sociologist why the right had felt it necessary to have all of these various groups fighting against the left instead of just centralizing the effort under the military, he explained,

> Together they make a complete system, a strong system of domination, control. The military, well, they called any opposition "communist" — and were thus officially fighting a civil war against guerrillas, against communism. The police and National Guard were [providing] local control, and working with the military. The civil patrols were to mobilize or rally the population. And the death squads took very specific targets and assassinated them.[§]

While division of labor makes sense, the point remains that the military could have delegated different responsibilities within its own ranks. I asked why the military did not simply take care of the targeted assassinations themselves. My interviewee pointed out that "they were the official military, and these others were illegal. . . . The military was concerned about its legitimacy, and used these [others] in the system of domination . . . for control."[§]

An established human rights advocate with expertise in El Salvador suggested there was indeed a level of "hypocrisy" within the military, such that its members worked to "keep the appearance of legality" while also "wanting to say, 'that was them'" and absolve themselves publicly of activities they were at least sympathetic to and at most involved with and directing.[§] Certainly the United States had given El Salvador's armed forces the incentive to "outsource" their more gruesome offenses to faceless groups whose acts could not be traced back to the State. Under the Carter administration, aid monies had been explicitly contingent upon respect for human rights and a visible commitment to democratic reform. This indeed made it very difficult for the El Salvadoran military to continue targeting labor unions and Christian Democrats and also receive the much-desired military aid from the United States. The murder of four U.S. churchwomen and subsequent withdrawal of aid was proof enough that the military simply could not have both.

The Reagan administration made a clear departure from the Carter doctrine's emphasis on human rights, and it immediately began asking Congress for additional aid monies for El Salvador. Democrats became increasingly suspicious that Reagan's policy in Central America was headed down the wrong path, and they began to create a new type of oversight role for Congress. Beginning at the 1982 budget cycle, any funding that was approved for El Salvador would trigger a biannual certification process, whereby "within thirty days after the foreign aid bill was signed into law and every six months thereafter," the president's administration would have to "certify" before Congress that "progress was being made towards" ending the State involvement in human rights violations, gaining authority over the military, holding elections, instituting land reform, and negotiating an end to the war with the guerrillas (LeoGrande 1998b:131–32). If the administration could not certify that the El Salvadoran government was making such progress, aid would not be granted.

The certification requirement was weak to the point of being impotent because it put the burden of proof on the administration rather than in the lap of Congress, so that the "oversight" was limited to just that. Nonetheless, had the armed forces continued their blatant disregard for human rights—such as leaving corpses in the streets, as had been so frequent during the Romero administration—the certification process would have been much more difficult if not impossible for the White House. D'Aubuisson and others on the far-right acknowledged themselves that the armed forces were constrained by frivolities like "human rights," and consequently were being forced to lose the war to communists. While the Congressional Democrats had hoped that the U.S. aid, conditioned upon certification, might help bring the human rights violations under control, it seems that it only gave further impetus for the far right, whose call for unmitigated repression had already been neglected by the moderate right, to organize their own means to their ends.

Thus it seems that the use of death squads—or the use of the identity of the deaths squad—was a tactic employed by El Salvador's right-wingers in order to "have their cake and eat it too." Wanting to maintain legitimacy in the eyes of their patron, the United States, did not mitigate in any way their simultaneous determination to not capitulate to the left. The United States was trying to promote its pro-democracy agenda by funding an antidemocratic military. PMGs gave the right wing a means both to continue the elimination of the left, fighting the war on their terms, while also to cash in on the aid from the United States.

The United States pro-democracy/pro-military strategy actually complicated things for El Salvador's hard-liners in two ways. First, the military lost its ability to overtly massacre the opposition if it wanted the money. The right found its way around this, led by Medrano and D'Aubuisson. But the pro-democracy emphasis was putting a second wrench in the works, as the right was also losing its ability to rely on its long tradition of election fraud to monopolize political power.

Despite the fact that political murders in the first months of 1981 averaged three hundred to five hundred weekly, and that in 1982 alone more than fifty-six hundred people were killed in the conflict (UN Security Council 1993:III:5), moderates continued efforts to establish a stable democracy forcing right-wingers to prepare for their own success in just such an arena. The continuation of elections and the increasing oversight of the United States and United Nations made traditional fraud difficult. Thus the right was forced not only to step up their repression against the opposition, but also to strengthen their own ability to run against the opposition in a fair election.

When D'Aubuisson went to Guatemala to first organize the PMGs, he established ties with some critical allies, including a Guatemalan named Mario Sandoval Alarcón. Sandoval was head of his country's right-wing Movimiento de Liberación Nacional (MLN), or National Liberation Movement (LeoGrande 1998b:159) and became a critical figure in the development of the far right in El Salvador. He advised D'Aubuisson on the limited longevity inherent to "death squads," advising that the tit for tat between the death squads and the guerrillas ("if they kill you, you kill back") was a short-term strategy at best. He told D'Aubuisson that without some degree of political organization, they were doomed to a short life span. "Sandoval supplied advice, raised money among right wing Miami exiles for the political activities of D'Aubuisson's cabal, helped smuggle weapons into El Salvador, and later supplied planes and pilots to ferry hit men in and out of the country" (Montgomery 1995:132; Pyes 1984:352). Thus Sandoval was an important link for D'Aubuisson, helping him round up the financial resources, much of which had left the country as the oligarchy fled to other parts of Central America or Miami, necessary for a truly expansive network of paramilitaries. But more important to the long-term success of D'Aubuisson's goals was the advice about forming a political organization.

In late 1981, as El Salvador was inching closer to the 1982 elections, D'Aubuisson and his network announced the formation of a new political party out of some previously organized groups, including "the Broad National Front, made up of private business associations, antireform groups of coffee growers and cattle ranchers, young executives, a women's association, and a right-wing nationalist youth organization; the old ORDEN network . . . and the civilian-military death-squad network that D'Aubuisson and the extreme right had organized" (Diskin and Sharpe 1986:63). Of course he also incorporated his traditional allies, the "landowners, middle-class professionals, and retired military officers" (Boyd 1982:1). The new party was named the Alianza Republicana Nacional (ARENA), or the National Republican Alliance, and it ran none other than D'Aubuisson as its presidential candidate. As he took to the campaign trail, D'Aubuisson developed an effective stump speech in which he energetically accused the Christian Democrats of being communists. His most infamous analogy involved the use of a machete and a watermelon. Hacking open the watermelon, he compared it to the Christian Democrats: "Green on the outside, Red on the inside" (LeoGrande 1998b:159). The party also condemned the human rights standards that they viewed as handcuffing El Salvadoran armed forces in their fight against the guerrillas. For ARENA, talk of reigning in the military to meet U.S. standards was only giving the guerrillas an edge (LeoGrande 1998b:160), and D'Aubuisson promised that if elected, ARENA would "let the Army go and finish off the communists in six month'" (Boyd 1982:1).

It is significant that ARENA was the only political party that would campaign openly, even preannouncing scheduled public events, during El Salvador's 1982 campaign season. Living in exile, a former leftist activist explained to a journalist, "in November 1980 we had one of [our] last public meetings. The paramilitaries came and hauled all the leaders of the 'Revolutionary Democratic Front' [FDR] away and killed them" (Boyd 1982:2). D'Aubuisson's death squads had definitively "cleared the field" of political competitors. Those who dared to run could not campaign at public rallies and events, as D'Aubuisson could.

The 1982 elections for an "interim government" were not quite decisive.

There were sixty seats to be filled by the array of parties. The FDR-FMLN boycotted the election. The Christian Democrats won twenty-four of the sixty seats, more than any other single party. But ARENA won nineteen and the PCN won fourteen, and three seats went to smaller right-wing parties (LeoGrande 1998b:161).[7] After much cajoling and negotiating on the part of the United States and the Christian Democrats, Alvaro Magaña was chosen to serve as president.[8]

Magaña's selection was based not so much on party or ideology as on the fact that he was acceptable to a broad range of actors (Stanley 1996:232; Montgomery 1995:161; Kidder 1983). Had the military remained aligned with ARENA in opposing any inclusion of the Christian Democrats in a shared-government arrangement, D'Aubuisson would have become president. It is entirely plausible that Magaña was acceptable to the military, despite its loyalty to D'Aubuisson, because of the fact that Magaña had previously served as president of Banco Hipotecario, a central bank in the country, and from that position had given "preferential loans to military officers." Such influence may have served him well in being named president (Kidder 1983:3). But other theories abound, including speculation that the fact that that military agreed to support Magaña only after the United States made it clear that D'Aubuisson was not a viable option (Stanley 1996:232; Montgomery 1995:161). D'Aubuisson was made president of the Constituent Assembly (Montgomery 1995:162), giving the central figure of the paramilitary network direct access to and power of the State.

Magaña was installed along with three vice presidents, representing the PDC, PCN, and ARENA. Despite spoken commitments to human rights and democracy and "economic recovery," the "National Unity" power-sharing pact was perhaps more of a hindrance than a help in making any real progress toward reform. Indeed, Magaña himself recognized the true seat of political power in the country, noting that "although he [was] officially commander in chief of the armed forces, he [saw] his role in staff meetings more as 'a friend giving advice.'" One observer noted that as president, Magaña had "only as much power as the people who want to give him power will give him" (Kidder 1983:3, 2).

## Undulations on a Road to Peace

Throughout the 1980s, El Salvador could be described much as Colombia might be today, a country plagued by a sort of split personality. At war with itself and yet holding democratic elections, the country was torn between irreconcilable forces. The far right still refused to concede any legitimacy or reform to the left, the left demanded genuine and transparent democracy and economic reform that included redistribution; the far right employed paramilitary groups to terrorize and eliminate the left, the leftists continually surprised their foes and proved the inadequacy of the armed forces; and the far right ran political candidates with close ties to the PMGs who accused even the most moderate of being communists, while the leftists refused to participate in elections held in a war zone and demanded the paramilitary engineers be held accountable for their crimes.

Peace talks started and sputtered over the decade but to no avail, largely because there simply was nothing with which mediators could build a bridge between the two sides. Neither had significant leverage over the other, and there was no common ground shared between the two. When Magaña initiated peace talks in 1982 under the advice of the United States, D'Aubuisson declared the negotiations to be "the most vile treason and an unqualifiably absurd policy" (LeoGrande 1998b:178), and the paramilitary groups cranked up their efforts a notch.[9] As in Colombia during the 1990s, the fact that the war raged around the electoral institutions of the State and that the PMGs continued to act, and to even greater extents, despite calls for peace talks, calls into considerable question the real significance of the elections, and whether those elected had any real political authority at all.

Despite this, the country continued down both tracks. Between 1982 and 1983, the country was both fighting a civil war and preparing for presidential elections, scheduled for 1984. Efforts on the part of the United States to professionalize the El Salvadoran military were of minimal if any success, as the traditional elements of military culture remained nearly unaffected. Loyalty to one's *tanda*, or cohort in military school, was of utmost importance, and promotion continued to be based entirely upon keeping *tandas* together rather than on performance or accountability, giving U.S. advisors very little leverage for rewarding progress or punishing failure. Military offensives continued to be broad attacks on primarily civilian areas, rather than specified strikes against identified guerrilla units. And while there was a decline in the number of those killed between 1982 and 1983, the number of disappeared rose significantly over the same period (Montgomery 1995:165–72).

Meanwhile, the United States was making repeated attempts to send the message that the human rights violations were becoming difficult to overlook. These efforts were capped with a visit to El Salvador by Vice

President George H. W. Bush, who was sent with a clear and unmistakable message. First, he "publicly condemned the death squads" (UN Security Council 1993:III, part 2:1–2), and then he presented the Magaña administration with two lists: the first, a list of names of high-ranking military officials with suspected (or confirmed) ties to paramilitary activity, including the commander of the Treasury Police, Nicolás Carranza; the head of the National Center for Analysis and Investigations, Aristides Márquez (Stanley 1996:229); and the "head of Assembly security," Héctor Antonio Regalado (Montgomery 1995:177; Stanley 1996:229). Washington wanted these individuals removed from their positions. The second list contained the litany of benefits the El Salvadoran military would reap from following through on dismantling or decapitating the PMGs. This list included "enough money from Congress 'to field 39 fully equipped counter-subversion battalions, 2 immediate reaction battalions, and an engineering battalion, . . . A-37 aircraft, transport aircraft, helicopters, augmented artillery, and naval patrol and landing crafts'" (Stanley 1996:229).

Bush's visit did have some effect. Soon after his visit, death squad activity did decline (see Stanley 1996:229). In fact, the Truth Commission concluded that Bush's visit and message was directly related to "a reduction in the number of violations" committed by the death squads (UN Security Council 1993:III, part 2:1–2). However, there were no significant nor meaningful personnel changes in the military leadership. Indeed, cabinet positions continued to be filled by D'Aubuisson minions, and the first list presented by Bush remained largely ignored (Montgomery 1995:177–78).

The impact of the Bush visit was perhaps mitigated by the fact that as paramilitary activity was curtailed, military activity picked up. In 1984, the El Salvadoran armed forces stepped up efforts in their counter insurgency and began high-intensity air raids thanks to U.S. advisors and helicopters. Categorizing civilians as "legitimate targets for attack" rather than as collateral losses they would prefer to avoid, the military began using "indiscriminate aerial bombings, massive artillery attacks and infantry advances," all of which resulted in a massive loss of life and internal displacement (UN Security Council 1993:III, part 2:1). The numbers of displaced quickly escalated, rising by more than 25 percent in only the first seven months of 1984. The increase was even more dramatic in areas that were under firm government control (Montgomery 1995:173), indicating that the raids were either poorly targeted or intended to terrorize and displace civilians rather than to crush the insurgency itself.

One positive force for peace came from perhaps a most unexpected place, the Pope. After the assassination of Archbishop Romero, the Catholic Church had refrained from naming another archbishop and had taken steps to ensure a more moderate role by the church's highest leadership in the country. But when Pope John Paul II spoke in San Salvador, just eighteen days before the third anniversary of Romero's assassination, he used his speech to reaffirm Archbishop Romero's efforts, focus, and service. The pontiff spoke out in favor of dialogue between the warring parties and even offered Arturo Rivera y Damas, the church's highest representative in the country at that time, as a possible mediator. The FDR-FMLN took advantage of that invitation in 1984, asking Rivera y Damas to present a "formal proposal for a meeting to the government" on their behalf (Montgomery 1995:176).[10]

Meanwhile, the Constituent Assembly was trying to encourage a peace process using the tools at its disposal. In 1983, the assembly passed the Amnesty and Citizen Rehabilitation Act (Decree 210), which "granted amnesty to any rebel who abandoned the armed struggle before 4 July" of that year (UN Security Council 1993:III:n.56) and began negotiations with the FDR-FMLN. The peace talks came to naught, as the government alleged that negotiations were futile if the FMLN refused to cooperate in the scheduled 1984 elections. The FMLN maintained that to disarm and try to participate in elections with no guarantee for their safety would be suicidal (Southerland 1983a:2). Indeed the death squad activity escalated around this time "primarily as a result of the continuing, though limited, dialogue between the peace Commission and the left" (UN Security Council 1993:III, part 2:3).

Despite the failed talks and the ongoing violence, work on a constitution and elections continued. Disagreement over agrarian reform delayed progress until the topic was finally put on the back burner. A new constitution was accepted in December 1983 without addressing land reform (Montgomery 1995:178), during a period when unemployment was estimated at 40 percent (Southerland 1983a:1), Internally displaced persons (IDPs) numbered more than 500,000 (UN Security Council 1993:III.2), and 120 civilians were murdered during the average week. By the time the Constitution was signed, more than 38,000 civilians had already been killed by either members of the security apparatus or the PMGs (Diskin and Sharpe 1986:67).

The delayed 1984 elections finally took place in March. The FMLN boycotted the elections, again on the grounds that truly democratic elections could not proceed under the conditions of violence that permeated the country (Montgomery 1995:216). The guerrillas managed to prevent any voting in "58 of 261 municipalities . . . a measure of the extent to which the FMLN had expanded" its realm of influence (Montgomery 1995:182). Regardless of the number of disenfranchised communities, the election went forward, and El Salvador finally got to celebrate a democratically elected civilian president after a half-century of fraud and military rule. In 1984, José Napoleón Duarte won with more than 53 percent of the vote in a runoff election against ARENA candidate Roberto D'Aubuisson, who garnered just over 46 percent of the vote. The following year, in elections for the Constituent Assembly (now known as the Legislative Assembly), the PDC again had success and won the majority. D'Aubuisson agreed to acquiesce to a realignment within ARENA, allowing Alfredo Cristiani to replace him as leader of the party (UN Security Council 1993:III, part 2:4, 5, 8).

The 1984 elections won international attention and praise, as news agencies broadcast images, to viewers around the world, of El Salvadorans standing in long lines ready to vote. And indeed the country had reason to celebrate; Duarte was a civilian, popularly elected president. But the election did not occur in a historical vacuum, nor did it signify any real change in the country's political environment. In terms of the violence, repression, and civil war, the election changed little, if anything. Christopher Dickey, who was reporting for the *Washington Post* at the time, perhaps best evaluated the election within the context of El Salvador in 1984:

> If you deal with the 1984 election as if the massacre of 1980 [in El Mozote] never happened, then the elections look pretty good. . . . But ask yourself what the elections represent if the military agreed to have them only after it eliminated ten thousand people. (Millman 1984:23)

El Salvador's Monsignor Ricardo Uriosted told a United States fact-finding mission in 1983, "Elections are but one note in the song of democracy. You Americans keep playing that note and expect us to hear a song" (Zuckerman 1983:12).

Indeed Duarte's campaign for president spoke volumes regarding the utter lack of substantive democracy in El Salvador. In a campaign that had perhaps foreshadowed the irresolute and ineffectual administration to come, Duarte reached out to the left and to the right. In one speech, he promised that if elected, he would not be the next "Alfonsín," a reference to Argentina's recent democratically elected president, who was carrying out his campaign vow to prosecute the country's grossest human rights violators. The promise sent a clear message to the military, that they had nothing to fear in a Duarte administration — that the system of impunity would be respected (Montgomery 1995:186–87). At the same time, Duarte signed a "social pact" in February 1984, promising "to end the repression and seek a political solution to the civil war" (Diskin and Sharpe 1986:71) indicating a willingness to open dialogue with the guerrillas rather than increase the military campaign. After his election, Duarte did make some movement toward holding paramilitary groups accountable via the country's justice system, but he simultaneously lived up to his anti-Alfonsín promise and made no significant changes to the military system (Montgomery 1995:186–87).

Toward the end of 1984, peace talks began again and the government met with representatives of the FDR-FMLN at La Palma in Chalatenango. Despite early hopes, the talks quickly fizzled out (Montgomery 1995:189). In addition, the economy worsened under Duarte so much so that despite the ever-present security forces and death squads, various organizations began demonstrating and demanding government action on their behalf. Duarte worked with the security apparatus to demobilize and repress strikes and protests, perhaps more than he worked to address the serious concerns being levied by the participants. At least one labor leader was disappeared during this time, and "13 days later his mutilated body appeared" (Montgomery 1995:192–93). Thus the election of Duarte brought little in terms of meaningful change.

Legislative elections were scheduled for 1988, with little to no progress having been made toward peace. In an attempt to pick up where the process had left off, Costa Rican president Oscar Arias initiated a process that would come to be known as the Esquipulas talks. Arias welcomed the United Nations to assist with military observation and negotiation in the region and convinced Duarte to meet with FDR-FMLN representatives again. Despite persistent efforts and outside intervention, the talks again came to naught (Montgomery 1995:209).

A new Amnesty Law was enacted in 1987, but it was the subject of wide criticism for not limiting the scope of its applicability (UN Security Council 1993:III, part 2:7).[11] There was a subsequent increase in the number of death squad murders over the previous year. The Governmental Commission on Human Rights wrote, "the fundamental right of every human being not to be unjustly deprived of life is brutally trampled in El Salvador by creatures possessed of the most irrational intolerance or wild fanatics who think they are entitled to crush and infringe the Republic's most sacred principles and juridical precepts" (IACHR 1988:3). The head of the Salvadorian Human Rights Commission (an NGO) was among those killed over the course of the year (UN Security Council 1993:III, part 2:7).

The following year, the Christian Democrats lost their majority when ARENA won the National Assembly (formerly the Constituent Assembly) and municipal elections. The FMLN had again refused to take part in the elections and reacted strongly against the ARENA win. Mayors and municipal officials were again targeted by the guerrillas, at least eight of whom were killed that year. The Truth Commission later determined that the PMG activity increased at least threefold, "averag[ing] eight victims a month" over the previous year (UN Security Council 1993:III, part 2:4, 8; Montgomery 1995:208 [on election]).

It seems that the elections provided the death squads with a new type of "cover." Not only could the squads themselves operate protected by their allies within the upper echelons of the armed forces, but also their elite allies now had cover, as well. Duarte's being at least nominally "in charge" put him at the top of the old cliché "the buck stops here." In 1983, Duarte had commented that the El Salvadoran political system had been based on the use of force for a very long time, and that "when he came to power as president [of the governing junta] in December 1980, he never had the authority to change the system." He said that "The structure of authority in [El Salvador] has been based on abuses . . . and to reform that you need enough power to assume complete responsibility" (Southerland 1983c:3). Indeed, the same assessment remained applicable throughout his full term as president between 1984 and 1989. Duarte was unable to follow through on most of his promises, including investigations into human rights violations allegedly committed by paramilitaries and security forces (Diskin and Sharpe 1986:77), because his presidency was defined by the constraints of his office — constraints that were imposed by the deep divide between the hard-liners and moderates, and the dominant strength of the hard-liners within the military.

By the late 1980s, the political mood across Central America was swinging toward peace, and representatives from the region's governments were negotiating a support system. In part the talks were aimed at building a system of joint accountability to keep each other on a path toward internal resolution and self-determination. The Esquipulas II Agreement was signed by the presidents of Central American countries, committing each of them to "the establishment of national reconciliation commissions in each country, an International Verification Commission and amnesty legislation" (UN Security Council 1993:III, part 2:7; Montgomery 1995:209–13).

In January 1989, the FMLN approached the government with a draft plan for using the upcoming March 1989 presidential elections as "a step for peace." The guerrillas suggested that election take place "under conditions which would allow its participation, the fairness of the tallying and acceptance of the outcome, and acceptance of the Army of El Salvador as the only armed force." The proposal was to postpone the election date in order to get the logistics in place, and in the meantime to get the military under control and include the Democratic Convergence, an amalgam of the Popular Social Christian Movement (MPSC), the Social Democrat Party (PSD), and the Nationalist Democratic Union (UDN) that had become a party in 1993 (Montgomery 1995:208, 254) on the election board (IACHR 1989:1; Montgomery 1995:213–14). The proposal was rejected by the government, and rather than serving as a "step for peace," the March elections took place under a hail of bullets and the shroud of nearly fifty murders (IACHR 1989:2). The ARENA candidate and member of the coffee oligarchy, Alfredo Cristiani, won the presidential election with 54 percent of the vote, and the Christian Democrats placed second with 36 percent. The relatively new but growing Democratic Convergence won 3.8 percent of the vote (Montgomery 1995:214).

Rhetoric surrounding the 1989 elections was not very different from that which had characterized earlier elections. D'Aubuisson campaigned with Cristiani and rallied the crowds with the ARENA hymn, "Tremble, Tremble, Communists . . . El Salvador will be the grave where the Reds meet their end." Before giving the stage over to Cristiani, D'Aubuisson criticized U.S. involvement in the country, declaring that "The foreigners are doing experiments on us like laboratory mice. . . . They never asked us if we wanted a corrupt, incompetent government. We've put up with it for ten years, experimenting on us as if we were rabbits. . . . We are never going to negotiate, whether the gringos like it or not" (Rosenberg 1991:264).

In November 1989, the guerrillas caught the country off guard when it began a well-orchestrated offensive that blew right into the capital city of San Salvador. The military tried to respond as they always had, using air strikes against civilian areas thought to be guerrilla strongholds. But when the FMLN retreated to avoid the air strikes and the civilian casualties that would result, they retreated into several elite neighborhoods in the city. Unwilling to strike against the upper-class residents, the military was caught, unable to oust the guerrillas as easily as they would have from poorer areas. Proving that U.S. advisors and training had changed little in terms of the El Salvadoran military's modus operandi, the Atlacatl Battalion followed the same course of action that had been used by the country's armed forces for decades. Rather than engaging the enemy in battle or confronting the guerrillas head-on, they circumvented battle by attacking civilian noncombatants. In the midst of the guerrilla offensive, the Atlacatl Battalion went to the rectory on the UCA campus — a site not involved in the guerrilla offensive. It was the residence of Father Ignacio Ellacuría, an outspoken advocate of peace negotiations and defender of the poor.[12]

Once the military gained entry to the residence (they first tried to force their way, but were then allowed in by the priests), the troops murdered the six priests living in the rectory, their housekeeper, and her sixteen-year-old daughter. Fathers Ignacio Ellacuría, Ignacio Martín-Baró, Segundo Montes, Amando López, Joaquín López y López, and Juan Ramón Moreno, Julia Elba Ramos, and sixteen-year-old Celina Mariceth Ramos were shot "in the early hours" of 15 November 1989 (UN Security Council 1993:IV.B:1). Another priest who had worked with the six Jesuits extensively and knew them personally later said that this attack was the "culmination of a process," not a "momentary madness." He said that while the military had allowed Archbishop Romero to speak for only three years, they had allowed the Jesuits to go on with only threats and bombings for fifteen years (Zin 1990). The guerrilla offensive provided an impetus (or perhaps excuse) to end the battle and assassinate Ellacuría and the other priests for their "subversive" advocacy of a negotiated settlement, and on behalf of the poor.

The assassination of the priests marks the beginning of the end of the violent conflict, but also the beginning of the country's struggle to address all that occurred during the war. The scene has become a sort of "living memory" and is a powerful illustration of the country's seemingly still open, if silent, wounds. Today there are eight rosebushes planted in the garden outside the rectory, one for each of the victims. They are planted in the area where five of the priests had been told to lie face down and were then shot. Down the garden path there is a small building housing photographs, clothes, letters, and possessions of the eight murder victims and of the four American churchwomen who had been murdered nine years prior, and a memorial to Archbishop Romero. There is a small room where the UCA keeps photo albums that document the lives and the assassinations of the six priests, the housekeeper, and her daughter. There are photos of their corpses as they were found — one in a small pool of blood trailing from his head, others still in their bathrobes or nightclothes or bloodied tee shirts, with matted hair and brain tissue lying inches away in the grass; the teenage girl dead on the floor, her mother still right beside her. The pictures are as gory as was the scene; the wounds are visible, the blood has not yet completely dried, and nothing has been moved or covered to cover up the reality. The room is an attempt to keep the memories and the wounds open, to remind the country that there has not been closure. Indeed, as I roamed the garden and the adjacent chapel, I encountered a sociology professor who showed me the photo albums and told me about the gardener who had planted the rosebushes in memory of the housekeeper, who was his wife, his daughter, and the priests. Motioning across the photo albums, the professor quietly but firmly declared that there "needs to be an accounting of what happened . . . there has to be truthful knowledge of what happened."§

In a sense there has been a truthful account of what happened. The Truth Commission gathered evidence and reported on the events leading up to the assassinations, including the meetings in which the murders were planned and the orders given. And after the Peace Accords were signed, the El Salvadoran justice system took real action on the case, eventually finding two officers guilty of their roles in "ordering the killings," and both received thirty-year sentences (LeoGrande 1998b:576). This momentous accomplishment in Salvadoran jurisprudence should not be overstated, however. While it was indeed significant, unusual, and precedent-setting, it should also be noted that the two who were convicted were exceptions. The vast majority of officers, soldiers, operatives, and civilians involved in similar atrocities never faced accountability. And "the price for getting the army to accept [Colonel] Benavides's conviction was that the rest of the participants be exonerated and that the investigation proceed no further" (LeoGrande 1998b:576). Consequently, the conviction of the two, while important in and of itself, was also a reflection of the larger political picture in El Salvador, one in which the military was not at all beholden to civilian officials and where obeying court orders was contingent upon bribery and backroom deal making.

The eight UCA victims were not the only targets of the right's response to the guerrilla offensive. Paramilitary groups targeted guerrillas and a broadly defined population of civilian "subversives." The IACHR reported "shelling of areas of civilian population in areas regarded as under FMLN influence," and attacks against FMLN combat hospitals. New (or perhaps previously unidentified) paramilitary groups emerged, including the Acción Revolucionario de Exterminio (ARDE), or the Revolutionary Extermination Action, a group that promised to "execute the FMLN traitors to our country." And Salvadoran "businessmen and members of ARENA" organized a new group known as the Patriotic Civilian Defense Forces, apparently to gather additional information on the "subversive" movement (IACHR 1989:3).

Continued military operations finally prompted the FMLN to begin withdrawing from its remaining capital city strongholds. Nonetheless, the offensive had severely compromised he government's position, particularly as the assassination of the priests had greatly undermined U.S. support. Thanks in large part to the proactive efforts on the part of the United Nations and the "Group of Friends" (Mexico, Colombia, Venezuela, and Spain), and some prodding by the United States, the FMLN and the administration of President Cristiani began talks again in 1990. Unlike in previous negotiations, this time the sides remained committed. The 1992 Chapultepec Accords brought an end to both wars, the official and unofficial. The agreement called for the complete demobilization of the National Guard and the Treasury Police (*Acuerdos* 1992:38), and for a National Civilian Police (PNC) to replace the former National Police.[13] BIRIs and security forces were to be disbanded and the military reduced in size by half, and UN Peacekeepers were to be given oversight responsibilities to ensure the demobilization process (LeoGrande 1998b:577; Montgomery 1995:246). A civilian ad hoc committee was charged with identifying members of the armed forces involved in human rights violations and providing a list of those to be removed entirely from military service. Finally, all military and intelligence agencies were to be reorganized under civilian authority (LeoGrande 1998b:577; Montgomery 1995:241; *Acuerdos* 1992:37–38). Perhaps most promising was the mandate for a special commission authorized to investigate the human rights epidemic that had plagued the country for so long, which would collect information and render findings on specific attacks and violations (Montgomery 1995:223–30).[14]

On paper, the accords were a tremendous win for the left. The FMLN, once disarmed and demobilized, was afforded rights as a legitimate political party. The agreement provided for land reform designed to provide for former combatants and long-term plot occupants, so as to distribute resources and reduce the number of landless peasants. The agreement also reformed the purpose of the military, restricting its role to "territorial security, revised the education of officers and provided for the purification of the officer corps" (Montgomery 1995:225). One interviewee, an official at the College for Strategic Studies in San Salvador, highlighted the importance of this shift, noting that "The job of the armed forces was to maintain order. Now it's defense."[§] The "caretaker" paternalistic role that had served as the very foundation for a legitimate anticommunist rhetoric and mania could not be entirely wiped out overnight, but it was greatly undermined by this fundamental revision and would weaken over time.

### "Se Fue"

An impassioned Christian Democrat who was intimately aware of the death squad campaign against his party during the civil war talked to me at length about the evolution of his country since the peace accords. Toward the end of our conversation, he noted, "There has not been a single death related to the war — revenge, politics — since we signed the Peace Accord. I am very proud of being Salvadorean."[§]

And despite a high rate of apolitical violence (gang warfare and an alleged social cleaning organization[§] are among the perpetrators) today in El Salvador,[15] the interviewee's assessment is accurate. Political assassinations and paramilitary activity rose during the negotiation process (Montgomery 1995:224), and the postaccord transition period did face challenges from right-wing mayors and groups unhappy with elements of the agreement, but the paramilitary violence stopped with the signing of the accord. It seems fairly incredible that after decades of unabashed impunity during which the PMGs literally terrorized the people of El Salvador, a peace agreement that did not meet the demands of the far right, and that in fact required some of the very reforms the death squads had been railing against for so long, was the mechanism that would bring their death campaign to an end. Members of El Salvador's left have a very different perspective on why this mechanism worked than do members of the right.

Salvador Sanchez Cerén, a significant figure within the FMLN both during the civil war and today, said that "the peace changed the army," introducing a "human rights doctrine. Thus the structure of the [PMGs] was dissolved. The structure of the paramilitaries, ORDEN, the White Hand — was disappearing with military reforms. The culture was also changing towards peace, human rights and so on" (Cerén 2003).

Salvador Samayoa attributes the abrupt end of the PMGs to the fact that they were so intimately intertwined with the State, so that when the peace accords were signed by the government and the military, they were, in essence, signed by the paramilitaries. "They were all the same, so when the government started agreeing to the peace, they all did." I expressed amazement that "at one time there are guerrillas and death squads and killing, and with nothing but peace accords, all that stopped. It was just ... the peace." According to Samayoa, the very fact that the violence had become so pervasive was in fact part of the explanation for the success of the peace accords, "Everyone was in danger of being killed." But he also acknowledged the importance of the United States in the successful demobilization of the right, saying that "the U.S. decided what would happen. And when the U.S. said peace — peace. The right got all its weapons, all its helicopters from the U.S., so ..." His implication was that the military had no choice in the matter once the United States was on board (Samayoa 2003).

A Christian Democrat who was integral in the development of the peace process had a similar view regarding the importance of the United States in the process, noting the roles of Presidents Carter and Reagan in pushing for democracy in the country. "You have to fight communism with democracy, not with repression."[§] But he also noted that there were rumors that the U.S. ambassador to El Salvador had a hand in the ultimate success of the peace accords, and the termination of PMG activity.

> Towards the time of the peace, when the U.S. wanted it to be finalized, the ambassador [from the United States] invited members of the oligarchy to a dinner at the embassy. At the dinner, he went around and handed each an envelope, containing intelligence that the U.S. had on each. He said, "Stop funding the killing now, or we go public with what we know."[§]

Holding a rather contrary perspective, a military spokesperson said that the peace was achieved because after twelve years of fighting, the "objective was achieved — there was support for the system,"[§] that is opposition to communism. This type of evaluation was typical from members of the military and the right. While interviewees from the left viewed the demise of the paramilitaries as a result of the weakening of the military mandated by the accords, explanations from the right fell along the lines that the FMLN had been defeated, making the paramilitary groups obsolete. Ignoring the well-known fact that the FMLN had extended an offer to negotiate before Duarte reached out to the guerrillas in 1984, a former senior officer within the security forces said that the peace was successful because "the guerrillas had to sign the peace — the communist world had fallen apart. The guerrillas could not get support arms, nothing from the USSR, nor Cuba, because they couldn't give anything. They asked Vietnam, North

Korea, China, but found no support. They had no alternative but to accept Duarte's invitation to negotiate."§ He acknowledged that D'Aubuisson had been totally opposed to negotiations with the FMLN, but he explained that ultimately D'Aubuisson and his forces were a different sort of beast of war than were the guerrillas. The PMGs "were a very small group of people, while the guerrillas were thousands. As a consequence, we had to officially disarm the guerrillas. But the death squad—they were such a small group." I asked whether the changes made to the military meant that the armed forces could no longer support the death squads, and he agreed, saying that "the accords changed the system of the military. The entire top leadership was dismissed. And the military is completely barred from any political activity at all. "§

Representative Carmen Alena Calderón de Escalon, a member of the ARENA party and member of the Directive Group of the Legislature in 2003, said that it was ARENA that began working for peace in 1989, and that the effort had been led by Cristianti. She described D'Aubuisson's role as leader and founder of ARENA and ORDEN, and that as the leader of ARENA, he had agreed with Cristiani regarding the peace negotiations. "D'Aubuisson . . . was very close to Cristiani, believed he was a man of great honor and valor, and absolutely supported him in the peace—the dialogue." I asked her what happened to members of ORDEN politically, after D'Aubuisson agreed to the dialogue. "Se fue [They went away]," she said, with an elegant wave of her arm. "¿Se fue, a donde?" I asked. "Those were military people," she said, "who did not agree to the change. They left the party and went to [another]. Se fue" (Calderón 2003).[16]

And indeed the evidence from El Salvador suggests that this is precisely what happened. Of course it is never quite so easy, but it is nearly astonishing that up to the time the accords were signed, paramilitary violence continued with impunity and free rein. Then the agreements were signed, and the activity stopped. It cannot be attributed to a system of justice, as none was exacted.[17] There were serious and dramatic reforms made to the military institutions, though those were not immediate and certainly did not result in the arrest or detention of any PMG members. Nor can it be attributed to a systematic demobilization or disarmament. A general amnesty was agreed to, and though there was an organized and systematic disarmament of the left, there was no such process for the right. It would appear as though even with the military reforms, the individuals who had been active in the PMGs could very well have continued on their path of destruction had they chosen to do so. But this assumes that the PMGs were autonomous, or even independent, self-contained groups driven by their own individual egos or desires for personal power, and it ignores their ties to the military and political identity.

The evidence collected for this study suggests that the demise of El Salvador's paramilitary groups was the result of three significant changes that came during or as a result of the Peace Accords: First, the international stage had changed. The USSR no longer existed, the cold war had ended, and the United States shifted support away from El Salvador's military and toward political institutions and processes, and this in turn limited the options available to the El Salvadoran government. The United States in and of itself was not a leg of the triad in El Salvador, but it was an "enabler" of the military in this case. Consequently, when the U.S. financial support for the military efforts dried up, it had repercussions for the triad and, more broadly speaking, the opportunity structure that had facilitated PMG emergence and sustenance. Second, as noted by some of the interviewees, the Peace Accords required the restructuring of the country's military. This domestic emphasis on ending the internal focus of the military meant a significant institutional evolution. This reform also contributed to a closed opportunity structure in the sense that the resources that had previously been available via connections in the military became closed off. Last, the leadership of ARENA and the far right became engaged in the political process, and the most visible PMG leader, Roberto D'Aubuisson, endorsed the peace talks. Support for continuing the violence declined as more hard-liners realized they could perpetuate their dominance via ARENA. Thus the division between the moderates and hard-liners slowly closed as more hard-liners got on board with the talks, further contributing to a closing opportunity structure for the PMGs.

One interviewee, a former member of the military, noted how important the military had been in the system of spoils enjoyed by El Salvador's conservatives. He said the military had been "corrupt," completely willing to "stop any reform, protect [the elite] control over the land, the money." He said that the only reason the elite was willing to go along with the peace accords was that "this is still power, just in a different way."[§] The purpose of the paramilitary groups was to perpetuate that system. Thus, if politicos had found a new means of protecting elite status, and if the PMGs had actually begun to threaten rather than promote the interests of the elite, they had become somewhat obsolete. The triad that nurtured the PMGs broke apart with the political leadership and economic elite turning toward ARENA to advocate for itself.

The advice given to D'Aubuisson by Guatemalan Mario Sandoval Alarcón was thus perhaps the first watershed moment in the evolution and ultimate preservation of El Salvador's far right, and the decisive factor in the inevitability of the paramilitary groups' demise. In ARENA, D'Aubuisson created the one source of power that the country's right wing had never really had: a political organization. Once it became clear that the opposition was willing, and maybe even able, to overthrow the wealthy and displace them from their socioeconomic home entirely, ARENA became a very useful tool and began drawing the support of the country's anti-FMLN activists. As ARENA gained more clout and exercised its muscle in elections and negotiations, it gained legitimacy among the country's hard-liners, who began to realize that they could make real gains (both domestically and internationally) without the death squads. Thus the success of ARENA on so many levels created an "out," a way for the former paramilitary leadership to continue on within the political arena, to maintain their power and their popular base, and to do all of this legitimately.[18] Indeed, LeoGrande asserts that the growing success of the left-wing Democratic Convergence party in the 1990 legislative elections "confirmed Cristiani's belief that ARENA's political health depended on ending the war" (LeoGrande 1998b:575). Thus the right wing was making calculated political decisions rather than strategic military ones in order to further its agenda.[19] When ARENA's leadership (and therefore former PMG leaders) chose this path, so chose their followers. Without the weapons, the financing, the recruits, the leadership, the purpose, and the impunity, paramilitaries simply cannot thrive. When El Salvador's triad began to evolve and take interest in other modes of political domination, the scaffolding supporting the death squads collapsed. The case of El Salvador thus provides some preliminary findings as to the process by which paramilitary groups dissolve, suggesting that the implosion of a triad is likely an important factor in that process and indicating the potential direction of future research.

Paramilitary groups are the political manifestation of profound uncertainty among a cross-section of a country's most resourced sectors. They emerge of out a process in which political dynamics create fissures between traditional allies and realignments among factions whose interests are served in their organization. The increasing global demand for States to avoid the appearance of sponsoring violence often plays a critical role in this process, forcing the newly aligned actors to work outside the official capacity of the State. The cases of Chiapas, Colombia, and El Salvador elucidate this process. This chapter summarizes the findings of the comparative case analysis presented here then briefly explores the international application of these findings using three contemporary conflicts from different parts of the world. We end with a discussion of the implications of this study's findings for the broader study of political violence.

## Cumulative Findings

Paramilitary groups are a product of changing political environments that create opportunities for some and extreme uncertainty for others. Elites with a vested interest in securing their wealth and privilege tend toward authoritarian structures that protect their interests, for instance one-party systems, power-sharing pacts, or military regimes. They support a State that has been traditionally capable of and willing to provide the exclusionary structures and repressive means to protect their interests. When a new threat arises demanding political reforms that would invariably weaken the elite's monopolization of economic resources, the wealthy turn again to the State, expecting it to repress or eliminate the threat. However, in the increasingly international political arena, the State no longer operates free of global pressures. Influential external forces may demand that the State take a new approach, perhaps to negotiate with or accommodate the new actor(s). In the cases studied here, global partners brandishing attractive aid and/or trade packages demanded the State curtail its traditionally violent repression. The State is caught between contradictory requirements of equally necessary supporters.

The State takes the moderate road, catering to the demands of its international donors. This leaves the reformers with a new sense of opportunity and the elite with a new sense of vulnerability. But while some are willing to support the reforms, others are unwilling to lose their status or wealth and begin looking for collaborators to organize their own security forces. They find willing allies in factions of the political elite who opposed the decision to pursue moderation and within the military who supported an all-out countersubversive strategy unrestricted by humanitarian concerns. But divisions within these sectors are not enough for paramilitary groups to emerge. These factions ally themselves and bring important resources to the table, but it is these divisions in conjunction with a confluence of additional factors that explain paramilitary emergence.

### Exclusive Political Systems

In each of the three cases discussed here, the elite had protected their economic largess for generations using a politically exclusive system. For Chiapas, the elite challenged the central tenet of the Mexican Revolution (land reform) by using local offices to undermine the implementation of national-level policies. In Colombia, the landholding elite had long controlled the majority of the country's wealth but suffered from their internal Liberal/Conservative battles. The elite both overcame their own internal divisions and solidified the exclusion of potentially reform-minded groups in the National Front, thus ensuring the protection of their concentrated control over status and privilege. Repression was used to ensure the Front's exclusivity. In El Salvador, the oligarchy had long relied on the military to violently repress any possible threat to their political dominance, which in turn secured their exclusive hold over the country's land and thereby wealth. The military regimes vacillated between moderate reforms and heavy-handed repression with enough frequency not only to ensure the exclusivity of the political system but also to undermine the ability of the most militant opposition groups to win widespread support. In each case, this system was entrenched such that the economic elite had come to rely on it nearly exclusively to protect their interests.

Thus in all three cases, the State was closely allied with the elite, ensuring that the wealth would remain sharply concentrated among the few. Theoretically, the opposition had essentially two means of expression: the first, try to organize and gain political access; the second, rebel. In reality, the State used an exclusive political system that forbade access to reform advocates and violent repression to prevent and stop uprisings.

### History of Arming Civilians in the Interest of the Elite

Thus when the State fails to deploy its long-standing tactics to protect the elite, and the sense of vulnerability to reform is heightened, the hard-liner factions look for a means by which they can protect themselves. Why turn to paramilitary groups rather than some other opposition strategy? The answer lies largely in the historical roots of each paramilitary groups. The foundations of paramilitarism, in terms of legitimacy, strategy, resources, and mobilization were readily available to the hard-liners in each case. Using PMGs was simply an extension of the same tactics these factions had always relied upon.

The legitimacy claimed by PMGs derives from a State history of providing arms to civilians specifically charged with protecting the land and wealth of the elite. Chiapas's White Guards, Colombia's Law 48, and El Salvador's Rural Police, National Guard, and later ORDEN were all designed to protect the interests of the elite and prevent organization or mobilization of "the masses." Thus in each of the three cases studied here, the interests of at least one faction of the State's security forces were indelibly tied to the interests of the landowners. All three countries authorized the arming of civilians in order to supplement the security details for landowners, and all three created security agencies intended to do the same. The evolution of the armed forces was, for each case, inextricably tied to the protection of the landed elite, usually via the repression of those who might threaten their property or interests. Because paramilitary groups evolved out of these legal organizations, they were the product of *legitimacy* rather than of "abnormal" or "nontraditional" modalities.

The Guardias Blancas, Law 48, and the roots of the National Guard and ANSESAL lent a powerful start-up mechanism for paramilitaries within uncertain environments. The resource mobilization hurdle faced by most grassroots organizations like social movements is nonexistent for paramilitaries because they are the product of an intertwining process that links the federal policy-making level of government with the leadership, mobilization, and money rallied at the local level. Policies like Law 48 link federal-level politics with local-level actors via common goals, and they make purpose and identity, arms, money, uniforms, and training much easier to marshal. Law 48 had consequences similar to the legal status of Chiapas's White Guards and El Salvador's Rural Police, National Guard units, and ANSESAL. They each motivated and mobilized civilian patrols around the needs of the elite. In doing so, they acknowledged the need for a supplemented security force, and indirectly the institutional inability to defeat the subversive threat. Consequently, in each case, when the State moved to declare the groups illegal, it had already lost legitimacy among the very groups it was trying to ban. For many in the civilian defense forces, this move only further verified the incapacity of the State they had been formed to fortify. Their legitimacy was thus not diminished by their illegality, smoothing their shift from state-sponsored to paramilitary group.

### Opposition Force Gains Ground

Historically, the success of the State tactics in preventing a viable political threat had precluded a need for PMGs. It is only when hard-liners were denied the right to legally use these tactics that they turned outside the State. For Chiapas, the growing popularity and presence of the PRD posed a real threat to PRI dominance, and that threat was compounded by the worldwide popularity of and attention to the Zapatista rebellion. Retracting laws allowing White Guards left them literally and physically without the type of defense (violent repression) to which they were accustomed. Conciliatory posturing by the federal government left the local elite and security forces further deserted in their determination to protect their status and wealth from reforms that would undoubtedly require democracy and redistribution.

In Colombia, the National Front excluded the masses from having a political voice and thus protected the elite from reform, but the pact simultaneously instigated guerrilla organizations to continue their battle for access to the political arena. The Front was supplemented by a counterinsurgency military campaign in a broader strategy of protecting the elite's interests. Feelings of insecurity and vulnerability among the country's wealthy were raised by the inability of the army to decisively defeat the guerrilla forces and were exacerbated by presidential administrations offering to negotiate with the guerrillas and subsequently rescinding the right to use armed civilian units.

For El Salvador, the size, support, and capability of the guerrilla forces, coupled with popular organizing and nonmilitant democratic organizations, posed a broad-based challenge to the system of military rule that had for so long protected the country's elite. Like in Colombia, the military appeared incapable of definitively defeating the guerrilla threat and stopping the popular organizations. Thus in each case, reform advocates found some opening in the system and exploited that opening with enough success to pose a real or perceived threat to the country's traditionally dominant forces. Meanwhile the change in policy regarding ORDEN could not undermine the level of support for its tactics among its backers and enthusiasts.

### Political Pressures Prevent Traditional Use of Force

In each of the three cases, the environment in which PMGs emerged was palpably influenced by international politics. Though the entry of international actors or influence was different in each case in terms of both mode and timing, the dynamic is comparable. "Global integration clearly alters traditional, State-level politics. If interstate relationships are becoming more important, then State decisions and practices are constrained by their relationships with other States." Such findings are consistent with two-level game theory. Smith notes in her work on globalization that "inter-State policies and institutions create new definitions of what domestic policies are acceptable" (Smith 2001b:2, vii). Similarly, Ron notes that the "wave of global democratization" leaves transitioning States needing to demonstrate their own legitimacy. Such transitioning States are thus caught in the "dialectic of legal repression," pulled between forces demanding repression and forces wanting proof of the State's legitimacy (2003:6–7). For Mexico, Colombia, and El Salvador, economic relationships with the United States and other global actors certainly became increasingly relevant in terms of how the respective countries addressed opposition and outright rebellion within their own borders. For scholars like Smith and Ron, the interaction between the State and the international community is not only one of maximizing interests, but also one defined by previously established, yet evolving constraints and opportunities (perhaps in the form of treaties, aid agreements, dependence on trade, and so on).

In Chiapas, the Zapatistas were winning international acclaim as the voice of the poor. Global sympathy for the EZLN and the very recent implementation of NAFTA made a traditional, repressive crackdown nearly impossible for moderates unwilling to sacrifice international support. The Mexican government had significant incentive to make the rebellion appear as benign as possible, and the government as "progressive" as possible. Both objectives precluded the option of a heavy-handed military response or overt repression and left the government with options that were less satisfactory to the PRI elite in Chiapas. In Colombia, international donors (the United States in particular) were pressuring the government to put an end to the extreme and severe military tactics that resulted in gross human rights violations. U.S. military aid was increasingly important to the country's counterinsurgency and counternarcotics efforts, but it was conditional upon meeting human rights standards.

Similarly in El Salvador, the Carter administration withheld aid in the absence of guarantees to protect human rights, an issue that again became relevant during the Reagan administration (particularly after the rape and murder of four American churchwomen). The desperately needed U.S. military support required the State to limit human rights violations by the military, placing constraints on counterinsurgency tactical options. Pressure by the United States for elections and land reform further intensified the vulnerability felt by the country's extreme right, fostering a determination to act proactively rather than be left susceptible to the whims of the international community.

### Factionalization within Political Elite, Economic Elite, and Military

The eventual decision to conform to international demands left the central actors within each political system factionalized. A significant faction of the elite who demanded immediate and violent reprisal against the subversives became frustrated and motivated. Similarly, in each country the pressure to respect the human rights of the guerrillas incensed factions of the military. Particularly in El Salvador, the division between moderates who were willing to make some accommodations and hard-liners who viewed such decisions with disdain was stark. Likewise, each case evidences a division within the political elite, some of whom saw accommodating international demands as necessary to the overall national agenda, others of whom saw it as detrimental to their own interests. Because policy makers eventually at least officially agreed to meet international demands, hard-liners were left without the option of relying on the State to protect their interests. These divisions laid the foundations for the triad and thus the opportunity structure for the PMG.

### Shared Grievance Creates New Alignment

The threat of a political opening, and therefore of subsequent reform to the system of exclusivity, provided a sense of grievance (vulnerability) across three critical groups, creating a cross-sectional alignment with the collective resources necessary to create a paramilitary group. The elite, of course, felt a sense of deep vulnerability. For the hard-liner faction, anything other than total defeat of the subversive threat meant unacceptable political and economic reforms that would have altered the exclusivity of the system. Among factions of the military, the grievance was, at its core, against the restrictions placed on their countersubversive campaigns by an internationally influenced State. In all three cases studied here, members of the military and their supporters expressed deep hostility at the human rights restrictions that limited their strategic deployment of force. Among members of the State, their own personal status and influence was largely a result of the exclusive political system. The power they wielded as allies of the elite and political officials could be lost was the political system to be reformed. While moderates were willing to make these reforms, hard-liners saw the sacrifice as too great.

The fact that the State was unwilling to use repression against a contemporary threat *when it had successfully done so in the past* left many of those whose status and wealth had been protected by the State's repression in the past feeling abandoned and disenfranchised. Consequently, the State's unwillingness to use force became juxtaposed against a long-standing tradition of doing just the opposite. Rather than viewing the use of violent repression as illegitimate, hard-liners and factions within the elite were more likely to see the State as illegitimate or constrained by external forces. Thus such factions view their own organization of a repressive organ as legitimately filling a void left by the State, and the use of PMGs as an extension of what the State had historically done.

### The Triad

In each of the cases analyzed here, factions of the military, the economic elite, and the political elite faced new political actors (such as the EZLN, FARC, FMLN, and so on) that posed a threat to their interests, and they found themselves with a powerful shared grievance. The trilateral alliance among these factions proved capable of mobilizing the leadership, arms, ideology, and sense of legitimacy necessary for the paramilitary group to emerge in a meaningful and effective way.

As noted earlier, the potential organization and success of a paramilitary group is in part determined by the repressive history and capacity of the State. A State's historical use of repression translates into a sense of legitimacy to do the same again. Thus, the historical *willingness* of the State to use repression is also important. A history of State repression is likely to provide the PMG with a sense of legitimacy in continuing tactics that have been successfully used in the past. This underlies the sense of the "right" to use repression.

In addition to this, the repressive capacity of the State is also important for PMG emergence because it is factions of the military who supply the training, arms, and at times leadership in the counterinsurgency campaign. Thus, the capacity of the State translates into the capacity of the paramilitary group. This is blatantly evident in Chiapas, Colombia, and El Salvador. From the simple proximity of paramilitary bases to army bases, to the overlap in personnel between official security forces and paramilitary groups, to the logistical cooperation and support, the importance of this connection to paramilitary groups is clear. Many of the attacks and massacres referenced throughout this study were successful because of military roadblocks being opened for paramilitary groups, or military blockades keeping help from reaching the victims. Furthermore, the direct role played by factions of the military in establishing and recruiting for paramilitary groups is evident: the MIRA in Chiapas recruited by local police, the Calima Front in Colombia initiated by the Third Brigade and Carlos Castaño, and D'Aubuisson's organizational efforts under ANSESAL.

Support offered by landowners, ranchers, and other wealthy civilians in establishing the paramilitary groups is also significant and consistent across the cases. For most of the paramilitary groups in Chiapas, the monies and access to land provided by local elite was instrumental. For the Castaño brothers in Colombia, the wealthy landowners and ranchers were critical not only for the start-up needs of funding and land on which to train, but also for the long-term support of the paramilitaries. Though the AUC later came to exploit the economic potential of the narcotics industry, it is evident that the landowners who were so desperate for protection from the guerrillas were a critical support base from the paramilitary's earliest days. In El Salvador, the deep connections between the country's elite and the security forces essentially parented the birth of the paramilitary groups. In all three cases, it was not only the resources of the wealthy that were critical, but also the *need* of the elite that was defining in paramilitary emergence. Abandoned by the State in the quest for repressive and decisive protection against reforms, the elite both needed and were willing to pay for the paramilitary organizations. Thus paramilitary emergence is the culmination of all of these variables coming together under certain circumstances. Each of these states had a politically exclusive system, armed civilians as part of a state-sponsored repressive machine, and an elite vulnerable to reform. But none of these factors in and of themselves is sufficient to explain paramilitary emergence: It is only with the confluence of all of the factors outlined here that we see PMGs emerge.

## Prevention and Dissolution

Unlike revolutionary groups, guerrilla groups, or even social movements, paramilitary groups enjoy impunity for their actions because of their extensive, if unofficial, connections within the apparatus of the State. Because revolutionary or social movements are entrenched directly in civil society and operate against the establishment, they tend not to enjoy a broad base of multilateral support from within the State's official institutional structures. Paramilitaries, being the "flip side of the coin" if you will, tend to rally support from all of those many sectors — within the State and civil society — who are determined to combat the opposition movement. Likewise, while movements, revolutionaries, and guerrillas tend to be disproportionately repressed or even persecuted by the State, paramilitaries are in just the opposite position, so that their illegal and extra-State activities are disproportionately supported or overlooked. Without the support of PRI leaders in Mexico like Samuel Sánchez Sánchez, or politicians in Colombia like Pablo Guarín, or Medrano's FUDI "party" in El Salvador, paramilitary groups would be themselves entirely outside the political system. But with such connections, the interests of the PMGs are protected, including their impunity.

In many cases of paramilitary violence, international efforts to quell the conflict arrive in the form of military aid to the State. Indeed, nearly all contemporary tools used to hold States accountable to international agreements, treaties, or to influence a change in policy are centered on the State: giving or withholding aid, giving or withholding recognition of a regime, offering or suspending loans, implementing or removing trade barriers. Yet paramilitaries operate in a space that is not readily acknowledged in political science, one where factions of civil society and factions of the state overlap. The extrainstitutional nature of paramilitary groups and the mutlilaterialism of their support networks have rendered State-centered approaches ineffective. For instance, in the case of Sudan, it is obvious that simply shunning a government tied to illicit organizations (the "stick" approach) fails to alleviate the violence. Yet international support for the State (the "carrot" approach) seems to yield similar results for at least two reasons.

First, the State is factionalized between moderates and hard-liners so that international support for the moderates is likely to be sidelined by the hard-liners and, at least partially, siphoned off to the PMGs. This was evident in the case of El Salvador, where U.S. support for the Christian Democrats was superficial at best and was entirely undermined by the domestic power of El Salvador's hard-liners. While U.S. aid may have been intended to fight the guerrillas, it often came under the direction of the country's hard-liners and was used for their purposes instead. U.S. aid has been funneled to similar purposes in Colombia.

Second, international efforts to support the regime fail to address the motivation behind paramilitary activity. Indeed, the overt support for moderate factions (the Christian Democrats in El Salvador) may instead serve to further intensify the vulnerability to reform felt by PMG supporters. Tina Rosenberg (1991) revealed the complete resentment felt by many El Salvadorans for the U.S. pursuit of democracy in their country, a resentment offset only by the sense of safety and loyalty incurred by D'Aubuisson and his death squads.

Thus, if we assume that some within the international community wish to genuinely support a moderate government in transition without simultaneously (however unwillingly) assisting paramilitary groups, what tools are politically viable? El Salvador, the only case studied here that has successfully ended paramilitary operations, provides some blueprints as to where future research might be directed and where future policies might find promise.

In essence, political and structural shifts began to slowly chip away at the opportunity structure that had given impetus to the paramilitary groups in El Salvador. As noted earlier, it was Guatemalan death squad leader Mario Sandoval Alarcón who advised D'Aubuisson to organize a political organization that could be sustained within mainstream politics, and indeed, organizing ARENA provided El Salvador's far right with a means for nonviolent domination of the political arena. This was a first and important shift in the political environment in El Salvador. The business elite who had been willing to support the PMGs found a new and less costly ally in ARENA, and they found their interests could be protected via political means rather than via PMGs. Meanwhile, the willingness of the stronger, political ARENA to negotiate led to peace accords that formalized changes in the military and undermined the ability of other members to support the PMGs.[1] Arguably this support had been slowly eroding with U.S. threats to withdraw aid, weakening interest in supporting the paramilitaries, and the reforms agreed upon in the accords added to this by weakening military factions' very ability to do so. These shifts, in no small part prompted by the success of ARENA, had a direct effect on the availability of both allies and resources for the PMG. Thus just as the opportunity structure facilitated PMG emergence, so its closure undermines PMG sustainability. What this process indicates is that structural and political shifts, a rise of new organizations, and the factions within the paramilitary leadership and sponsoring populations are all potential explanatory factors in PMG dissolution. Only future research can tease out the precise dynamics at play, but certainly El Salvador indicates that the closure of the opportunity structure and structural shifts that facilitate political interests be successfully protected within the political system are important factors in PMG dissolution.

## Contemporary PMGs in Global Perspective

Obviously it is methodologically impossible to generalize from this study, and I make no claim otherwise. Nonetheless, the cases studied here offer significant insights into the nature of paramilitary groups, the process of emergence, and the potential strategies a State may embrace in order to demobilize such organizations. As noted in the introduction to this book, paramilitary groups like Arkan's Tigers were active in the Serbian onslaught against the Bosnians, paramilitary groups played a central role in the escalation of violence in Baghdad, Iraq, during 2006 and 2007, and the Janjaweed continue their campaign of victimization against civilians in Darfur, Sudan. The specifics of these contemporary situations indicate that the triad model of PMG emergence offers promise for understanding cases well beyond those studied in depth here.

### The Former Yugoslavia

Arkan's Tigers were perhaps among the most violent and feared of the Serbian paramilitary groups. Active in Croatia and Bosnia, and evidence suggests later Kosovo (Gertz 1992; "UN War Crimes" 1999; HRW 2001d), the Tigers, whose formal name was the Serb Volunteer Guard (or SDG) are attributed with a slew of massacres including the "executions in November 19991 of seven unarmed Hungarian civilians" (Gertz 1992). Arkan was indicted by the International Criminal Tribunal for the Former Yugoslavia (ICTY) in 1997 for crimes committed in the early 1990s; he himself was assassinated before he could stand trial ("Serb Volunteer Guard" 2000; ICTY 1997). Throughout the early 1990s, there were suspicions and suppositions that Arkan and his Tigers had the support of Milosevic and officials within his upper echelon. The fact that the paramilitary group operated in tandem with the needs of the former Yugoslavian leader and Serb forces indicated that at the very least, the group operated without condemna-

tion. Evidence suggested that there were also additional levels of cooperation. For instance, in 1995, an estimated twenty thousand refugees were
arrested by the Serbian Ministry of Internal Affairs, and taken to Arkan's
paramilitary base camp in Erdut ("Serb Volunteer Guard" 2000). There
were also reports that Serbia's security force was "involved in organizing
and armed" the Tigers along with other Serbian PMGs (HRW 2001d).

Such evidence of unofficial cooperation between the Milosevic regime
and Arkan's paramilitary group was confirmed in 2003 by a former secretary to Arkan. The woman, known before the ICTY as witness B129, testified to the court that the SDG was in direct communication with, and took
commands from, the two chiefs of state security under Milosevic, Jovica
Stanisic and Franko Simatovic. The secretary also testified that "weapons
and gasoline" were provided to the PMG directly by the army, via General
Dusan Loncar. While smuggling and stealing contributed directly to the
funds of Arkan's Tigers, so did the financial assistance of "wealthy businessmen and other members of the Milosevic government." Thus the testimony provided by this former employee of the paramilitary confirms what
had long been suspected by international journalists and NGOs: Arkan's
Tigers, though disavowed publicly by Milosevic himself, even at his trial
at the Hague, had direct ties to individuals within the official apparatus of
the State (Simons 2003).

### Iraq

In Iraq in the years after the U.S. invasion, Baghdad's death squads
wreaked havoc on an already chaotic situation while facing no accountability. Eerily reminiscent of the situation in El Salvador during the 1980s,
the "unity" government of Nouri al-Maliki continued to receive support
from the United States and attempted to pursue a democratic system of
government while paramilitaries operated seemingly without challenge in
the capital. Throughout 2006, reports of dozens of corpses showing signs
of torture crossed international wires weekly. Some were decapitated,
most bound, many having been tortured with power drills or other such
devices. Victims were sometimes killed with a single gunshot to the head,
while others' skulls were crushed with cement blocks (Poole 2006; "Baghdad Bombed" 2006).

While journalists reported multiple PMGs operating in Iraq's capital
city, the most renowned and powerful was the Madhi Army. With an estimated 10,000 members (Poole 2006), the Madhi Army was led by Moqtada

al-Sadr, a Shiite leader and vehement opponent of the U.S. presence in Iraq. Through al-Sadr, the PMG benefited from extremely well-placed political officials who provided a wide range of access to institutions and additional resources. For instance, allies within the Ministry of Transportation allegedly allowed members of the Madhi Army access to gasoline stations where "soldiers" reportedly made profits for the PMG by charging customers for more gasoline than was dispensed (Poole 2006). The Ministry of Health, which also had ties to the Madhi paramilitary group, allegedly inflated the number of corpses found in Baghdad in an effort to "get the Americans out of the country" ("Slaughter" 2006). The ministry was also linked to Madhi attacks inside hospitals, which were described in one report as "a sectarian killing ground to attack Sunni Muslims" ("Iraq Hospitals" 2006). Thus as in the cases studied with more depth here, political elites divided. Some moderates were willing to cooperate with the United States and pursue democratic reforms, while hard-liner factions opposed both U.S. involvement and democratic reforms. Unable to pursue their preferences through institutional means, the hard-liners cooperated unofficially to support organizations like the Madhi Army.

Perhaps the most critical ally to the PMGs in Iraq was the Ministry of Interior. Thanks to allies within this office, the PMGs, including the Madhi Army, were able to tap into the official police and military units for personnel and other resources. In October 2006, the 2nd National Police Division, organized specifically for the purposes of regaining control of Baghdad and curbing death squad violence, was demobilized and sent for "retraining." Significant numbers of forces within the division were alleged to have operated as or in conjunction with death squads (Hess 2006). During the same month, fifty or sixty bodies were found around the city on a daily basis ("Baghdad Bombed" 2006). The country's police force was linked to paramilitaries, allegedly benefiting the PMGs with not only personnel but also the funding and training given by the United States (Caryl and Hastings 2006).

Meanwhile, political allies of the Madhi Army served as a critical component of al-Malaki's support base ("Rival Militias" 2006). It is relationships like this that guarantee the impunity the PMGs need to carry out their violence. Of course, this relationship also puts the prime minister in an awkward position: If he met the demand of his military ally, the United States, to dismantle the PMGs, he would alienate one of his most critical domestic allies.

## Sudan

The ongoing paramilitary onslaught of Sudan's Janjaweed began in 2003, and has since cost at least 180,000 lives. The Janjaweed have also displaced 2.5 million Sudanese and driven an estimated 200,000 to seek refugee status outside the country (HRW 2005). The PMG coalesced after the government agreed to a power-sharing agreement with the SLA/M, the Sudanese Liberation Army/Movement. The entrenched political system that reserved political access and economic benefits for the Arab Sudanese had been long targeted by the SLA and its allies, who demanded economic redistribution and political equality. The international community pushed for peace between the SLA and the regime in Khartoum, but for many of the Arab Sudanese the reforms were not an acceptable means of resolving the conflict. The preferred method was simple elimination of the enemy (HRW 2004b).

The Janjaweed are only the most recent incarnation of Sudan's extra-State militias. Regimes have armed their civilian allies against perceived threats at least since the 1960s, beginning with the "muraheleen," armed by President Nimeiri (1969–85). Such groups traditionally operated without much centralization; this changed dramatically in 2003 when the reality of a power-sharing arrangement became more ominous (Lindijer 2004; HRW 2004a). Since that time, the collaboration between the paramilitary and factions within the government has become increasingly evident. Former members of the Janjaweed testified that their orders "always c[a]me from the government" ("Sudan 'Backs'" 2006), and Human Rights Watch has verified that a significant number of the Janjaweed units were physically sharing bases with certain military units. There is also long-standing evidence that the Sudanese air force was used to provide air cover for the Janjaweed attacks, which were typically carried out by men on camelback (HRW 2004a, b, c). In addition, the PMG benefited from the support of some local politicians, who supported recruitment efforts and used government funds to compensate the PMG members (HRW 2004a:3). Additional support came from several elite tribal leaders who were quite obviously well resourced (some having multiple residences). Among these were Hamid Dawai and Abdullah abu Shineibat, both emirs from the Beni Halba tribe (HRW 2004a:2).

Thanks to the support network, the Janjaweed in Sudan has enjoyed broad impunity, just as in the cases of Chiapas, Colombia, and El Salvador. Police officers were instructed "not to interfere with [the Janjaweed] in any way" (HRW 2004b:4). The PMG has literally been able to carry out a massive genocidal campaign, obliterating entire villages, kidnapping and raping women and girls, mutilating and murdering men and boys, and burning homes and businesses to the ground after looting them of anything valuable with no repercussion whatsoever. In addition, the lack of "formal" ties to the State allowed the government to acknowledge the countersubversive "common cause" of the PMG and the military, while also denying any links between the two at all. Such positioning allowed the Janjaweed to claim legitimacy much as Castaño did for Colombia's AUC even while existing illegally.

OF COURSE use of the triad model of paramilitary emergence to analyze any of these cases is preliminary at best. While PMGs have emerged in these cases, the fact that the conflicts are ongoing creates a prohibitive environment for research. Documents are still classified, intelligence information is not accessible, and in the case of Sudan, the government has denied investigators access to Darfur itself. Thus it is impossible to know all of the information necessary to evaluate the applicability of the model. This having been said, the political nature of the PMGs and the resources at their disposal suggests the applicability of the model presented here, as well as the benefit of pursuing additional research into these and other cases.

## Paramilitaries and the State of Democracy

In the introduction to this book, I noted that paramilitaries challenge the typologies comparativists have traditionally relied upon in that they are neither entirely "state" nor entirely "civil society" actors. Rather they are the product of interests shared across factions of groups within both arenas. PMGs therefore occupy a political space that has characteristics of both the state and civil society but is not accurately characterized as either, and has attributes unique unto itself as well. Understanding the paramilitary phenomenon requires traversing this political space, and therefore not limiting inquiry with either a "top-down" or "bottom-up" approach. Indeed to understand phenomena such as paramilitary groups, we need to use an approach that allows us to investigate and analyze those actors who have a foot in each arena, and who network with members of both.

In his 2006 work on the world of narcotics and crime in Latin American favelas, Enrique Desmond Arias advocated that scholars recognize the deficiencies of the "state-society model of politics" and embrace a "networked model of politics in which state and civic institutions are given less weight than the formal and informal ties that bring together like-minded state officials, civic actors, and, in some cases, criminals" (202). I concur. The evidence on paramilitary emergence and subsequent implications for paramilitary devolution similarly suggest that the model juxtaposing state and civil society is incapable of conceptualizing the space in between. As a theoretical tool, the model cannot account for the multitude of actors, many of whom are innately political, who transcend both boundaries, who traverse both arenas, and who oftentimes dominate the unofficial but increasingly important political landscape.

Ultimately, a consolidated democracy is one where members of civil society and members of the state interact freely and fairly. Often, the road to consolidation is ridden with conflict. In 1968, Samuel Huntington argued that political instability was a consequence, in part, of "rapid social change and the rapid mobilization of new groups into politics" (4). In many ways, the phenomenon of paramilitary violence is a varied expression of the same instability and conflict Huntington was studying. They are a backlash against expanding access to the state led by sectors who have traditionally monopolized access and who fear marginalization. Paramilitary groups therefore both reflect the lack of such consolidation and impede further attempts to achieve it. A deep understanding of the process by which consolidation succeeds or fails hinges in part on our ability to understand the political dynamics underlying the emergence of groups like PMGS, whose political activity occurs primarily in this "space in between" the state and civil society.

# NOTES

## Introduction

1   The lack of consistent, analytic meaning underlying the use of terminology is
    clearly exemplified in Schulze and Smith (2000), for instance, in which the au-
    thors discuss the challenges to "decommissioning" Northern Ireland's paramil-
    itaries using cross-national comparison. The authors compare the case of the
    paramilitaries in Northern Ireland with the "guerrillas" in El Salvador, "paramili-
    taries" in Lebanon, and the "rebels" in Mozambique. Presumably, all of these
    groups share some substantive characteristics (for instance, the use of violence
    for political ends). Haider-Markel and O'Brien (1997) refer to armed, antigov-
    ernment militia groups in the United States as paramilitary groups. Similarly,
    in an important study of violent political actors, Payne (2000) categorizes para-
    military groups as a type of "uncivil movement," though she argues that uncivil
    movements are not always right-wing and do not always work in support of a sta-
    tus quo. For instance, she describes the Nicaraguan Contras as "paramilitary,"
    though they were engaged in an effort to overthrow the Sandinista government.
    Studies such as these, with their diverse use of the term, demonstrate the need
    for political scientists to be more deliberate and rigorous in the terminology and
    conceptualization upon which we build models and theories, and upon which
    politicians often build public policy.

2   In the sense that PMGs "promote exclusionary policies," they are consistent with
    Payne's conceptualization of an "uncivil movement" (1). However, paramilitary
    groups should not be understood as a subset of "uncivil movements" (see note
    1 above) in that they have very specific characteristics not always held by uncivil
    movements as defined by Payne. For instance, uncivil movements may try to over-
    throw the state, while a paramilitary group fights to protect the status quo as
    propagated by the state.

3   This is not to suggest that I agree with Kaldor's suggestion that PMGs are a rela-
    tively new phenomenon. Quite the contrary; militant groups throughout U.S.
    history, the KKK for instance, may indeed have been paramilitary groups, and I
    suggest further research on this. Despite disagreeing with Kaldor on this point,
    her conceptualization and analysis of the phenomenon make unquestionably
    important contributions to our understanding of this type of violence.

4   For a note on the relationship between movements and revolutions, see, for
    example, Goodwin and Jasper (2003:3), McAdam, McCarthy, and Zald (1996:9),
    Tarrow (1996:10, 24), and Giugni, McAdam, and Tilly (1998:xviii). For more on
    countermovements, see Zald and Useem (1987).

5   See also Sluka, who reviews and comments on other studies that have found that
    U.S. "client states" were the most frequent setting of paramilitary emergence

during the 1970s. Such studies have concluded that "the global rise in state terror has been mainly or fundamentally the result of U.S. foreign policy" (Sluka 2000:8). Sluka quotes Edward Herman (1982), who found that "'the death squad is a manifestation of U.S. influence. Torture and the death squad are as U.S.-related-American as apple pie' (1982:132)" (Sluka 2000:8).

6  In the past, selection of cases on the dependent variable has raised suspicion among some scholars regarding a study's ability to speak to any type of causal relationship (King, Keohane, and Verba 1994). However, recent scholarship has demonstrated that while such concerns are quite relevant for statistical studies, where the objective is to generalize the findings that emanate from a sample to a broader population, they are not necessarily relevant for case study research, where the objective is to establish the necessity and/or sufficiency of variables, and the ways in which those variables work. Methodological consensus now rests with the beneficial nature of case selection based on the dependent variables for research intended to "identif[y] the potential causal paths and variables leading to the dependent variable of interest" (George and Bennett 2005:23). Patterns of agreement, cases selected to limit variation on the dependent variable, enable the researcher to uncover conditions *necessary* for the outcome of interest (Mahoney and Rueschemeyer 2003:18, 342, 351; George and Bennett 2005:23, 32–33; Ragin 2000:60).

7  Studies of the political dynamics of the State have traditionally been either structural or process-oriented in their approach. Structuralist explanations often focus on the configuration of actors (for instance, coalitions and divisions) and the consolidation of power (which actors have it and which actors legitimate it) in a given situation as explanatory factors for decision or event outcomes (Rueschemeyer, Stephens, and Stephens 1992). Process-oriented approaches focus on the "actors' manipulation of their own and their adversaries' cognitive and normative frames" (Kitschelt 1992:1028). For process-oriented scholars, the strategic options available to actors is therefore not narrowly limited by structural restraints and can actually be expanded or constrained by one's own actions or those of other actors (Kitschelt 1992:1028–33; Shin 1994).

8  See McAdam, McCarthy, and Zald 1996, especially pages 1–8, for more on this structural dynamic and the opportunity structure for movements.

9  If this distribution of political power and the structural alignment of relationships was different, it is possible that hard-liners might be successfully marginalized and reforms undertaken without PMG emergence. Though this question is beyond the scope of this study, it is deserving of additional exploration.

10  See, for instance, McAdam 1988; and Snow, Zurcher, and Ekland-Olson 1980.

Chapter 1

1  For example, claims of fraud in the election of 1988 brought tremendous upheaval and conflict in Mexico. On the night of the election, some representatives from the Partido Acción Nacional, National Action Party (PAN), were in the

Federal Election Registry (RFE) to watch the votes come in on computer monitors. "'We knew there were two systems — the real data and one displaying data designed to show that the PRI [Partido Revolucionario Institucional] was winning. We had some ideas about passwords, and we tried them and one of them got us in to the real system,' details José Gómez Urquiza. . . . The screen showed Cárdenas (of the PRD) sweeping ten Mexico City and state districts from the PRI and their own party. A hurried meeting of RFE officials was noticed in the rear of the . . . room. Then the screens went dead. The RFE reported that the system had crashed. . . . The system remained 'crashed' for a week while tens of thousands of ballots marked for Cárdenas were found smoldering in garbage dumps or floating down central Mexican rivers." Salinas was declared president with about 50 percent of the vote (Ross 1995:335–36; Wheaton 1998:16).

2   The account of the proximity of the armed forces and police is supported by the testimonies of survivors and by analyses of reporters and human rights observers. In particular, see Kampwirth 1998, and Ramírez Cuevas 1997b.

3   In December 1999, two former state-level government officials were tried and found guilty on charges relative to the Acteal massacre. The first was sentenced for failing to take action against the perpetrators and the second for "carrying firearms restricted to the use of the military." The earlier convictions of two dozen individuals (including the former mayor of Chenalho) were "revoked" and said to require further investigation for alleged technicalities (SIPAZ 2000e:8). In 2002, a Mexican court sentenced eighteen of the alleged perpetrators to prison sentences of thirty-six years, though it was widely believed among the human rights community that "the true authors of the massacre are still at large" ("Sentences" 2002).

4   Some estimates are that the church controlled one-third of Mexico's total landmass early in the country's independence (Levy and Székely 1983:41).

5   The name "White Guards" is alleged to hark back to the "private police" used by wealthy landowners in Russia after the 1917 Russian Revolution to prevent their land from being redistributed. The groups should not be confused with "*pistoleros*," who usually operated alone or with one partner (rather than in groups) and were hired for the purpose of protecting the landowner himself and his home. According to Hidalgo (1997), while White Guards were hired to protect tracts of property, *pistoleros* were comparable to bodyguards and were generally at the side of the landowner (Hidalgo 1997:1–2).

6   The investigation was carried out by the Comisión Nacional de Derechos Humanos (CNDH), or the National Commission on Human Rights.

7   It should be noted that not all communities fared the same regarding land redistribution. There were periods during which the promises of land were fulfilled and communities benefited from government programs in a more timely fashion than others. While some communities won land over a two-year period, others persisted in their petitions for more than five or six years (See Collier and Quaratiello 1999:47–49).

8   One such model city was discovered by the Mexican army one year prior to the offensive, according to a declassified U.S. Defense Intelligence Agency intelligence report (Doyle 2004:9).

9   Absalón was kidnapped by the EZLN in their offensive and was held until 16 February. During that time, he was tried by the EZLN and found "guilty by the Justice Tribunal of the Zapatista Army of National Liberation of 'having obliged the Indians of Chiapas to rise up in arms.'" His sentence was a life term of service ("hard labor") in an Indian community, but the sentence was commuted "'condemning (Absalón) to live until the end of his days with the pain and shame of having received the pardon and the good will of those he had killed, robbed, kidnapped, and plundered'" (Ross 1995:184).

10  Like the CNDH, the IFE began with strong links to the PRI and would gain only limited autonomy in future changes. Despite the intent to prevent election fraud, according to a PRD report done a few years after the implementation of the IFE and a new voter registry, "only 15 percent of the names of 600,000 people who have died in Mexico [between] 1991 [and 1993] have been deleted from the registration list" (Council 1993:19).

11  Whether this is due to a decline is public support for the PRI or to a decline in election fraud cannot be determined from statistical electoral data presented here.

12  Others have argued that Zedillo's new approach was actually a direct response to the demands of Chase Manhattan Bank following the U.S. bailout of the Mexican economy. In 1994, the Mexican economy crashed. President Clinton secured US$50 billion for Mexico in January 1995. Reports are that "On January 13, 1995, Riordan Roett, head of the 'Emerging Market Group' of the Chase Manhattan Bank, issued a memo to President Ernesto Zedillo calling on Mexico 'to eliminate the Zapatistas to demonstrate their effective control of the national territory and security policy.'" It was early February when President Zedillo broke the cease-fire agreement and sent in the army to arrest EZLN leadership and sympathizers (Wheaton 1998:14).

## Chapter 2

1   Twenty-six members of the Chinchulines were later arrested for the attack (HRW 1997:37).

2   Auténticos Coletos has been openly critical of the bishop and has allegedly vandalized the church in San Cristóbal. Hidalgo writes that the group is "funded and organized by the local PRI deputy, Jorge Mario Lescieur Talavera" (1997:4).

3   Specific criticisms of Bishop Ruiz and the catechists claim that their political activism has linked the church to political beliefs, making it difficult for their followers to make any distinction at all. DPJ also refers to the PRD as the "Partido del Reino de Dios" (Party of the Kingdom of God).

4   Subcommandante Marcos, the most frequent spokesperson for the EZLN, has spoken to the insinuation that the Zapatistas are somehow linked to a religion.

"We have no links to Catholic religious authorities, nor with those of any other creed. . . . Among the ranks, the majority are Catholic, but there are also other creeds and religions. . . . We are not religious, nor are we against religion. We respect beliefs, but each one of us is in the battle for our poverty. There are catechists among us, as well as Seventh Day Adventists" (from *Tiempo,* in Collier and Quaratiello 1999:66).

5   The troop level was not diminished until after President Vicente Fox took office in 2000 and began shifting the government's approach to Chiapas from "military logic [to] embracing political logic" (Weiner 2000:1; Greste 2000, 2001; "Mexican Army" 2001).

6   The PFP is a specialized force composed of individuals from both the "Army and other federal agencies" governed by the Interior Ministry. The force was implemented in 1999 under Zedillo and has been used in a variety of special tasks, including ending the student occupation of the UNAM and serving in Chiapas as "the guardians of the jungle." The PFP works closely with the army, particularly at army road checkpoints where identification is checked, was authorized to use surveillance and other investigatory tools, and given national jurisdiction (SIPAZ 2000c).

The PSP fall under the Ministry of Government but are "under the command of the presidents of the municipalities where they are" stationed. Their primary responsibility is crime prevention; investigation of crimes is left to federal and "judicial" police (HRW 1997:20).

7   The general was "relieved of his duties" just one month prior to the Acteal massacre. A farewell party for the general was held at the governor's home and was attended by Paz y Justicia members, including Sánchez Sánchez and Torres López. Ruis Ferro resigned the governorship following the Acteal massacre (Arronte, Gustavo, and Lewis 2000:125; Cheung 1998a).

8   Movement scholars speak of the "biographical availability" of activists, meaning that certain individuals have the economic resources and career/family flexibility to volunteer time and resources for a cause (see McAdam 1988). PMG recruits have a different sort of biographical availability in that they are economically vulnerable and open to the financial benefits and status offered by the triad.

9   Clearly such "recruitment" tactics could serve as a source of real tension within the group, particularly between those members who are ideologically supportive of the cause and those who are there either under force or out of desperate need for income. Such internal dynamics are beyond the scope of this study, but they deserve further investigation. Social movement scholars have found that the internal workings of a social movement, from internal polarization, to the degree of exclusivity of the group, to the range of cognitive and emotional commitment of members, can influence the longevity and cohesion of a movement organization (see, for instance, Mansbridge 2003; and Jasper 2003). Such variables are likely to be relevant for PMGs, as well, and may be investigated in future research.

## Chapter 3

1  Citations for IACHR 1999 include a roman numeral, referring to the document chapter, followed by a number that refers to the corresponding denoted paragraph, as numbered in the document.

2  Gran Colombia's life span began in 1819, before the "official" independence of Colombia, due to Bolívar's conviction that victory was only a matter of time (Bushnell 1993:50). The boarders of Gran Colombia shifted over time, once including modern day Venezuela and Colombia, then later incorporating Panama and Ecuador (Bushnell 1993:58–64; Bergquist, Peñaranda, and Sánchez 1992:11–24).

3  The UNHCHR calls such tactics "'lucky catch' roadblocks."

4  Monetary conversions are made using Xe.com: Universal Currency Converter.

5  It is worth noting that the "guerrillas sometimes demand ransom payments before returning the bodies of kidnap victims who died in captivity. For example, relatives of a merchant kidnapped . . . in Caldas . . . paid the FARC nearly $2,000 (5.9 million pesos) to recover his body" (USDOS 2003:12). Castaño emphasizes in numerous interviews and writings his frustration and resentment of the FARC for not returning his father's remains (Aranguren 2001; IACHR 2000a:1.7).

6  Carlos Castaño claims that he began his personal vendetta against Escobar in 1989, upon becoming "an anonymous informant for the government." Eventually, Carlos told his brother Fidel what he'd been doing and persuaded Fidel to give up the alliance with Escobar. They organized "Perseguidos por Pablo Escobar" (People Persecuted by Pablo Escobar), commonly known as the "Pepes," and worked together with officials against Escobar (Dudley 2002:24; Ruiz 2001:204).

7  Despite the skepticism of guerrillas after the failed UP experiment, some members of the EPL agreed to demobilize during Trujillo's administration (1990–94) to form a new political party known as Esperanza, Paz y Libertad (Hope, Peace and Liberty). Similarly, in 1990 a political branch of the M-19 known as the Alianza Democratica (Democratic Alliance) organized (IACHR 1993:II.4–5). But little had changed in the political environment, and again amnesty was not protected by the State. In 1990, the presidential candidate running under the Alianza Democratica banner was assassinated, and cases of Esperanza members being harassed and killed were reported (IACHR 1993.VI.5).

8  The prohibition lost its muscle when amnesty in the form of "suspended sentences for belonging to unlawful armed groups" was later extended to individuals who remained active in paramilitaries (IACHR 1993:II.8).

9  Despite rumors that Fidel was not killed but went into hiding, Carlos Castaño vehemently asserted that his brother was killed and buried on his own private property (Dudley 2002:10–13).

## Chapter 4

1  The *personero* received several death threats and was notified by several people testifying to paramilitary/military collusion that there were plans to kill him before the end of his term in office. Nonetheless, he continued taking testimonies

and documenting violations until the threats became increasingly dire. He eventually fled from Puerto Asís (HRW 2001c:35).

2 The bookkeeper reports that most times the payments were delivered in cash, and that occasionally she was responsible for such deliveries, or the recipients would pick up the cash at her boss's home. In the same testimony, she reported to the local *personero* that on one occasion, she had had to use the local wire service to get money to a 24th Brigade major's wife. The *personero* did later "confirm this transaction by consulting the Servientrega [wire service] records" (HRW 2001c:22).

3 Ironically, other paramilitary groups have been lauded by local supporters for "prohibit[ing] the sale of black-market gasoline, accomplishing something the authorities have been unable to do on other parts of the same highway" (Wilson 2002c:3).

4 For further examples, see also USDOS 1999:2.

5 In the spring of 2005, the government began the "Productive Projects for Peace" program. Using government and private resources, the plan was to provide jobs for former AUC soldiers. Jobs provided to former paramilitaries included legitimate agriculture (with land donated to the program by the private sector), "ranching, agro-industry and eco-tourism." In Valle de Cauca department, "the 557 Calima Bloc fighters . . . benefit[ed] from a 300 hectare farm in Palmira on which chicken, ranching and farming projects [were to be] implemented" (Rivas 2005a:2).

6 The United States later offered support in the training of the criminal investigators and prosecutors who would be involved in the Peace and Justice Law defendants ("Colombia: First" 2005).

7 Michael Farhling "said that the [law] 'does not honor the right to truth'" ("Shameful" 2005). The lack of public confidence in the process is evident in grassroots efforts to seek information. "Public tribunals of opinion" have been organized around the country to "allow victims, survivors and witnesses of atrocities to speak out, and to gather evidence and draw public attention to human rights crimes, although their decisions are non-binding" (Vieira 2005a).

## Chapter 5

1 "In the early years of the [twentieth century]" the *catorce* was a "core" of a larger group made up of an estimated sixty-five families (Dunkerley 1982:7).

2 Some suggest that this is not only due to the inability to rely on fraud, but also to the fact that the upper class had never organized the party structure necessary to run a candidate in a competitive election. The personal ambitions of individuals complicated matters, as too many "competed with one another for a relatively limited conservative electorate" (Stanley 1996:45).

3 In a twist of irony, after Martínez resigned he moved to Honduras, where he was "soon afterwards hacked to death with a machete by his *mayordomo*." (Dunkerley 1982:34).

4    The interviewee claimed that the churches and universities saw the FMLN as a *"causa noble,"* and therefore provided money, which then provided for the weapons[§].

5    Diskin reports that the arms used by one of the guerrilla groups were primarily "captured (and some were even bought) from the military. Of the arms and supplies that did come from outside, many were bought on the open market by the FMLN" (Diskin and Sharpe 1986:80). Diskin suggests that reports of a black market movement of arms, particularly from Nicaragua and Cuba, were "grossly distorted" in order to support the rhetoric being used in Washington to support military aid to the Central American country.

6    Dunkerley notes that CONDECA was intended to protect the anticommunist dictators across the region from the growing guerrilla movement and that it "served as a critical prop for the PCN" in El Salvador through the 1970s (Dunkerley 1982:75).

7    There is evidence to suggest that the United States CIA was involved to some extent with collecting or analyzing intelligence information for the El Salvadoran agencies. One aide to a CIA agent told a U.S. journalist in 1984 that the CIA kept reports and even photographs, so that "'we knew exactly what we were doing, who was who,' he add[ed] that many of the subjects were later assassinated by Death Squads" (Nairn 1984:24). Medrano himself confirmed that the CIA provided assistance by informing ANSESAL about "the activities of Salvadorans working or studying abroad" (Nairn 1984:24). This information not only connects the United States to the targeting of "death squad" victims, but also indicates the precision with which the PMGs acted. Their violence was not random or intended to create mass and untargeted terror but rather intended to affect a precise number of individuals and groups.

8    ORDEN began as part of yet another government attempt at structuring a means of controlled public "input" into the political system, a counterinsurgency instrument designed to draw peasant support toward the state and away from the nascent guerrilla groups (Stanley 1996:69; Montgomery 1995:55–56). Medrano described the organization's goals as to "'indoctrinate the peasants regarding the advantages of the democratic system and the disadvantages of the communist system.'" Medrano described the plan as intended to "'catechize'" the people and said "'It was almost like a religion.'" (Nairn 1984:23).

9    The remains of the two victims were eventually found and described as "'almost unrecognizably mutilated'" (Stanley 1996:82).

10   Thus we see that the "biographical availability" of some of the lowest-level recruits is similar to what we saw in Chiapas and Colombia. Again, whether the differing agendas of recruits (for some, ideology, for others, income) provided a source of contention within the group is beyond the scope of this study, but it is an interesting question.

11   The use of the mass media to sway public opinion in favor of the far right was a strategy the hardliners would continue to use. In 1979 D'Aubuisson used televi-

sion ads to indict alleged "communists," reading names taken from old ANS-ESAL records to the viewership. Medrano later told a journalist that D'Aubuisson was using the television time to instruct troops, "'pointing out the Communists so the troops would kill them. . . . He had good information. He was speaking the truth'" (Nairn 1984:29). And indeed the troops did as expected, their victims including Attorney General Zamora, who was accused by D'Aubuisson only days before his assassination (LeoGrande 1998b:49). Some of the information used by D'Aubuisson was allegedly provided by the United States CIA (Nairn 1984:20).

12 A leading Christian Democrat told me that D'Aubuisson had also operated a "kidnapping ring to raise money, comparable to the drug trade in Colombia." This allegation was supported by Carlos Antonio Borja Letona, an ARENA representative in the House of Deputies in 2003 and a former member of the National Association of Enterprises. Borja Letona reported that while Duarte was president, the members of the business community knew that paramilitaries were kidnapping entrepreneurs for money, and that the concern was raised with Duarte himself (Borja Letona 2003).

## Chapter 6

1 Owners would have received 25 percent of the value of the land (as noted in tax reports) in cash, and the other 75 percent would have been paid in "government bonds, which could only be reinvested in industry," a provision designed to encourage industrialization within the broader economy (Dunkerley 1982:158).

2 U.S. military aid had been suspended after the kidnapping, rape, and murder of three nuns and a young, female Catholic lay worker, all from the United States (UN Security Council 1993:II.4). However, the military aid was soon reinstated and continued regardless of the miserable failure on the part of El Salvador to meet U.S. congressional standards regarding human rights. For example, see LeoGrande 1998b:179–80; Diskin and Sharpe 1983:68; Dickey 1983:21.

3 The group was also responsible for the 1989 assassination of six Jesuit priests, their cook, and her daughter (UN Security Council 1993:II.4; III.B:1).

4 The Truth Commission, in an attempt to describe the extremity of the violence during 1980, in its report on the six FDR victims observed that "The climate of violence and insecurity prevailing in the country at the time was such that, had it not been for who the victims were, the place and time of the abduction, the type of operation and the public outrage it caused, it would have been just one more in the long list of abuses that were occurring at the time" (UN Security Council 1993:IV.B.2:3).

5 The commission notes that there have also been theories that it was the National Guard that carried out the attack, despite the fact that the Anti-Communist Brigade "claimed responsibility" (UN Security Council 1993:IV.B.2:5).

6 The commission findings are consistent with information revealed by Sarávia in a notebook obtained by authorities in May 1980. The records were in D'Aubuisson's possession when he was arrested and held briefly for his role in a plot to over-

throw the governing junta. The findings are also consistent with a confession offered by Avila in 1982 (Pyes 1984:352). Sarávia later moved to the United States, eventually residing in Modesto, California, when charges were brought against him by family members of Romero. The Fresno Court ruled that the plaintiffs faced significant vulnerability to retaliatory violence, even in 2004, and allowed the proceedings while protecting their anonymity. On 3 September 2004, Judge Oliver Wanger ruled that Sarávia was indeed responsible for Romero's death in his complicity in planning the assassination and in providing the shooter "with a gun, payment, and transportation" ("Man Liable" 2004:1). The judge further found Sarávia guilty of crimes against humanity, finding that the assassination of Archbishop Romero was intended to and did in fact have ramifications beyond the death of one individual, reverberating politically throughout the country with violent consequence (Simon 2004).

7　The success of ARENA despite the fact that it had been in existence only a few months was due at least in part to the significant support it enjoyed from U.S. friends. McCann Erikson, a U.S.-based public relations firm, provided campaign advice, as did other conservative supporters (LeoGrande 1998b:159).

8　Diskin points out that in 1982, the FDR had the legal right to run candidates in the election provided they could submit a petition of "three thousand signatures." But after the postelection manhunt in 1980 that had resulted in the deaths of multiple FDR leaders, the military had collected a list of the remaining FDR leaders and put them on a "traitor's list." Diskin concludes that it was only logical that the FDR would not run in 1982, since "three thousand signatures on a petition would have amounted to a convenient 'death list'" (Diskin and Sharpe 1986:64).

9　The FDR was particularly targeted. In October, seventeen "labor leaders and politicians affiliated with parties in the FDR coalition" were disappeared. Eight of them were later found in the possession of the armed forces (LeoGrande 1998b:178).

10　Diskin notes that the FDR-FMLN had actually tried to use Rivera y Damas in 1981 to start negotiations, but when Rivera y Damas brought the proposal to "Vice-President George Bush and William Clark (then number two in the State Department)," the U.S. leaders "said they were not interested." Later that same year, the FDR-FMLN sent a letter directly to President Ronald Reagan relaying their "disposition to undertake them [negotiations] at any time," but again there was no follow through). Diskin explains the guerrilla willingness to negotiate based on reports that as early as 1982, the guerrillas had concluded that the "military victory would be too costly," and that alienating itself or El Salvador from the good graces of the United States would preclude access to the funding that might be available for reconstruction after the war (Diskin and Sharpe 1986:60–61, 81).

11　Decree Law No. 805, the Law of Amnesty, which became applicable as of 5 November 1987, "grant[ed] absolute and lawful amnesty to all persons, national and foreign, who have acted as the immediate or proximate perpetrators or accomplices in the commission of political crimes or common crimes related to political or common crimes perpetrated prior to October 22 [1987] of this year in which no fewer than twenty persons were involved." Those who voluntarily disarmed and "renounce[d] violence" within two weeks after the enactment of the Law of Amnesty were also eligible. Commission in certain crimes excluded one from eligibility, however, including participating in the assassination of Archbishop Romero or of Herbert Anaya, former chair of the Governmental Human Rights Commission, kidnapping for "personal gain," or drug trafficking (IACHR 1988:5).

12   Ellacuría had been targeted by the right before; his offices had been bombed three times, including after he had first advocated "dialogue" between the government and the guerrillas (Zin 1990).

13   There were initial problems with this aspect of the agreement. The National Police actually expanded after the demobilization began, as "former members of BIRIs, the National Guard and the Treasury Police were incorporated and its training center was still graduating from 60 to 100 officers monthly" (Montgomery 246). After pressure from the United Nations, the National Police was finally shut down and there was a complete shift to the PNC forces.

14   A truth commission was created by the Peace Accords to investigate and publish findings regarding acts of violence, particularly human rights violations, carried out during the conflict. The published report identified those involved in orchestrating and implementing some of the most well-known murders, including the assassination of the archbishop, the four American churchwomen, the Jesuit priests, mother, and daughter at UCA, and the El Mozote massacre. Many of the findings were challenged by various sectors, including the military (Montgomery 1995:243), demonstrating that there is still a great deal of contention regarding the interpretation of the facts of the conflict.

15   La Sombra Negra is alleged to have murdered young men and has published its own newsletter criticizing the State and the post-Peace Accords political environment in El Salvador. According to one of my sources, the group has left the corpses of their victims in rural areas and appears to have political undertones.[§] One of the 1995 newsletters put out by the organization expressed specific frustration with the justice system in the country and claims to *Hacia la justicia por medio de la muerte* [move toward justice through death]" (La Sombra Revista 1995).

16   The PPR is the Popular Republican Party, a splinter party from the right that has yet to gain the necessary 3 percent of votes to obtain representation in the Legislative Assembly ("Frustration" 2003; CNN World/Election Watch 2005; "Elections" 2004).

17   Former defense ministers General Jose Guillermo Garcia and Carlos Eugenio Vides Casanova were both convicted of human right violations, including torture, in a West Palm Beach, Florida, court in 2002. They were ordered to pay $54.6 million to three plaintiffs who suffered at the hands of the men under the

ministers' command, a decision upheld in 2005 by the Eleventh Circuit Court of Appeals ("El Salvador" 2004; "$54 million" 2006). Roberto D'Aubuisson died of throat cancer on 21 February 1992 (LeoGrande 1998b:577).

18 A similar analysis can be made regarding the guerrillas and the success of the Democratic Convergence party in 1990. The party, which we have already noted had won only 3.8 percent of the vote in the previous presidential elections (Montgomery 1995:214) won "12 percent of the vote . . . and eight seats in the new National Assembly. The success of the Convergence showed the guerrillas that the electoral system offered real possibilities for the left" (LeoGrande 1998b:575).

19 Payne's book *Uncivil Movements* (2000) provides a more in-depth and systematic analysis of the relationship between democratic institutionalization and the use of those institutions by violent groups. In her discussion of the "pathologies of democracy" (10–14), in particular, Payne explores not only how these groups may come to use the institutions of government and evolve in the process, but also how they may come to affect the institutions themselves and the broader transition to democracy.

### Conclusion

1 The suggestion that Cristiani and other far-right principals negotiated and agreed to the peace hints that Rustow's theory of elite accommodation (1970) may help explain why the peace accords were implemented in El Salvador, making his model tangentially relevant to the demise of the PMGs. However, D'Aubuisson was not a direct part in the negotiations, and he was unquestionably the head of the PMG organizations. In fact it seems that two different sets of the elite participated in the democratic shift in El Salvador at two different points in time. The party and government leaders took part in the negotiations, making concessions that did bring an end to the conflict and laid the groundwork for democracy. The concessions of the paramilitary groups came after the establishment of the accords, a seeming acquiescence to the already established compromises.

# WORKS CITED

"1200 Colombian Paramilitary Militiamen Disarmed." 2005 (4 Sept.). Xinhau General News Service. *LexisNexis Academic*, 1 Mar. 2006 ⟨http://web.lexis-nexis .com⟩.

"209 Extra Colombian Paramilitaries Surrender Arms." 2005 (7 Aug.). Xinhau General News Service. *LexisNexis Academic*, 27 Feb. 2006 ⟨http://web.lexis-nexisz .com⟩.

"$54 Million Verdict Upheld against Salvadoran Generals Found Responsible for Torture." 2006 (6 Jan.). Center for Justice & Accountability (San Francisco, Calif.). Online Posting. 5 Mar. 2006 ⟨center4justice@cja.org⟩.

"60 in Colombia Are Said to Die during Battles." 2002 (4 May). *New York Times*, 6 May 2002 ⟨www.nytimes.com/2002_headlines+&pagewanted=print& position=top⟩.

ACCU (Autodefensias Campesinas Cordoba y Uraba). 2002 (2 May). Estado Mayor de las Autodefensias Campesinas Cordoba y Uraba. "Las ACCU informamos a los Colombianos." 26 Sept. 2002 ⟨www.colombialibre.org/publicaciones⟩.

ACCUBEC (Autodefensias Campesinas Cordoba y Uraba, Bloque Élmer Cárdenas). 2003a (3 Oct.). Unpublished letter from Comandante José Alfredo Berrío-Alemán, Bloque Élmer Cárdenas, AUC, to the CAMIZBA non-governmental organization. 16 Dec. 2003 ⟨www.accubec.org/comunicadoes/3092003.htm⟩.

―――. 2003b. "Autodefensas en Colombia." 18 Dec. 2003 ⟨www.accubec.org/ biblioteca/autodefensas.htm⟩.

―――. 2003c. "La Guerra en Urabá." 18 Dec. 2003 ⟨www.accubec.org/biblioteca/ guerra.htm⟩.

*Acuerdos de El Salvador: En el Camino de la Paz.* 1992. New York: United Nations.

AI (Amnesty International). 1980. *Recommendations of an Amnesty International Mission to the Government of the Republic of Colombia.* London: Amnesty International. (AI Index: AMR 23/04/80.)

―――. 1988. *El Salvador: "Death Squads": A Government Strategy.* New York: Amnesty International Publications. (AI Index: AMR 29/21/88.)

―――. 1989. *Colombia: Human Rights Developments, Death Squads on the Defensive?* New York: Amnesty International.

―――. 1996 (14 Oct.). "Mexico: Amnesty International Gravely Alarmed at Sharp Increase in Human Rights Violations against Civil and Human Rights Activists." (AI Index: AMR 41/064/1996, 14/10/96.) 20 May 2002 ⟨www.amnesty .org/802568F7005C4453⟩.

―――. 1998. "Annual Report: AI Report 1998: Mexico." 30 Apr. 2001 ⟨www.amnesty .org/ailib/aireport/ar98/amr41.htm⟩.

―――. 1999. "Colombia: Defenders Forced to Flee." *On the Front Line: Regional*

*Action Network on Human Rights Defenders.* 11 June 2002 ⟨www.amnesty
.org/802568F7005 C4453/0/216D8F42C817B4978025690000693410⟩.

———. 2001a (9 Feb.). "Colombia: Colombian Paramilitaries Declare International
Human Rights Organization a 'Military Target.'" 28 Aug. 2001 ⟨www.amnesty-us
.org/news/2001/colombia 02092001.html⟩.

———. 2001b. "Colombia: Annual Report 2001." 28 Aug. 2001 ⟨www.web.amnesty
.org/web/ar2001.nsf/webamrcountries/Colombia?OpenDocument⟩.

———. 2001c (July–Dec.). "Colombia, Justice: The Road to Protection." *On the Front
Line: Bulletin on Human Rights Defenders* 5, no. 2: 4–6.

Allison, Rebecca. 1999 (29 Mar.). "The Killer Who Laughs as His Victims Suffer."
*Western Daily Press. LexisNexis Academic,* 8 Oct. 2007 ⟨http://www.lexisnexis.com⟩.

Alonso, Marcelo. 1984. *Central America in Crisis.* Washington: The Washington
Institute, Task Force on Central America.

Anaya, Federico. 2000. "The Historical and Sociological Context of the Armed
Forces." In *Always Near, Always Far: The Armed Forces in Mexico,* ed. Ernesto
Ledesma Arronte, Gustavo E. Castro Soto, and Tedford P. Lewis. S.A de C.V.
Mexico, D.F.

Anderson, Thomas P. 1992. *Matanza: The 1932 "Slaughter" That Traumatized a
Nation, Shaping US-Salvadoran Policy to This Day.* 2nd ed. Willimantic, Conn.:
Curbstone Press.

Aranguren Molina, Mauricio. 2001. *Mi Confesión: Carlos Castaño revela sus secretos.*
Colombia: Printer Colombiana S.A.

Arias, Enrique Desmond. 2006. *Drugs and Democracy in Rio de Janeiro: Trafficking,
Social Networks, and Public Security.* Chapel Hill: University of North Carolina
Press.

Arronte, Ernesto Ledesma, Gustavo E. Castro Soto, and Tedford P. Lewis, eds. 2000.
*Always Near, Always Far: The Armed Forces in Mexico.* Impretei, S.A de C.V. Mexico,
D.F.

"Asesinado Secuestrador de Richard Boulton: Colombia AUC se Atribuyen
Asesinato." 2002 (4 Sept.). *El Mundo.* 4 Apr. 2004 ⟨www.ultimasnoticias.com.ve/
ediciones/2002 /09/04/p45n1.htm⟩.

Aubry, André, and Angélica Inda. 1997 (23 Dec.). ". . . Quiénes son los
'paramilitares'"? *La Jornada.* 1 Feb. 2001 ⟨www.jornada.unam.mx/1997
.dic97./9712223/aubry.html⟩.

———. 1998a. "Who Are the Paramilitaries?" *NACLA Report on the Americas* 31,
no. 5: 8.

———. 1998b (30 July). "No Hay Paramilitares en Chiapas." *La Jornada.* 1 Feb. 2001
⟨www. jornada.unam.mx/1998/jul98/980730/inda.html⟩.

AUC (Autodefensas Unidas de Colombia). 1997. "Constitucion de la Autodefensas
Unidas De Colombia." 28 Aug. 2001 ⟨www.colombialibre.org/pag_prin/
organizacion/constitucion.htm⟩.

———. 1998. "Estatuto de Constitucion y Regimen Disciplinario." 28 Aug. 2001
⟨www. colombialibre.org/pag_prin/organizacion/. . .⟩.

———. 1999. "Origen, Evolución y Proyección de las Autodefensas Unidas de Colombia." 28 Aug. 2001 ⟨www.colombialibre.org/pag/prin/organizacion/ organizacion_ institucional.htm⟩.

Avilés, Jaime. 1997 (21 Dec.). "Ruiz Ferro y los paramilitares: Relaciones al Desnudo." *La Jornada*. 1 Feb. 2001 ⟨www.jornada.unam.mx/1997.dic97./9712221/ mas-aviles.html⟩.

"Baghdad Bombed as Iraq Toll Mounts." 2006 (11 Oct.). *Turkish Daily News*. *LexisNexis Academic*, 17 Oct. 2006 ⟨http://web.lexis-nexis.com/universe⟩.

Baker, Pauline, and John Ausink. 1996. "State Collapse and Ethnic Violence: Toward a Predictive Model." *Parameters: US Army War College Quarterly* 26, no. 1: 19–31.

Balboa, Juan. 1998 (31 July). "Entrenan como paramilitares a 200 Tzeltales: Pobladores." *La Jornada*. 1 Feb. 2001 ⟨www.jornada.unam.mx/1998/ ago98/980801/entrenan.html⟩.

Base de Datos Políticos de las Américas. 1999. "Resultados Electorales Para La Camara de Diputados/1961–1991." Georgetown University and the Organization of American States. 27 Apr. 2001 ⟨www.georgetown.edu/pdba/Elecdata/Mexico/ mex61-91.html⟩.

———. 2000. "México: 1994 Deputy Election Results/Proportional Representation." Georgetown University and the Organization of American States. 20 Mar. 2006 ⟨http://pdba.georgetown. edu/Elecdata/Mexico/Dip94RP.html⟩.

Beers, Rand, and Francis X. Taylor. 2002 (13 Mar.). "Narco-Terror: The Worldwide Connection between Drugs and Terror." Testimony before the United States Senate Committee of the Judiciary Subcommittee on Technology, Terrorism, and Government Information. 12 Mar. 2006 ⟨http://yale.edu/lawweb/avalon/sept_11/ taylor_007.htm⟩.

Bell, Gustavo. 2000 (7 Mar.). "The Creation of the Colombian State: An International Perspective." Presentation given at the American University, sponsored by the School of International Service and the Kennedy Political Union. Washington, D.C.

Bell, Martin. 1999 (6 June). "I Know He's a War Criminal, but I Can't Help Liking Him." *Mail on Sunday. LexisNexis Academic*. 8 Oct. 2007 ⟨http://www.lexis-nexis .com⟩.

Benítez Manaut, Raúl. 2000. "The Mexican Armed Forces at the End of the 20th Century." In *Always Near, Always Far: The Armed Forces in Mexico*, ed. Ernesto Ledesma Arronte, Gustavo E. Castro Soto, and Tedford P. Lewis. S.A de C.V. Mexico, D.F.

Bergquist, Charles. 1992. "The Labor Movement (1930–1946) and the Origins of the Violence." In *Violence in Colombia: The Contemporary Crisis in Historical Perspective*, ed. Charles Bergquist, Ricardo Peñaranda, and Gonzalo Sánchez. Wilmington, Del.: Scholarly Resources.

Bergquist, Charles, Ricardo Peñaranda, and Gonzalo Sánchez, eds. 1992. *Violence in Colombia: The Contemporary Crisis in Historical Perspective*. Wilmington, Del.: Scholarly Resources.

"Between Peace and Justice; Colombia." 2005 (23 July). *The Economist. LexisNexis Academic.* 27 Feb. 2006 ⟨http://web.lexis-nexis.com⟩.

"Bishop Samuel Ruiz: Apostle of the Poor." 1999 (Mar.). *National Outlook: On-Line.* Outlook Media. 26 Jan. 2001 ⟨www.ozemail.com.au/`wfnev/mar99Ruiz.htm⟩.

"Boletín La Opinión No. 68: CIACH: Chiapas, Mexico." 1997 (20 Aug.). Centro de Información y Análisis de Chiapas, A.C. 4 Sept. 2001 ⟨www.spunk.org/library/places/mexico/sp001837.txt⟩.

Borja Letona, Carlos Antonio. 2003 (12 Mar.). Personal interview. San Salvador.

Boyd, Joseph. 1982 (10 Mar.). "Salvador Death-Squad Leader Becomes Right's Hope." *Christian Science Monitor.* 6 Feb. 2005 ⟨http://www.csmonitor.com/cgibin/wit_article.pl?tape/82/031055.txt⟩.

Bushnell, David. 1992. "Politics and Violence in Nineteenth-Century Colombia." In *Violence in Colombia: The Contemporary Crisis in Historical Perspective*, ed. Charles Bergquist, Ricardo Peñaranda, and Gonzalo Sánchez. Wilmington, Del.: Scholarly Resources.

———. 1993. *The Making of Modern Colombia: A Nation in Spite of Itself.* Berkeley: University of California Press.

Bussey, Jane. 1990 (26 June). "Mexico's Human Rights Record Faces Popular Challenge." *Christian Science Monitor.* 1 Mar. 2005 ⟨www.csmonitor.com/cgi-bin/wit_article.pl?tape/90/omexi⟩.

Calderón de Escalon, Carmen Alena. 2003 (11 Mar.). Personal interview. San Salvador.

Campbell, Bruce B., and Arthur D. Brenner. 2000. *Death Squads in Global Perspective: Murder with Deniability.* New York: St. Martin's Press.

Carter Center, The. 1993. "Electoral Reform in Mexico." Final Report. Unpublished.

———. 2001. "Observing the 2000 Mexico Elections." Final Report by Marcela Szymanski. Unpublished.

Caryl, Christian, and Michael Hastings. 2006 (16 Oct.). "Death Squads On Line." *Newsweek. LexisNexis Academic.* 17 Oct. 2006 ⟨http://web.lexis-nexis.com/universe⟩.

Castro, Gustavo. 1999 (Aug.). "Población Desplazada en Chiapas." CIEPAC. Aug.

Castro Caicedo, Germán. 1996. "Los Paramilitares." In *En Secreto.* 28 Aug. 2001 ⟨www.colombialibre. org/reportajes/entrevistas_report1.htm⟩.

Centro de Derechos Humanos Fray Bartolomé de las Casas. 1999 (Nov.). "The Tip of the Iceberg: Update on the Human Rights Situation in Chiapas: A Special Report for the United Nations High Commissioner on Human Rights." 18 Mar. 2006 ⟨http://www.laneta.apc.org /cdhbcasas/Informes/InfoUpdate.html⟩.

Cerén, Salvador Sanchez. 2003 (13 Mar.). Personal interview. San Salvador.

Cevallos, Diego. 1998 (6 Apr.). "Conflict-Mexico: Accusations Shower down on Bishop Samuel Ruiz." Inter Press Service. 26 Jan. 2001 ⟨www.oneworld.org/ips2⟩.

———. 1999 (30 Apr.). "Rights-Mexico: Report Links Paramilitaries with Ruling Party." Inter Press Service. 26 January 2001. ⟨www.oneworld.org/ips2/may99/20_23_086.html⟩.

Chamé, Nolberto. 2001 (Mar.). "Insta Aguiar al gobierno atender conflicto religioso." *Cuarto Poder.*

Chernick, Marc W. 1998. "The Paramilitarization of the War in Colombia." *NACLA Report on the Americas.* 31, no. 5: 28–33.

Cheung, Michele. 1998a. "The Paramilitaries' Paymasters: Fishers of Men." *Dark Night Field Notes.* N.p.: Dark Night Press. 12/13:37–38.

———. 1998b. "The Paramilitary Groups and the Army: Chiapas Campaign Plan —'94." *Dark Night Field Notes.* N.p.: Dark Night Press. 12/13: 38–42.

"Chiapas: La Guerra en Curso." 1998. Centro de Derechos Humanos "Miguel Agustín Pro Juárez," A.C. Mexico City.

Ching, Erik. 2004. "Patronage and Politics under General Maximiliano Hernández Martínez, 1931–1939." In *Landscapes of Struggle: Politics, Society, and Community in El Salvador*, ed. Aldo Lauria-Santiago and Leigh Binford. Pittsburgh: University of Pittsburgh Press.

CNN World/Election Watch. 2005. "El Salvador." 13 Mar. 2005 ⟨http://edition.cnn.com/WORLD/election.watch/americas/el.salvador3.html⟩.

Cockcroft, James D. 1989. *Neighbors in Turmoil: Latin America.* New York: Harper and Row.

Collado, Héctor. 2001 (16 Mar.). "Entrevista a Carlos Castaño, Comandante de las Autodefensas Unidas de Colombia." Urgente Digital. 28 Aug. 2001 ⟨www.colombialibre. org/reportajes/urgente_digital. htm⟩.

Collier, George A., with Elizabeth Lowery Quaratiello. 1999. *Basta! Land and the Zapatista Rebellion in Chiapas.* Oakland, Calif.: Food First Books.

Collier, David, James Mahoney, and Jason Seawright. 2004. "Claiming Too Much, Warnings about Selection Bias." In *Rethinking Social Inquiry: Diverse Tools, Shared Standards*, ed. Henry E. Brady and David Collier. Lanham, Md.: Rowman and Littlefield.

"Colombia: AUC Calls Halt to Demobilizations." 2005 (11 Oct.). Intelligence Research, Latin American Weekly Report. *LexisNexis Academic.* 27 Feb. 2006 ⟨http://web.lexis-nexis.com⟩.

"Colombia: AUC Chiefs Explain Political Ties." 2005 (5 Aug.). Intelligence Research, Latinnews Daily. *LexisNexis Academic.* 1 Mar. 2006 ⟨http://web.lexis-nexis.com⟩.

"Colombia: AUC Probes Official Willingness to Accommodate." 2005 (26 July). Intelligence Research, Latin American Weekly Report. *LexisNexis Academic.* 27 Feb. 2006 ⟨http://web.lexis-nexis.com⟩.

"Colombia: AUC Suspends Demobilization." 2005 (7 Oct.). Intelligence Research, Latinnews Daily. *LexisNexis Academic.* 27 Feb. 2006 ⟨http://web.lexis-nexis.com⟩.

"Colombia: AUC Talks to Continue." 2005 (27 May). Intelligence Research, Latinnews Daily. *LexisNexis Academic.* 1 Mar. 2006 ⟨http://web.lexis-nexis.com⟩.

"Colombia: Court Clears Way for Uribe's Reelection." 2005 (25 Oct.). Intelligence Research, Latin American Weekly Report. *LexisNexis Academic.* 27 Feb. 2006 ⟨http://web.lexis-nexis.com⟩.

"Colombia: 'Demobilization' Totters as Murillo Is Charged." 2005 (31 May).

Intelligence Research, Latin American Weekly Report. *LexisNexis Academic*. 1 Mar. 2006 ⟨http://web.lexis-nexis.com⟩.

"Colombia: Don Berna Calls for Progress with Government." 2005 (25 Oct.). Intelligence Research, Latinnews Daily. *LexisNexis Academic*. 27 Feb. 2006 ⟨http://web. lexis-nexis.com⟩.

"Colombia: First Public Test Case for 'Justice and Peace' Law." 2005 (30 Aug.). Intelligence Research, Latin American Weekly Report. *LexisNexis Academic*. 27 Feb. 2006 ⟨http://web.lexis-nexis.com⟩.

"Colombia: Government Acknowledges Demobilization Problems." 2005 (24 Oct.). Intelligence Research, Latinnews Daily. *LexisNexis Academic*. 27 Feb. 2006 ⟨http://web.lexis-nexis.com⟩.

"Colombia: Murillo Surrenders; Demobilization Restarts." 2005 (31 May). Intelligence Research, Latinnews Daily. *LexisNexis Academic*. 1 Mar. 2006 ⟨http://web.lexis-nexis.com⟩.

"Colombia: Paramilitary Chief Rules Out Extradition." 2005 (6 June). Inteligence Research, Latinnews Daily. *LexisNexis Academic*. 1 Mar. 2006 ⟨http://web .lexis-nexis.com⟩.

"Colombia: Paramilitary Demobilization Rescheduled." 2005 (22 Nov.). Intelligence Research, Latinnews Daily. *LexisNexis Academic*. 27 Feb. 2006 ⟨http://web .lexis-nexis.com⟩.

"Colombia: Paramilitary Groups Rush to Demobilize." 2005 (12 July). Intelligence Research, Latin American Weekly Report. *LexisNexis Academic*. 1 Mar. 2006 ⟨http://web.lexis-nexis.com⟩.

"Colombia: Paramilitary's 'Dissolution' a Tactical Ploy." 2002 (19 July). Strategic Forecasting. 14 Apr. 2004 ⟨www.tools4change.org/encamino/stratfor_paras .htm⟩.

"Colombia: Vicente Castaño Demobilizes." 2005 (5 Sept.). Intelligence Research, Latinnews Daily. *LexisNexis Academic*. 1 Mar. 2006 ⟨http://web.lexis-nexis.com⟩.

"Colombia Authorizes Warrantless Arrests, Citing Terror Fight." 2002 (12 Sept.). *New York Times*. 18 Sept. 2002 ⟨www.nytimes.com/2002/0_1?tntemail⟩.

"Colombia Declares State of Emergency Amid Violence." 2002 (12 Aug.). *New York Times*. 12 Aug. 2002 ⟨wysiwyg://31/http://www.nytimes.com/reuter_headlines = &pagewanted=print&position=bottom⟩.

"Colombian Government, Rebels Talk Peace." 2003 (15 July). CBSnews.com. 5 Apr. 2004 ⟨www.cbsnews.com/stories/2003/07/15/world/main563444.shtml⟩.

"Colombia Not Pursuing Drug Trafficker Wanted by Germany." 2005 (25 May). *Financial Times Information. LexisNexis Academic*. 1 Mar. 2006 ⟨http://web .lexis-nexis.com⟩.

"Colombian Paramilitary Leader Poses Peace Referendum." 2005 (16 Mar.). *Financial Times Information. LexisNexis Academic*. 1 Mar. 2006 ⟨http://web .lexis-nexis.com⟩.

"Colombian Peace Commissioner Uneasy over Fate of Paramilitary Leader." 2005

(12 Apr.). *Financial Times Information. LexisNexis Academic.* 1 Mar. 2006 ⟨http://
web.lexis-nexis.com⟩.

"Colombian Seeking a Deal in U.S. Drug Case." 2002 (26 Sept.). *New York Times.*
27 Sept. 2002 ⟨www.nytimes.com/2002/0_.1?ntemail1⟩.

"Colombia's Paramilitary Transforms into Guerrilla Force." 2000. Stratfor.com.
16 Oct. 2000 ⟨www. stratfor.com/latinamerica/analysis/0006222320.htm⟩.

"Colombia's Rightists Back Talks with Marxists." 2002 (31 May). *New York Times.*
Reuters. 31 May 2002 ⟨www.nytimes.com/2002_headlines=&pagewanted=print&
position=top⟩.

"Colombia Steps Up Emergency Powers." 2002 (10 Sept.). *New York Times.* 11 Sept.
2002 ⟨www.nytimes.com/aponli_ysheadlines⟩.

"Colombia Talks Shaken." 2002 (1 Feb.). *New York Times.* 7 Feb. 2003 ⟨wysiwyg://101/
http://www.nytimes.com/2003/_1?tntemail1=&pagewanted=print&position=top⟩.

Commission for the Study of the Violence. 1992. "Organized Violence." In *Violence
in Colombia: The Contemporary Crisis in Historical Perspective*, ed. Charles
Bergquist, Ricardo Peñaranda, and Gonzalo Sánchez. Wilmington, Del.:
Scholarly Resources.

Concha, Miguel. 1997 (8 Nov.). "El conflicto de la zona norte." *La Jornada.* 28 Jan.
2001 ⟨http://www.jornada.unam.mx/1997/nov97/971108/concha.html⟩.

CONPAZ (Coordinación de Organismos no Gubernamentales por la Paz de
Chiapas). 1997. Centro de Derechos Humanos Fray Bartolomé de las Casas,
Convergencia de Organismos Civiles por la Democracia. *Militarization and
Violence in Chiapas.* Servicios Informativos Procesados, A.C.

Cooper, Marc. 2001 (1 Mar.). "Plan Colombia." *Nation.* 1 June 2005 ⟨http://www
.thenation.com/doc.mhtml?i=20010319&s=cooper⟩.

Council of Freely Elected Heads of Government and The Carter Center. 1993.
"Electoral Reform in Mexico." Occasional Paper Series, 4:1 (unpublished).

Coverdell, Paul. 2000 (29 Mar.). Speech (United States Senate). 1 Apr. 2006 ⟨http://
www.ciponline.org/colombia/032997.htm⟩.

"Crecerá el pie de fuerza: Redacción Judicial." 2002 (12 Aug.). *El Espectador.* 12 Aug.
2002 ⟨www.elespectador.com/judicial/nota7.htm⟩.

Crighton, Elizabeth, and Martha Abele MacIver. 1991 (Jan.). "The Evolution of
Protracted Ethnic Conflict: Group Dominance and Political Underdevelopment
in Northern Ireland and Lebanon." *Comparative Politics* 22:127–42.

"Declaración de Principios." 2001 (Apr.). Partido Revolucionario Democrática.
10 July 2002 ⟨www.prd.org.mx/historia/documentos⟩.

"Defensor del Pueblo denuncia ataque paramilitar a corregimiento de Yondó." 2002
(19 Aug.). *El Teimpo.* 19 Aug. 2002 ⟨http://eltiempo.terra.com.co/coar/noticias_
NTER_Friendly-PRINTER _FRIENDLY-120056.html⟩.

"Demobilization of 9,000 Paramilitaries Planned in Colombia." 2005 (7 June).
*Financial Times Information. LexisNexis Academic.* 1 Mar. 2006 ⟨http://web
.lexis-nexis.com⟩.

Desarrollo, Paz y Justicia. 1997. *Ni Derechos Ni Humanos en la Zona Norte de Chiapas.*
Tila, Chiapas, Mexico: Desarrollo, Paz y Justicia.

Devereux, Stephen, and John Hoddinott. 1993. *Fieldwork in Developing Countries.*
Boulder, Colo.: Lynne Rienner Publications.

Dickey, Christopher. 1983 (26 Dec.). "Behind the Death Squads." *New Republic* 189,
no. 26: 16–21.

Diskin, Martin, and Kenneth E. Sharpe. 1986. "El Salvador." In *Confronting
Revolution: Security through Diplomacy in Central America*, ed. Morris J.
Blachman, William M. LeoGrande, and Kenneth Sharpe. New York: Pantheon
Books.

"DoD News Briefing, ASD PA Clarke and Maj. Gen. McChrystal." 2003 (26 Mar.).
Department of Defense. 27 May 2005 ⟨http://www.defenselink.mil/transcripts/
2003/t03272003_t0326asd.html⟩.

"Doubts Exist about Demobilization of Colombia Paramilitaries." 2006 (6 Feb.).
*Financial Times Information. LexisNexis Academic.* 27 Feb. 2006 ⟨http://web
.lexis-nexis.com⟩.

Doyle, Kate. "Rebellion in Chiapas and the Mexican Military." 2004 (20 Jan.).
National Security Archive Electronic Briefing Book no. 109. 29 June 2005
⟨http://www.gwu.edu/~nsarchiv/NSAEBB/NSAEBB109⟩.

Dudley, Steven. 2001 (16 Oct.). "AUC Paramilitaries." Audio report on *Morning
Edition*, National Public Radio.

———. 2002 (24 Nov.). "Deadman's Bluff." *Washington Post Magazine.*

Dunkerley, James. 1982. *The Long War: Dictatorship and Revolution in El Salvador.*
London: Junction Books.

"Elections in El Salvador." 2004. *Election World.* 13 Mar. 2005 ⟨http://www
.electionworld.org/elsalvador.htm⟩.

"El Salvador: Carlos Eugenio Vides Casanova and Jose Guillermo Garcia." 2004
(8 Sept.). Center for Justice and Accountability ⟨http://www.cja.org/cases/
romagoza.shtml⟩.

"En Guerrero hay 'un triángulo rojo,' el de la guerrilla: Acosta Chaparro." 2004.
*Revista Proceso, Cinco Años de Impunidad* no. 4. 15 May 2001 ⟨www.proceso.com
.mx/especiales/aguasblancas/texto04. html⟩.

Estadistica de las Elecciones Federales de 1997. 2001a. Eleccion de Diputados
Federales por El Principio de Representacion Proporcional. Instituto Federal
Electoral. 10 July 2001 ⟨www.ife.org.mx/wwworge/tablas/rpent.htm⟩.

———. 2001b. Eleccion de Diputados Federales por El Principio de Mayoria Relativa.
Instituto Federal Electoral. 10 July 2001 ⟨www.ife.org.mx/wwworge/tablas/mrent
.htm⟩.

Estadistica de las Elecciones Federales de 2000. 2001a. Eleccion de Diputados
Federales por El Principio de Representacion Proporcional. Instituto Federal
Electoral. 10 July 2001 ⟨www.ife.org.mx/comp_test/reportes/centrales/
DiputadoRP.html⟩.

———. 2001b. Eleccion de Diputados Federales por El Principio de Mayoria Relativa. Instituto Federal Electoral. 10 July 2001 ⟨www.ife.org.mx/comp_test/reportes/centrales/DiputadoMR.html⟩.

"Estado de Chiapas." Map. CIEPAC. 28 Mar. 2006 ⟨http://www.ciepac.org/images/maps/chiapas.gif⟩.

Evans, Peter B., Harold Karan Jacobson, and Robert D. Putnam, eds. 1993. *Double-Edged Diplomacy: International Bargaining and Domestic Politics*. Berkeley: University of California Press.

Evans, Sara. 1980. *Personal Politics*. New York: Vintage Books.

"FFMM proponen creación de nuevas zonas bajo control military." 2002 (23 Sept.). *El Espectador*. 23 Sept. 2002 ⟨www.elespectador.com/politica/nota1.htm⟩.

Figueroa Ibarra, Carlos. 1991. "Guatemala: The Recourse of Fear." In *Vigilantism and the State in Modern Latin America: Essays on Extra-Legal Violence*, ed. Martha K. Huggins. New York: Praeger.

Flores Mérida, Antony. 2001 (2 Mar.). "Inicia Campaña contra intolerancia religiosa." *El Observador de la Frontera Sur*. 5.

"Foreigners of Conscience: The Mexican Government's Campaign against International Human Rights Observers in Chiapas." 1999. Global Exchange; Miguel Agustín Human Rights Center; Mexican Commission for the Defense and Promotion of Human Rights; "All Rights for Everyone" Human Rights Network. San Francisco: Global Exchange.

Forero, Juan. 2000 (5 Dec.). "Rightist Squads in Colombia Beating the Rebels." *New York Times*, A14. 28 Aug. 2001 ⟨www.colombialibre.org/reportajes/entrevistas_report1.htm⟩.

———. 2002a (19 May). "Rightist's Hard Line Appeals to War-Weary Colombians." *New York Times*. 19 May 2002 ⟨www.nytimes.com/2002_dlines⟩.

———. 2002b (13 Aug.). "Colombia President Declares Limited State of Emergency." *New York Times*. 13 Aug. 2002 ⟨wysiwyg://10/http://www.nytimes.com/2002/0_/13Colo. html?pagewanted=print&position=top⟩.

———. 2002c (9 Mar.). "Rebel Tactics Intimidate Colombia Candidates." *New York Times*. 9 Mar. 2002 ⟨wysiwg://6/http://www.nytimes.com/2002/...O.html?todaysheadlins =pagewanted=print⟩.

———. 2002d (10 Aug.). "Shifting Colombia's Aid: U.S. Focuses on Rebels." *New York Times*. 11 Aug. 2002 ⟨wysiwyg://17http://www.nytimes.com/2002/0_COLO. html?page wanted=print&position=bottom⟩.

———. 2002e (8 Sept.). "Burdened Colombians Back Tax to Fight Rebels." *New York Times*. 8 Sept. 2002 ⟨wysiwyg://15/http://www.nytimes.com/2002/0_yheadlines=&page wanted= print&position=top⟩.

———. 2002f (25 Aug.). "Colombia Counters Rebels with Troops and Music." *New York Times*. 25 Aug. 2002. ⟨wysiwyg://9/http://www.nytimes.com/2002/08_ COLO .html?pagewanted=print& position=bottom⟩.

———. 2004 (25 Apr.). "Paramilitary Chief Tied to Drug Trade Gains Power in

Colombia." *New York Times.* 25 Apr. 2004 ⟨www.nytimes.com/2004/04/25/
international/americas . . .⟩.

———. 2005a (23 June). "Colombia Passes Disputed Law Disarming Death Squads."
*International Herald Tribute. LexisNexis Academic.* 1 Mar. 2006 ⟨http://web
.lexis-nexis.com⟩.

———. 2005b (23 June). "New Colombia Law Grants Concessions to Paramilitaries."
*New York Times. LexisNexis Academic.* 1 Mar. 2006 ⟨http://web.lexis-nexis.com⟩.

———. 2005c (1 Aug.). "Report Adds to Criticism of Colombian Disarmament Law."
*New York Times. LexisNexis Academic.* 27 Feb. 2006 ⟨http://web.lexis-nexis.com⟩.

"The Frustration of the Right-wing Sector." 2003 (19 Mar.). *Proceso.* 13 Mar. 2005
⟨http://www.uca.edu.sv/publica/proceso/proci1041.html⟩.

Funes, Nelson. 2003 (12 Mar.). Personal interview. San Salvador.

Gaitan Mahecha, Bernardo. 1966. *Mision Historica del Frente Nacional de al violencia
a la democracia.* Bogotá, D.E.: Editorial Revista Colombiana.

Garcia de León, Antonio. 1985. *Resistencia y utopía: Memorial de agravios y crónicas
de revueltas y profecías acaecidas en la provincia de Chiapas durante los últimos
quinietos años de su historia.* Mexico: Ediciones Era.

George, Alexander L., and Andrew Bennett. 2005. *Case Studies and Theory
Development in the Social Sciences.* Cambridge: MIT Press.

Gertz, Bill. 1992 (1 Dec.). "Serbian Warlord Called 'Criminal' by U.S. Officials."
*Washington Times. LexisNexis Academic.* 8 Oct. 2007 ⟨www.lexis-nexis.com⟩.

Giugni, Marco, Doug McAdam, and Charles Tilly. 1998. *From Contention to
Democracy.* Lanham, Md.: Rowman and Littlefield.

"Gobierno aclara que reclutamiento de soldados campesinos se hará bajo estrictas
medidas de vigilancia." 2002 (22 Aug.). *El Tiempo* 23 Aug. 2002 ⟨www.eltiempo
. terra.com.co/coas/noticias/1233348.html⟩.

Golden, Tim. 1994a (26 Feb.). "Rebels Battle for Hearts of Mexicans." *New York
Times.* 5.

———. 1994b (20 Feb.). "Mexican Rebel Leader Sees No Quick Settlement." *New York
Times,* 3.

Gómez, Hernán. 2004 (21 Nov.). "Así Nacieron Las autodefensas Unidas de
Colombia" ⟨www.accubec. org/biblioteca/asinacieron.htm⟩.

Gonzales, Michael J. 2002. *The Mexican Revolution: 1910–1940.* New Mexico:
University of New Mexico Press.

Green, W. John. 2003. *Gaitanismo, Left Liberalism, and Popular Mobilization in
Colombia.* Gainesville: University Press of Florida.

Greste, Peter. 2000 (23 Dec.). "Mexico Shuts Chiapas Army Base." *BBC News.* 29 June
2005 ⟨http://news.bbc.co.uk/1/hi/world/americas/1084282.stm⟩.

———. 2001 (21 Apr.). "Mexican Army Leaves Chiapas." *BBC News.* 29 June 2005
⟨http://news.bbc.co.uk/1/hi/world/americas/1288865.stm⟩.

Guillermoprieto, Alma. 2000 (27 Apr.). "Colombia: Violence without End?" *New York
Review of Books.*

Gusmorino, Paul A., III. 1996 (13 May). "Main Causes of the Great Depression."

*Gusmorino World Online.* 4 July 2004 ⟨http://www.gusmorino.com/pag3/great_depression/index.html⟩.

Gutiérrez Roa, Élber. 2002 (12 Aug.). "Gobierno declara Conmoción Interior." *El Espectador.* 12 Aug. 2002 ⟨www.elespectador.com/politica/nota1.htm⟩.

Haider-Markel, Donald P., and Sean P. O'Brien. 1997 (Sept.). "Creating a 'Well Regulated Militia': Policy Responses to Paramilitary Groups in the American States." *Political Research Quarterly* 50, no. 3: 551–65.

Hall, Peter A. 2003. "Aligning Ontology and Methodology in Comparative Politics." In *Comparative Historical Analysis in the Social Sciences,* ed. James Mahoney and Dietrich Rueschmeyer. New York: Cambridge University Press.

Hedges, Chris. 1983 (30 Sept.). "Salvador-Labor Friction Reaches Flash Point as Union Leaders Abducted." *Christian Science Monitor.* 8 Feb. 2005 ⟨http://www.csmonitor.com/cgi-bin/witarticle.pl?tape/83/093059.txt⟩.

————. 1984 (17 May). "Christian Democrats Seek Purge of 4 Officers." *Christian Science Monitor.* 6 Feb. 2005 ⟨http://www.csmonitor.com/cgi-bin/wit_article.pl?tape/84/051726.txt⟩.

Hendricks, Tyche. 2004 (25 Aug.). "Fresno Suit Hearing Recalls Salvadoran Cleric's Slaying in '80." *San Francisco Chronicle.* 4 Sept. 2004. ⟨www.cja.org/cases/Romero%20Press /SF%20chron%208.25.04.htm⟩.

Herman, Edward. *The Read Terror Network: Terrorism in Fact and Propaganda.* Boston: South End Press.

Hernández Castillo, R. Aída. 2001. *Histories and Stories from Chiapas: Boarder Identities in Southern Mexico.* Austin: University of Texas Press.

Hernández Navarro, Luis. 1998. "The Escalation of the War in Chiapas." *NACLA Report on the Americas* 31, no. 5: 7–10.

Hess, Pamela. 2006 (4 Oct.). "Analysis: Baghdad's Corrupt Police." 17 Oct. 2006 ⟨http://web.lexis-nexis.com/universe⟩.

Hidalgo, Onésimo. 1997 (5 Nov.). "La Guerra Encubierta A Traves de Pistoleros, Guardias Blancas y Paramilitares." CIEPEC Boletin no. 79. 7 June 2005 ⟨www.ciepac.org/bulletins/oldboletins/bolec79.htm⟩.

————. 1998 (May). "Los Evangélicos en el Conflicto Actual de Chiapas." CIEPEC. 7 June 2005 ⟨http://www.ciepac.org/analysis/evangelicos.htm⟩.

Hidalgo, Onésimo, and Gustavo Castro. 1997 (Oct.). "Militarizacion y Paramilitarizacion en Chiapas." CIEPAC. 7 June 2005 ⟨www.ciepac.org/analysis/militar.html⟩.

"Historia de la Autodefensa." 2003. Unpublished interview with Carlos Castaño and Ivá Roberto Duque (also known as Ernesto Báez). 14 Dec. 2003 ⟨www.accubec.org/historia/historiadelasauc.htm⟩.

"Historia de un Secuestro." Globovision 2002. 4 Apr. 2004 ⟨www.globovision.com/eltema/2002.06/boulton/index.shtml⟩.

"Hombre, Líder, Presidente: Vota Fox Presidente." 2000. Maya Ayarzagoitia. Mexico.

Hommes, Rudolf. 1999. "Regulation and Deregulation in Colombia: Much Ado about Nothing?" In *Competition Policy, Deregulation, and Modernization in Latin America.* Boulder, Colo.: Lynne Rienner Publishers.

HRW (Human Rights Watch). 1997. *Implausible Deniability: State Responsibility for Rural Violence in Mexico*. [New York]: Human Rights Watch.

———. 1999a. *Systemic Injustice: Torture, 'Disappearance,' and Extrajudicial Execution in Mexico*. New York: Human Rights Watch.

———. 1999b. "Mexico." *World Report, 1999*. 26 Apr. 2005 ⟨www.hrw.org/wr2k/americas-07.htm⟩.

———. 1999c. "Colombia." *World Report 1999: Human Rights Developments*. 18 Mar. 2006 ⟨www.hrw.org/worldreport99/americas/colombia.htm⟩.

———. 2000a. "Colombia." *World Report, 2000*. 28 Aug. 2001 ⟨www.hrw.org/wr2k/americas-03.htm⟩.

———. 2000b (Feb.). *Colombia: The Ties That Bind: Colombia and Military-Paramilitary Links*. 26 Jan. 2001 ⟨www.hrw.org/reports/2000/colombia/⟩.

———. 2000c. "The Individuals Involved in the Ethnic Cleansing of Bijeljina." 28 Nov. 2007 ⟨www.hrw.org/reports/2000/bosnia/Bosn005-05.htm⟩.

———. 2001a. "Colombia." *World Report, 2001*. 28 Aug. 2001 ⟨www.hrw.org/wr2ka/americas/colombia.html⟩.

———. 2001b (4 Apr.). "Civil and Political Rights: Colombia and Indonesia." 28 Aug. 2001 ⟨www.hrw.org/pres/2001/04/un_oral11.0405.htm⟩.

———. 2001c. *The "Sixth Division": Military-Paramilitary Ties and U.S. Policy in Colombia*. New York: Human Rights Watch.

———. 2001d. "Milosevic and the Chain of Command in Kosovo." 28 Nov. 2007 ⟨www.hrw.org/press/2001/07/chain-of-command.htm⟩.

———. 2003 (22 Aug.). "Colombia's Checkbook Impunity: A Briefing Paper." Nov. 2003 ⟨http://hrw.org/backgrounder/americas/checkbook-impunity.pdf⟩.

———. 2004a. "Darfur Destroyed: Additional Evidence of Government Working Hand in Glove with Janajweed." 4 Dec. 2006 ⟨http://hrw.org/2004/sudan0504/7.htm⟩.

———. 2004b. "Darfur Destroyed: Summary." 4 Dec. 2006 ⟨http://hrw.org/2004/sudan0504/2.htm⟩.

———. 2004c. "Sudan: Janjaweed Camps Still Active." 4 Dec. 2006 ⟨http://hrw.org/english/docs/2004/08/27/darfur9268_txt.htm⟩.

———. 2005 (Apr.). "Sexual Violence and Its Consequences among Displaced Persons in Darfur and Chad." Background chapter. 1 June 2005 ⟨http://hrw.org/backgrounder/africa/darfur0505/1.htm#Toc100979339⟩.

Huggins, Martha K., ed. 1991. *Vigilantism and the State in Modern Latin America: Essays on Extra-legal Violence*. New York: Praeger.

Huntington, Samuel. 1968. *Political Order in Changing Societies*. New Haven: Yale University Press.

IACHR (Inter-American Commission on Human Rights). 1978. "Report on the Situation of Human Rights in El Salvador." 1 Apr. 2006 ⟨http://www.cidh.oas.org/countryrep/ElSalvador78eng/TOC.htm⟩.

———. 1981. "Informe Sobre la Situación de los Derechos Humanos en la Republica de Colombia." 17 Sept. 2001 ⟨www.cidh.oas.org/countryrep/Colombia 81sp/Indice.htm⟩.

————. 1985. "El Salvador." *Annual Report*. 17 June 2004 〈www.iachr.org/annualrep/
84.85eng/chap.4a.htm〉.

————. 1986. "El Salvador, Guatemala, and Haiti." *Annual Report*. 17 June 2004
〈www.iachr.org/annualrep/85.86eng/chap4.a.htm〉.

————. 1987. "El Salvador." *Annual Report*. 17 June 2004 〈www.iachr.org/annualrep/
86.87eng/chap.4a.htm〉.

————. 1988. "El Salvador." *Annual Report*. 17 June 2004 〈www.iachr.org/annualrep/
87.88eng/chap4a.htm〉.

————. 1989. "El Salvador." *Annual Report*. 17 June 2004 〈www.iachr.org/annualrep/
88.89eng/chap.4a.htm〉.

————. 1993. "Second Report on the Situation of Human Rights in Colombia." 17 Sept.
2001 〈www.cidh.oas.org/countryrep/93ColS&E/EngHaiti.htm〉.

————. 1997a. (12 Aug.). "Press Communique." 17 Sept. 2001 〈www.cidh.oas.org/
Comunicados/English/1997/Pres%2014-21.htm〉.

————. 1997b (14 Mar.). "Human Rights Developments in the Region: Introduction."
*Annual Report 1996*. 6 Sept. 2001 〈www.cidh.oas.org/annualrep/96eng/96ench5.htm〉.

————. 1997c (14 Mar.). "Reports on Individual Cases." *Annual Report 1996*. 6 Sept.
2001 〈www.cidh.oas.org/annualrep/96eng/96ench3d.htm〉.

————. 1999a. "Third Report on the Human Rights Situation in Colombia." 10 Feb.
2001 〈www.cidh.oas/org /countryrep/colom99en〉.

————. 1999b. "Colombia." *Annual Report*. 6 Sept. 2001 〈www.cidh.oas.org/
annualrep/99 eng/Chapter5a.htm〉.

————. 2000a. "Report n. 57/00, case 12.050; La Granja, Ituango." 4 Sept. 2001
〈www.cidh.org/annualrep/2000eng/colombia12050.htm〉.

————. 2000b. "Colombia." *Annual Report*. 4 Sept. 2001 〈www.cidh.oas.org/
annualrep/2000 eng/chap.4a.htm〉.

————. 2001 (10 Oct.). "Report n. 75/01, case 12.266; El Aro, Ituango." 3 Aug. 2003
〈www.iachr.org/annualrep/2001eng/Colombia 12266.htm〉.

————. 2004. "Case of 19 Tradesmen v. Colombia: Judgment of July 5, 2004." 10 Sept.
2007 〈www.corteidh.or.cr/docs/casos/articulos/seriec_109_ing.doc〉.

ICTY (International Criminal Tribunal for the Former Yugoslavia). 1997 (23 Sep).
"The Prosecutor of the Tribal against Zeljoko Raznjatovic, Also Known as 'Arkan':
Indictment." 1 Dec. 2007 〈http://www.un.org/icty/indictment/english/ark-
ii970930e.htm〉.

Iliff, Laurence. 2000 (29 Jan.). "Church of the Indians: Many in Chiapas Fear That
Commitment to the Dispossessed is Threatened." *Dallas Morning News*. 26 Jan.
2001 〈www.ksda.com/religion_news/Mayan%20Mexico,%20where%20Indian%20
and%20Eu. . .〉.

"Iraq Hospitals Run by Death Squads." 2006 (5 Oct.). LexisNexis Academic. 17 Oct.
2006 〈http://web.lexis-nexis.com/universe〉.

Jasper, James. M. 2003. "The Emotions of Protest." *Sociological Forum* 13(3). Reprinted
in *The Social Movements Reader: Cases and Concepts*, ed. Jeff Goodwin and James M.
Jasper. Malden, Mass.: Wiley-Blackwell Publishing.

Jenkins, J. Craig, and Charles Perrow. 1977. "Insurgency of the Powerless: Farm Worker Movements (1946–1972)." *American Sociological Review* 42:249–68.

Jorgensen, Danny L. 1989. *Participant Observation: A Methodology for Human Studies.* Thousand Oaks, Calif.: Sage Publications.

Kaldor, Mary. 2001. *New and Old Wars: Organized Violence in a Global Era.* Stanford, Calif.: Stanford University Press.

Kampwirth, Karen. 1998. "Peace Talks, but No Peace." *NACLA Report on the Americas* 31, no. 5: 15–19.

Kern, Kathy. 1998 (13 Oct.). "Chiapas, Mexico: Development, Peace and Justice." Christian Peacemaker Teams. 4 Sept. 2001 ⟨www.prairienet.org/ept/archives/1998/oct98/0013.html⟩.

"Key to Improving Human Rights: 'Bring Army under Civilian Control.'" 1983 (3 Aug.). *Christian Science Monitor.* 8 Feb. 2005 ⟨http://www.csmonitory.com/cgi-bin/wit_article. pl?tape/83/080343.txt⟩.

Kidder, Rushworth M. 1983 (13 Apr.). "Salvador's Magana: Consensus Builder or Military Pawn?" *Christian Science Monitor.* 8 Feb. 2005 ⟨http://www. csmonitor. com/cgi-bin/wit_article.pl? tape/83/041336.txt⟩.

King, Gary, Robert O. Keohane, and Sidney Verba. 1994. *Designing Social Inquiry: Scientific Inference in Qualitative Research.* Princeton: Princeton University Press.

Kirk, Robin. 1998. "A Meeting with Paramilitary Leader Carlos Castaño." *NACLA Report on the Americas* 31, no. 5: 28–33.

Kirk, Jerome, and Marc L. Miller. 1986. *Reliability and Validity in Qualitative Research.* London: Sage Pulibcations.

Kitschelt, Herbert. 1992. "Political Regime Change: Structure and Process-Driven Explanations." *American Political Science Review* 86, no. 4: 1028–34.

"Kosovo; Citizen Arkan." 1993 (6 Feb). *Economist. LexisNexis Academic.* 8 Oct. 2007 ⟨http://www.lexis-nexis.com⟩.

"La Actuacion de Paramilitares en el Estado de Guerrero Agrava la Situacion de Derechos Humanos en Esa Region." 27 Dec. 1998. 24 May 2005 ⟨http://members .aol.com/mapulink1/mapulink-1e/pi-ntcs-15.html⟩.

LaFranchi, Howard. 1996a (1 July). "Who Were Those Masked Men? Mexico Is Worried." *Christian Science Monitor.* 1 Mar. 2005 ⟨www.csmonitor.com/cgi-bin/wit-article.pl?script/96/07/01/070196.intl.intl.6⟩.

———. 1996b (3 Sept.). "New 'Bad' Guerrillas Threaten a Shaky Mexican Recovery." *Christian Science Monitor.* 1 Mar. 2005 ⟨www.csmonitor.com/cgi-bin/wit-article .pl?script/96/09/03 /090396.intl.intl.4⟩.

Lane, Ruth. 1997. *The Art of Comparative Politics.* Boston: Allyn and Bacon.

*La Sombra Revista.* 1995. No. 1.

Lauria-Santiago, Aldo. 2004. "Land, Community, and Revolt in Late Nineteenth-Century Indian Izalco." In *Landscapes of Struggle: Politics, Society, and Community in El Salvador*, ed. Aldo Lauria-Santiago and Leigh Binford. Pittsburgh: University of Pittsburgh Press.

LeoGrande, William M. 1998a (Spring). "From Havana to Miami: U.S. Cuba Policy as a Two-Level Game." *Journal of InterAmerican Studies and World Affairs* 40:67–86.

———. 1998b. *Our Own Backyard: The United States in Central America, 1977–1992.* Chapel Hill: University of North Carolina Press.

Levy, Daniel, and Gabriel Székely. 1983. *Mexico: Paradoxes of Stability and Change.* Boulder, Colo.: Westview Press.

Lijphart, Arend. 1977. *Democracy in Plural Societies: A Comparative Exploration.* New Haven: Yale University Press.

Lindijer, Koert. 2004 (25 Oct.). "Analysis: Reining in the Militias." BBC News on-line. 4 Dec. 2006 ⟨http://news.bbc.co.uk/2/hi/africa/3594520.stm⟩.

Lobe, Jim. 1990 (5 Feb.). "Rights-Colombia: US Groups Demand Crackdown on Paramilitaries." One World News, Inter Press Service. 28 Aug. 2001 ⟨www .oneworld.org/ips2/feb99/04_27_005.html⟩.

Mahoney, James, and Dietrich Rueschemeyer. 2003. *Comparative Historical Analysis in the Social Sciences.* Cambridge: Cambridge University Press.

Mairesse, Marianne. 2002 (May). "Kidnapped: Our Photographer's Shocking Story." *Marie Claire*, 85–88.

Mancuso, Salvatore. (2002) "Las ACCU le decimos que sí una negociación seria y pacificadora, de cara a Colombia y al mundo." 26 Sept. 2002 ⟨www.colombialibre .org⟩. Path: Publicaciones de interés general.

"Man Liable for Salvador Archbishop"s Murder." 2004. *New York Times.* 4 Sept. 2004 ⟨www.nytimes.com/aponline/national/AP-Salvador-Slain-Bishop.html⟩.

Mansbridge, J. J. 2003. "Ideological Purity in the Women's Movement." From *Why We Lost the ERA* (1986). Reprinted in *The Social Movements Reader: Cases and Concepts*, ed. Jeff Goodwin and James M. Jasper, 147–53. Malden, Mass.: Blackwell Publishing.

Marín, Carlos. 1998 (4 Jan.). "Plan del Ejército en Chiapas, desde 1994: Crear bandas paramilitares, desplazar a la población, destruir las bases de apoyo del EZLN . . ." *Proceso* no. 1105. Unpublished document of the EZLN. 1 Feb. 2001 ⟨http://spin .com.mx/~floresu/FZLN/archivo/paramilitares⟩.

Martínez, Alexander. 2002 (26 Sept.). "Incierto futuro de paramilitares tras pedido de extradición de EU." *El Espectador.* Colombian Human Rights Network. 26 Sept. 2002 ⟨colhrnet.igc.org/archive/news.esp.2002.htm⟩.

Marx, Gary. 2003 (8 May). "Colombian Militia Scoffs at Peace; Militia Leader Has No Plans to Give Up." *TheState.com.* 5 Apr. 2004 ⟨www.thestate.com/mld/thestate/ news/world/58139⟩.

McAdam, Doug. 1982. *Political Process and the Development of Black Insurgency, 1930–1970.* Chicago: University of Chicago Press.

———. 1988. *Freedom Summer.* New York: Oxford University Press.

———. 1996. "Conceptual Origins, Current Problems, Future Directions." In *Comparative Perspectives on Social Movements*, ed. Doug McAdam, John D. McCarthy, and Mayer N. Zald. New York: Cambridge University Press.

McAdam, Doug, John D. McCarthy, and Mayer N. Zald, eds. 1996. *Comparative Perspectives on Social Movements: Political Opportunities, Mobilizing Structures, and Cultural Framings*. New York: Cambridge University Press.

McAdam, Doug, and David A. Snow. 1997. *Social Movements: Readings on Their Emergence, Mobilization, and Dynamics*. Los Angeles, Calif.: Roxbury Publishing.

"Mexican Army Leaves Chiapas." 2001 (21 Apr.). BBC News. 29 June 2005 ⟨http://news.bbc.co.uk/1/hi/world/americas/1288783.stm⟩.

"Mexico." 1996. *World Fact Book*. Washington, D.C.: Central Intelligence Agency. CD-ROM edition.

"Mexico." 2005 (16 June). *World Fact Book*. Washington, D.C.: Central Intelligence Agency. 30 June 2005 ⟨http://www.cia.gov/cia/publications/factbook/geos/mx.html#People⟩.

"Mexico: Snipers Attack Zapatista Supporters." 1997 (8 Nov.). Comité chrétien pour les droits humains en Amérique latine. 26 Jan. 2001 ⟨kafka.uvic.ca/˜vipirg/SISIS/emerg/nov08mex.html⟩.

Meyer, David S., and Suzanne Staggenborg. 1996. "Movements, Countermovements, and the Structure of Political Opportunity." *American Journal of Sociology* 101, no. 6: 1628.

Migdal, Joel. 1987. "Strong States, Weak States: Power and Accommodation." In *Understanding Political Development*, ed. Myron Weiner and Samuel Huntington. Prospect Heights, Ill.: Waveland Press.

———. 1988. *Strong Societies and Weak States: State-Society Relations and State Capabilities in the Third World*. Princeton: Princeton University Press.

"Military Moves in Chiapas." 1998 (7 May). 29 Jan. 2001 ⟨www. americas.org/news/nir/19980507⟩.

Millman, Joel. 1984 (20 Oct.). "Reagan's Reporters." *Progressive* 48, no. 10: 20–24.

"Missing Colombian Paramilitary Leader Alive, Says Brother." 2005 (5 June). *Financial Times Information. LexisNexis Academic*. 1 Mar. 2006 ⟨http://web.lexis-nexis.com⟩.

Mitchell, Timothy. 1991 (Mar.). "The Limits of the State: Beyond Statist Approaches and Their Critics." *American Political Science Review* 85, no. 1: 77–96.

Molinski, Dan. 2005 (16 Nov.). "Two Dozen Leftist Colombian Rebels Disarm in Ceremony." *LexisNexis Academic*. 27 Feb. 2006 ⟨http://web.lexis-nexis.com⟩.

Montgomery, Tommie Sue. 1981. "The Black Southern Student Sit-in Movement, an Analysis of Internal Organization." *American Sociological Review* 46:744–67. Reprinted in Doug McAdam and David A. Snow, eds., 1997, *Social Movements: Readings on Their Emergence, Mobilization, and Dynamics*. Los Angeles, Calif.: Roxbury Publishing.

———. 1995. *Revolution in El Salvador: From Civil Strife to Civil Peace*. Boulder, Colo.: Westview Press.

Mueller, Carol. 1994. "Conflict Networks and the Origins of Women's Liberation." In *New Social Movements: From Ideology to Identity*, ed. Enrique Larana, Hank Johnston, and Joseph R. Gusfield. Philadelphia: Temple University Press.

Munck, Gerardo L. 2004. "Tools for Qualitative Research." In *Rethinking Social Inquiry: Diverse Tools, Shared Standards*, ed. Henry E. Brady and David Collier. Lanham, Md.: Rowman and Littlefield.

Munoz, Sergio. 1998 (10 May). "Samuel Ruiz Mediating for Peace and Social Justice in Chiapas, Mexico." *Los Angeles Times*. 26 Jan. 2001 ⟨http://flag.blackened.net/revolt/mexico/comment/ruiz_interview.html⟩.

Murphy, Dan. 2001 (5 Sept.). "Reforms Falter for Mexican Indians." *Christian Science Monitor*. 1 Mar. 2005 ⟨www.csmonitor.com/2001/0905/p6s1-woam.html⟩.

Nairn, Allan. 1984. "Behind the Death Squads." *Progressive* 48, no. 5: 1, 20–29.

Nelson Goodsell, James. 1980 (10 Mar.). "El Salvador Junta on the Offensive." *Christian Science Monitor*. 6 Feb. 2005 ⟨http://www.csmonitor.com/cgi-bin/wit_article.pl?tape/80/031037.txt⟩.

Nesmith, Susannah. 2002 (10 Oct.). "Colombia Military Claims Questioned." *Washington Post online*. 11 Oct. 2002 ⟨wysiwyg://13//http://www.washingtonpost.com/wp-dyn/articles/A4536-2002Oct10.html⟩.

Nordlinger, Eric. 1981. *On the Autonomy of the Democratic State*. Cambridge: Harvard University Press.

"Number of Paramilitaries Keeps on Growing." 2006 (7 Feb.). Intelligence Research, Andean Group Report. *LexisNexis Academic*. 27 Feb. 2006 ⟨http://web.lexis-nexis.com⟩.

OAS (Organization of American States). 2003. *Basic Documents Pertaining to Human Rights in the Inter-American System*. Washington, D.C.: Organization of American States.

O'Donnell, Guillermo. 1979. *Modernization and Bureaucratic-Authoritarianism: Studies in South American Politics*. Berkeley: Institute of International Studies, University of California.

———. 1988. *Bureaucratic Authoritarianism: Argentina, 1966–1973, in Comparative Perspective*. Berkeley: University of California Press.

O'Donnell, Guillermo, and Philippe C. Schmitter. 1986. *Transitions from Authoritarian Rule: Tentative Conclusions about Uncertain Democracies*. Baltimore: John Hopkins University Press.

Oppenheimer, Andres. 1996. *Bordering on Chaos: Guerrillas, Stockbrokers, Politicians, and Mexico's Road to Prosperity*. Boston: Little, Brown.

Ortiz Sarmiento, Carlos Miguel. 1992. "The 'Business of the Violence': The Quindío in the 1950s and 1960s." In *Violence in Colombia: The Contemporary Crisis in Historical Perspective*, ed. Charles Bergquist, Ricardo Peñaranda, and Gonzalo Sánchez. Wilmington, Del.: Scholarly Resources.

"Paramilitar acusa a subteniente del Ejército en Antioquia de nexos con su grupo." 2002 (5 Oct.). *El Tiempo*. 06 Oct. 2002 ⟨http://eltiempo.terra.com.co/coar/noticias_NTER_ FRIENDLY-PRINTER_FRIENDLY-163892.html⟩.

"Paramilitaries Gamble with Rejection of Peace Process." 2005 (12 Apr.). Intelligence Research, Andean Group Report. *LexisNexis Academic*. 1 Mar. 2006 ⟨http://web.lexis-nexis.com⟩.

Payne, Leigh A. 2000. *Uncivil Movements: The Armed Right Wing and Democracy in Latin America*. Baltimore: John Hopkins University Press.

"Paz y Justicia para Colombia." 2001. Colombia Support Network. 28 Aug. 2001 ⟨www.colombiasupport.net⟩.

Pearce, Jenny. 1990. *Colombia: Inside the Labyrinth*. London: Latin America Bureau.

Peters, Gretchen. 2002 (10 May). "Rebels Gain Ground in Guerrero." *Christian Science Monitor*. 1 Mar. 2005 ⟨www.csmonitor.com/2002/0510/p07s01-woam.html⟩.

Pizarro, Eduardo. 1992. "Revolutionary Guerrilla Groups in Colombia." In *Violence in Colombia: The Contemporary Crisis in Historical Perspective*, ed. Charles Bergquist, Ricardo Peñaranda, and Gonzalo Sánchez. Wilmington, Del.: Scholarly Resources.

———. 1999. "Clouds over Colombia." *NACLA Report on the Americas* 33, no. 2: 6–9.

Poole, Oliver. 2006 (22 Sept.). "Shia Killers Rake in Pounds 500,000 a Day from Crime, says US." *Daily Telegraph*. LexisNexis Academic. 4 Dec. 2006 ⟨http://web.lexis-nexis.com⟩.

PPDH. 2004a. Programa Presidencial de los Derechos Humanos y Derecho Internacional Humanitario Vicepresidencia de la República. "Observatorio de los Derechos Humanos en Colombia: Secuestros." 2 May 2004 ⟨www.derechoshumanos.gov.co/observatorio/indicadores/diciembre/secuestrosdic.pdf⟩

———. 2004b. "Observatorio de los Derechos Humanos en Colombia: Masacres." 2 May 2004 ⟨www.derechoshumanos.gov.co/observatorio/indicadores/diciembre/masacresidic.pdf⟩.

———. 2004c. "Observatorio de los Derechos Humanos en Colombia: Homicidios." 2 May 2004 ⟨www.derechoshumanos.gov.co/observatorio/indicadores/diciembre/homicidiodic.pdf⟩

———. 2004d. "Los Derechos Humanos en el Departamento de Antioquia." 2 May 2004 ⟨www.derechoshumanos.gov.co/observatorio/departamentos/separataantioquia.pdf⟩.

Pratt, Timothy. 2000 (Apr.). "The Drug War's Southern Front: Colombia, Cocaine, and U.S. Foreign Policy." *ReasonOnline*. 18 Mar. 2006 ⟨http://reason.com/0004/fe.tp.the/shtml⟩.

PRD (Partido de la Revolución Democrática). 2002a. "La Reputura Con el PRI." 10 July 2002 ⟨http://www.cen-prd.org.mx/historia/ruptura.php⟩.

———. 2002b. "Los Primeros Años del PRD: Resistir al Salinismo." 10 July 2002 ⟨www.cen-prd.org.mx/historia/salinismo.php⟩.

PRODH. 1997. Miguel Agustín Pro Juárez Human Rights Center, A.C. "Human Rights Violations in Mexico." 28 Apr. 2005 ⟨www.sjsocial.org/PRODH/english/publications/publications/index_publications.htm⟩.

"Proponen vigilancia para militares al mando en zonas de rehabilitación." 2002 (23 Sept.). *El Espectador*. 23 Sept. 2002 ⟨www.elespectador.com/politica.nota2.htm⟩.

Purnell, Jennie. 1999. *Popular Movements and State Formation in Revolutionary*

*Mexico: The Agraristas and Cristeros of Michoacán.* Durham: Duke University Press.

Putnam, Robert D. 1988. "Diplomacy and Domestic Politics: The Logic of Two-Level Games." *International Organization* 42, no. 3: 427–60.

Pyes, Craig. 1984 (13 Oct.). "Who Killed Archobishop Romero?" *Nation* 239, no. 11: 1, 350–54.

Ragin, Charles. 1987. *The Comparative Method: Moving beyond Qualitative and Quantitative Strategies.* Berkeley: University of California Press.

———. 2000. *Fuzzy-Set Social Science.* Chicago: University of Chicago Press, 2000.

Ramírez Cuevas, Jesús. 1997a (23 Nov.). "Chiapas, mapa de la contrainsurgencia." *La Jornada.* 18 Mar. 2006 ⟨www.jornada.unam.mx/1997/nov97/971123/mas-mapa.html⟩.

———. 1997b (30 Dec.). "Jamás atendió la policía estatl los llamados de auxilio: Testigos." *La Jornada.* 7 June 2001 ⟨www.jornada.unam.mx/1997/dic97/971230/testigos.html⟩.

"Rebels Holding 2 Journalists Tell Colombian Army to Leave State." 2003 (29 Jan.). *New York Times.* 29 Jan. 2003. 7 Feb. 2003 ⟨wysiwyg://95/http://www.nytimes.com/2003/0_1?tntemail1=&pagewanted=print&position=top⟩.

"Reclutarán a 20 mil campesinos para cuidar a más de 500 poblaciones." *El Tiempo* 22 Aug. 2002 ⟨www.eltiempo.terra.com.co/coar/noticias.1222245.html⟩.

"Redacción Judicial: Reclutarán 20.000 'soldados campesinos.'" 2002 (22 Aug.). *El Espectador* ⟨www.elespectador.com/judicial/nota6.htm⟩.

Reel, Monte. 2005 (21 Aug.). "Law Seen as Soft on Militias in Colombia; Critics Say Effort at Demobilization Is Deeply Flawed." *Washington Post. LexisNexis Academic.* 27 Feb. 2006 ⟨http://web.lexis-nexis.com⟩.

Reid, Michael. 2001a (25 Apr.). "Diálogos de pas, actos de guerra." *El Espectador.* Apr. 2001 ⟨www.elespectador.com/the_economist/nota4.htm⟩.

———. 2001b (26 Apr.). "La Maldición de las autodefensas." *El Espectador.* Apr. 2001 ⟨www.elespectador.com/the_economist/nota5.htm⟩.

"Reinsertados del Bloque Cacique Nutibara de las AUC reciben apoyode la Corporación Democracia." 2003 (18 Dec.). *El Tiempo.* 22 Dec. 2003 ⟨www.colombialibre.org/detalle_col.php?banner=Caminos%2⟩.

Reno, William. 1998. *Warlord Politics and African States.* Boulder, Colo.: Lynne Rienner Publishers.

"República Mexicana." 2004 (9 Feb.). Map. 2 Oct. 2005 ⟨www.ciepac.org/images/maps/mexico.gif⟩.

Reyes Ramos, María Eugenia. 1992. *Relaciones de poder y dominio en el movimiento magisterial Chiapaneco.* Tuxtla Gutiérrez, Mexico: Universidad Autónoma de Chiapas.

"Rival Militias Threaten Stability of Iraq's Shiite South." 2006 (26 Oct.). *LexisNexis Academic.* 6 Nov. 2006 ⟨http://web.lexis-nexis.com/universe⟩.

Rivas G., Enrique. 2004 (2 May). "Enviado Especial, Montañas de Colombia." *El Espectador.* 27 May 2004 ⟨www.colombialibre.org/ver_imp.php?Varid=5234⟩.

———. 2005a (15 Mar.). "Colombian Private Sector to Play Key Role in Reintegrating Demobilized Fighters." Financial Times Information. *LexisNexis Academic.* 1 Mar. 2006 ⟨http://web.lexis-nexis.com⟩. First published as "Economic Projects for 'Paras' Get Under Way." *El Espectador.* 13 Mar. 2005.

———. 2005b (9 Aug.). "Colombian Paramilitary Leader Says Ex-fighters Should Form a National Guard." British Broadcasting Corporation. *LexisNexis Academic.* 1 Mar. 2006 ⟨http://web.lexis-nexis.com⟩. First published as "The Ideal Is to Create a National Guard." *El Espectador.* 7 Aug. 2005.

Rojas R., Carlos Eduardo. 1994. "La Violencia llamada 'Limpieza Social.'" Colombia: CINEP.

Rojas Sánchez, Martha. 2002 (30 Sept.). "SOS en Saravena y Arauquita: 80 por ciento de estudiantes va a la guerrilla o a raspar coca." *El Espectador.* 30 Sept. 2002 ⟨www.elespectador.com/2002/20020930/judicial/nota1.htm⟩.

Roldán, Mary. 2002. *Blood and Fire: La Violencia in Antioquia, Colombia, 1946–1953.* Durham: Duke University Press.

Romero, Simon. 2006. "World Briefing: Americas: Colombia: Paramilitary Chief's Remains Identified." *New York Times.* 18 Nov. 2006 ⟨www.query.nytimes.com/gst/fullpage.html?res...⟩.

Ron, James. 2003. *Frontiers and Ghettos: State Violence in Serbia and Israel.* Berkeley: University of California Press.

Rosenberg, Tina. 1991. *Children of Cain: Violence and the Violent in Latin America.* New York: Penguin Books.

Ross, John. 1995. *Rebellion from the Roots: Indian Uprising in Chiapas.* Monroe, Maine: Common Courage Press.

———. 2000. *The War against Oblivion: Zapatista Chronicles, 1994–2000.* Monroe, Maine: Common Courage Press.

RSF (Reporters Sans Fronteirs). 2002. "Colombia — Annual Report 2002." 5 Apr. 2004 ⟨www.rsf.org/article.php3?id_article=1383⟩.

Rueschemeyer, Dietrich, Evelyne Huber Stephens, and John D. Stephens. 1992. *Capitalist Development and Democracy.* Chicago: University of Chicago Press.

Ruiz, Bert. 2001. *The Colombian Civil War.* Jefferson, N.C.; McFarland.

Rustow, Dankwart. 1970 (Apr.). "Transitions to Democracy: Toward a Dynamic Model." *Comparative Politics* 2, no. 3: 337–63.

Safford, Frank, and Marco Palacios. 2002. *Colombia: Fragmented Land, Divided Society.* New York: Oxford University Press.

Salazar, Alonso. 1991. *Born to Die in Medellín.* London: Latin American Bureau.

Samayoa, Salvador. 2002. *El Salvador: La Reforma Pactada.* San Salvador: UCA Editores.

———. 2003 (5 Mar.). Personal interview. San Salvador.

"San Andres Accords." 2006 (Feb.). Ejército Zapatista de Liberación Nacional. 29 June 2005 ⟨http://www.ezln.org/san_andres/documento_1.en.htm⟩.

Sánchez, Gonzalo. 1992. "The Violence: An Interpretative Synthesis." In *Violence in Colombia: The Contemporary Crisis in Historical Perspective*, ed. Charles Bergquist,

Ricardo Peñaranda, and Gonzalo Sánchez. Wilmington, Del.: Scholarly Resources.

Sanford, Victoria. 2003. "Leaning to Kill by Proxy: Colombian Paramilitaries and the Legacy of Central American Death Squads, Contras, and Civil Patrols." *Social Justice* 30, no. 3: 63–81.

Schairer-Vertannes, Rachel. 2001. "The Politics of Human Rights: How the World Has Failed Burma." *Asia-Pacific Journal on Human Rights and the Law* 2, no. 1: 77–118.

Schneider, Cathy Lisa. 1995. *Shantytown Protest in Pinochet's Chile*. Philadelphia: Temple University Press, 1995.

———. 2000 (Fall). "Violence, Identity, and Spaces of Contention in Chile, Argentina, and Colombia." *Social Research* 67, no. 3: 773–802.

Schulz, Donald E., and Edward J. Williams, ed. 1995. *Mexico Faces the 21st Century*. Westport, Conn.: Praeger.

Schulze, Kirsten E., and M. L. R. Smith. 2000. "Decommissioning and Paramilitary Strategy in Northern Ireland: A Problem Compared." *Journal of Strategic Studies* 23, no. 4: 77–106.

Scott, David Clark. 1994a (14 Apr.). "Chiapas Ranchers Vow to Take Law into Their Own Hands." *Christian Science Monitor*. 1 Mar. 2005 ⟨www.csmonitor.com/cgi-bin/wit-article.pl?tape/94/apr/day14/14061⟩.

———. 1994b (11 Sept.). "Chiapas Rebellion Sparks Indian Dissent across Mexico." *Christian Science Monitor*. 1 Mar. 2005 ⟨www.csmonitor.com/cgi-bin/wit-article.pl?tape/94/feb/day11/11042⟩.

Scott, James C. 1972. "Patron-Client Politics and Political Change in Southeast Asia." *American Political Science Review* 66, no. 1: 91–113.

"Se creará Red Nacional para salida del conflicto armado." 2002 (23 Sept.). *El Espectador*. 23 Sept. 2002 ⟨www.elespectador.com/paz/nota1.htm⟩.

Selee, Andrew. 1999 (Winter). "From Elite Violence to State Violence: The Origins of Low-Intensity Conflict in Chiapas, Mexico." *UCLA Journal of Latin American Studies*. 29 Jan. 2001 ⟨www.generation99.org/journal/Chiapas.htm⟩.

"Sentences Handed Down for Chiapas Attack." 2002 (13 Nov.). BBC News. 29 June 2005 ⟨http://news.bbc.co.uk/1/hi/world/americas/2469509.stm⟩.

Serafino, Nina. 2000 (4 May) "Colombia: Conditions and U.S. Policy Options." *CRS Report to Congress [excerpt]*. 1 Apr. 2006 ⟨http://www.globalsecurity. org/military/library/report/crs/crscolom.htm⟩.

"Serb Volunteer Guard." 2000 (1 Feb.). FAS: Intelligence Resource Program. 28 Nov. 2007 ⟨www.fas.org/irp/world/para/sdg.htm⟩.

"Se reunifican las AUC." 2002 (10 Sept.). *La Semana*. 10 Sept. 2002 ⟨www.semana.com/archiva/articulosView.jsp?id=65325⟩.

"'Shameful' Colombian Congress Forces through Justice and Peace Law." 2005 (27 June). *Financial Times Information. LexisNexis Academic*. 1 Mar. 2006 ⟨http://web.lexis-nexis.com⟩.

Sharpe, Kenneth E. 1981 (18 Aug.). "El Salvador: The Myth of the Center." *Christian*

*Science Monitor.* 6 Feb. 2005 ⟨http://www.csmonitor.com/cgi-bin/wit_article
  .pl?tape /81/081824.txt⟩.

Sherman, John W. 1997. *The Mexican Right: The End of Revolutionary Reform,
  1929–1940.* Westport, Conn.: Praeger.

Shin, Doh Chull. 1994. "On the Third Wave of Democratization: A Synthesis and
  Evaluation of Recent Theory and Research." *World Politics* 47 (Oct.): 135–70.

Silva, Patricio. 2002. "Searching for Civilian Supremacy: The Concertación
  Governments and the Military in Chile." *Bulletin of Latin American Research* 21,
  no. 3: 375–95.

Simon, Scott. 2004 (4 Sept.). "Judge Rules against Accused Plotter in Romero
  Killing." *Weekend Edition.* With Aryeh Neier. National Public Radio. 4 Sept. 2004
  ⟨www.npr.org/features/feature.php?wfId=3889722⟩.

Simons, Marlise. 2003 (25 Apr.). "Hidden Witness Tells of Smuggling in Milosevic's
  Regime: Paramilitaries Took Orders from Secret Policy: Secretary." *New York
  Times. LexisNexis Academic.* 8 Oct. 2007 ⟨http://www.lexis-nexis.com⟩.

SIPAZ (Servicio Internacional para la Paz). 1996 (Sept.). "Bachajon — The Cost of
  Impunity." *SIPAZ Report.* 18 Mar. 2006 ⟨http://www.sipaz.org/informes/vol1no2/
  vol1 no2e.htm⟩.

———. 2000a (Nov.). "We Live Displaced: A Suffering People Cries Out for an
  Answer." *SIPAZ Report* 5, no. 4. 26 Jan. 2001 ⟨www.sipaz.org/vol5no4/feate.htm⟩.

———. 2000b (Aug.). "The Children of Low Intensity War." *SIPAZ Report* 5, no. 3: 4–7.

———. 2000c (Aug.). *SIPAZ Report* 5, no. 3: 1–8, 11.

———. 2000d (May). "Chiapas: Scene of a Religious Conflict?" *SIPAZ Report* 5, no. 2:
  4–6.

———. 2000e (Mar.) "Tense Beginning to the New Century in Chiapas." *SIPAZ Report*
  5, no. 1: 8–10.

Siverts, Henning. 1981. *Stability and Change in Highland Chiapas, Mexico.* Bergen,
  Norway: University of Bergen.

Skidmore, Thomas E., and Peter H. Smith. 1992. *Modern Latin America*, 3rd ed. New
  York, Oxford: Oxford University Press.

Skocpol, Theda, and Margaret Somers. 1994. "The Uses of Comparative History in
  Macrosocial Inquiry." In *Social Revolutions in the Modern World*, ed. Theda
  Skocpol. New York: Cambridge University Press.

"Slaughter in Baghdad." 2006 (Sept. 23). *Economist. LexisNexis Academic.* 4 Dec.
  2006 ⟨http://web.lexis-nexis.com/universe⟩.

Sluka, Jeffrey A., ed. 2000. *Death Squad: The Anthropology of State Terror.*
  Philadelphia: University of Pennsylvania Press.

Smith, Jackie. 2001a. "Introduction to Special Issue: Globalization and Resistance."
  *Mobilization* 6, no. 1: v–viii.

———. 2001b. "Globalizing Resistance: The Battle of Seattle and the Future of Social
  Movements." *Mobilization* 6, no. 1: 1–19.

Snow, David A., Louis A. Zurcher Jr., and Sheldon Ekland-Olson. 1980. "Social
  Networks and Social Movements: A Microstructural Approach to Differential
  Recruitment." *American Sociological Review* 45:787–801. Reprinted in Doug

McAdam and David A. Snow, eds. 1997. *Social Movements: Readings on Their Emergence, Mobilization, and Dynamics.* Los Angeles, Claif.: Roxbury Publishing.

Solarz, Stephen. 1983 (19 July). "El Salvador: The Case for Negotiation." *Christian Science Monitor.* 8 Feb. 2005 ⟨http://www.csmonitor.com/cgi-bin/wit_article .pl?tape/83/071929.txt⟩.

Southerland, Daniel. 1981a (13 Mar.). "Salvador's Army Draws Verbal Fire for Role in Killings." *Christian Science Monitor.* 6 Feb. 2005 ⟨http://www.csmonitor.com/ cgi-bin/wit_article.pl ?tape/81/031339.txt⟩.

———. 1981b (18 Mar.). "Salvador's Morales Ehrlich: Can the Middle Hold?" *Christian Science Monitor.* 8 Feb. 2005 ⟨http://www.csmonitor.com/cgi-bin/wit_ article.pl?tape/81/031838.txt⟩.

———. 1981c (5 May). "Captain Flees Salvador When He's Told, 'You're Next.'" *Christian Science Monitor.* 6 Feb. 2005 ⟨http://www.csmonitor.com/cgi-bin/wit_ article.pl?tape/81/050504.txt⟩.

———. 1983a (3 June). "El Salvador's Elusive Peace." *Christian Science Monitor.* 8 Feb. 2005 ⟨http://www.csmonitor.com/cgi-bin/wit_article.pl?tape/83/060341.txt⟩.

———. 1983b (6 June). "El Salvador: Fewer Murders, but Death Squads Roam Freely." *Christian Science Monitor.* 8 Feb. 2005 ⟨http://www.csmonitor.com/ cgi-bin/wit_article.pl?tape/83/060646.txt⟩.

———. 1983c (7 June). "In El Salvador, Being a Politician Means Risking Your Life." *Christian Science Monitor.* 8 Feb. 2005 ⟨http://www.csmonitor.com/cgi-bin/wit_ article.pl?tape/83/060745.txt⟩.

———. 1983d (5 Aug.). "Salvadorean Labor Leaders Say Land Reform Is Stalled." *Christian Science Monitor.* 8 Feb. 2005 ⟨http://www.csmonitor.com/cgi-bin/wit_ article.pl?tape/83/08059.txt⟩.

Staggenborg, Suzanne. 1997. "The Consequences of Professionalization and Formalization in the Pro-Choice Movement." In *Social Movements: Readings on Their Emergence, Mobilization, and Dynamics*, ed. Doug McAdam and David A. Snow. Los Angeles, Calif.: Roxbury Publishing.

Stahler-Sholk, Richard. 1998. "The Lessons of Acteal." *NACLA* 31, no. 5: 11–14.

Stanley, William. 1996. *The Protection Racket State: Elite Politics, Military Extortion, and Civil War in El Salvador.* Philadelphia: Temple University Press.

Stavenhagen, Rodolfo. 2001. "Prospects for Peace in Chiapas." Panel discussion at the Woodrow Wilson Center, Washington, D.C. 21 June.

"Sudan 'Backs' Janjaweed Fighters." 2006 (30 Oct.). BBC News. 4 Dec. 2006 ⟨http:// news.bbc.co.uk/2/hi/africa/6060976.stm⟩.

Sweeny, John P. 1999 (25 Mar.). "Tread Cautiously in Colombia's Civil War." Heritage Foundation Backgrounder. 1 Apr. 2006 ⟨www.heritage.org/Research/ LatinAmerica/BG1264.cfm⟩.

Tanner, Marcus. 1999 (29 Mar.). "Assault on the Serbs: The Laughing Butcher of Bosnia Sent South 'to Defend' Kosovo." *Independent. LexisNexis Academic.* 8 Oct. 2007 ⟨http://www.lexis-nexis.com⟩.

Tarrow, Sidney. 1989. *Democracy and Disorder: Protest and Politics in Italy, 1965–1975.* Oxford: Oxford University Press, 1989.

———. 1996. "States and Opportunities: The Political Structuring of Social Movements." In *Comparative Perspectives on Social Movements*, ed. Doug McAdam,
John D. McCarthy, and Mayer N. Zald. New York: Cambridge University Press.

Thomas, Troy S., Stephen D. Kiser, and William D. Casebeer. 2005. *Warlords Rising:
Confronting Violent Non-State Actors*. Lanham, Md.: Lexington Books.

"Undemobilized Paramilitary Blocs Control Bulk of Drug Crops — Colombian
Weekly." 2005 (7 Nov.). *Financial Times Information. LexisNexis Academic*. 27 Feb.
2006 ⟨http://web.lexis-nexis.com⟩.

UNHCHR (United Nations High Commissioner for Human Rights). 2001a (13 Feb.).
"Question of the Violation of Human Rights and Fundamental Freedoms in Any
Part of the World: Written Statement, Submitted by the Colombian Commission
of Jurists, a Non-governmental Organization in Special Consultative Status."
United Nations Economic and Social Council. E/CN.4/2001/NGO/136. 18 Mar.
2006 ⟨http://daccessdds.un.org/doc/UNDOC/GEN/G01/111/60/PDF/G0111160
.pdf?OpenElement⟩.

———. 2001b (8 Feb.). "Organization of Work: Report of the United Nations High
Commissioner for Human Rights on the Human Rights Situation in Colombia."
United Nations Economic and Social Council. E/CN.4/2001/15. 5 Jan. 2009
⟨http://daccessdds.un.org/doc/UNDOC/GEN/G01/110/61/PDF/G011061.
pdf?OpenElement⟩.

———. 2002 (28 Feb.). "Organization of the Work of the Session: Report of the
United Nations High Commissioner for Human Rights on the Human Rights
Situation in Colombia." United Nations Economic and Social Council. E/
CN.4/2002/17. 10 Aug. 2002 ⟨http://daccessdds.un.org/doc/UNDOC/GEN /
G02/111/15/PDF/G0211115.pdf?OpenElement⟩.

UN Security Council. 1993. "From Madness to Hope: The 12-Year War in El Salvador:
Report of the Commission on the Truth for El Salvador." Annex. S/25500 (1993):
187–92. "Truth Commissions: Reports: El Salvador." *United States Institute of
Peace Library*. 24 Feb. 2003 ⟨www.usip.org/library/tc/doc/reports/el_salvador /tc_
es_03 151993_VI_VII.html⟩.

"UN War Crimes Tribunal Names Arkan as Suspect." 1999 (31 Mar.). Deutsche
Presse-Agentur. *LexisNexis Academic*. 8 Oct. 2007 ⟨http://web.lexis-nexis.com⟩.

"Uribe as Peace President." 2005 (2 Aug.). Intelligence Research, Andean Group
Report. *LexisNexis Academic*. 27 Feb. 2006 ⟨http://web.lexis-nexis.com⟩.

USDOS (United States Department of State). 2000. "1999 Country Reports on
Human Rights Practices — Colombia." Washington, D.C.: United States
Department of State. 28 Aug. 2001 ⟨www.state.gov/www/globabl/human _
rights/1999_hrp_report /colombia.html⟩.

———. 2002a. "Country Reports on Human Rights Practices — 2001: Colombia."
Washington, D.C.: United States Department of State. 5 Aug. 2002 ⟨www.state
.gov/g/drl/rls/hrrpt/2001/what/8326pf. htm⟩.

———. 2002b (25 Sept.). "Taken Questions: Office of the Spokesman." (Press
conference.) 5 Apr. 2004 ⟨www.state.gov/r/pa/prs/ps/2002/13716.htm⟩.

————. 2003. "Country Reports on Human Rights Practices — 2002: Colombia."
Washington, D.C.: United States Department of State. Nov. 2003 ⟨www.state
.gov/g/drl/rls/hrrpt/2002/18325pf.htm⟩.

Utria, Miguel. 2001 (14 Feb.). "Gobierno Está Arrodillado ante la Guerrilla: Castaño."
*El Heraldo.* 28 Aug. 2001 ⟨www.colombialibre.org/reportajes/entrevistas_report1
.htm⟩.

Valencia, Leon. 2002. "La Historia con los Paras." *Adiós a la Política, Bienvenida la
Guerra: Secretos de un Malogrado Proceso de Paz.* Bogotá: Intermedio. 26 Sept.
2002 ⟨www.colombialibre.org/⟩. Path: Pulicaciones de interés general.

Van Cott, Donna Lee, ed. 1994. *Indigenous Peoples and Democracy in Latin America.*
New York: St. Martin's Press.

Vargas Meza, Ricardo. 1998. "The FARC, the War, and the Crisis of the State." *NACLA
Report on the Americas* 31, no. 5: 22–27.

Vieira, Constanza. 2005a (29 June). "Rights: Colombian Atrocity Survivors Vow to
Struggle for Justice." IPS-Inter-Press Service/Global Information Network.
*LexisNexis Academic.* 1 Mar. 2006 ⟨http://web.lexis-nexis.com⟩.

————. 2005b (23 Sept.). "Colombia: U.N. Lashes out at Paramilitary Demobilization
Law." IPS-Inter Press Service/Global Information Network. *LexisNexis Academic.*
27 Feb. 2006 ⟨http://web.lexis-nexis.com⟩.

Vivanco, Jose Miguel, and Maria McFarland Sanchez-Moreno. 2005 (16 Mar.). "A Bad
Plan in Colombia; Rewarding Outlaws." *International Herald Tribute. LexisNexis
Academic.* 1 Mar. 2006 ⟨http://web.lexis-nexis.com⟩.

Volman, Dennis. 1984 (8 May). "Salvador Death Squads, a CIA Connection?"
*Christian Science Monitor.* 6 Feb. 2005 ⟨http://www.csmonitor.com/cgi-bin/
win_article.pl?tape/84/050846.txt⟩.

"The Wars Within: Counterinsurgency in Chiapas and Colombia." *NACLA Report on
the Americas.* 31.5 (1998): 6.

"Week's Top Story — Colombian Government Warns It Would Begin Military
Strikes." Noticias Financieras/Groupo de Diarios America. 4 Nov. 2005.
*LexisNexis Academic.* 27 Feb. 2006 ⟨http://web.lexis-nexis.com⟩.

Weiner, Tim. 2000 (4 Dec.). "Mexico's New Leader Swiftly Seeks Peace in Chiapas."
*New York Times.* 29 June 2005 ⟨http://www.nytimes.com/2000/12/4/
world/04MEXI.html? ex=1120190400&en=cfcfe76e2. . .⟩.

————. 2002 (1 July). "Mexico Secrets: Envelope Holds Ghosts of 70's." *New York
Times.* 2 July 2002 ⟨www.nytimes.com/2002_1MEXI.html?pagewanted=print&
position=top⟩.

"We'll Never Give Up Our Claim, Says Thug Arkan." 2007. *Daily Mail. LexisNexis
Academic.* 8 Oct. 2007 ⟨www.lexis-nexis.com⟩.

Wheaton, Rev. Philip E. 1998. "Unmasking the Powers in Mexico: The Zapatistas'
Prophetic Alternative to the New World Order." Washington: EPICA.

White, Robert E. 1999 (12 Sept.). "El Salvador's Lessons Unlearned: Heading for
Trouble in Colombia." *Washington Post.* 29 Mar. 2004 ⟨www.unc.edu/depts/
diplomat/AD_Issues/amdipl_16/warburg_11/white_trouble.html⟩.

———. 2000 (8 Feb.). "Shades of Vietnam: The Wrong War." *Washington Post*. 29 Mar. 2004 ⟨www.unc.edu/depts/diplomat/AD_Issues/amdipl_16/warburg_11/white_ wrong_prt.htm⟩.

Wilkie, James W., ed. 1999. *Statistical Abstract of Latin America*. Vol. 35. Los Angeles: UCLA Latin American Center Publications.

Wilson, Scott. 2001a (12 Mar.). "Colombia's Other Army: Growing Paramilitary Force Wields Power with Brutality." *Washington Post*. 28 Aug. 2001 ⟨www.colombialibre .org/reportajes/entrevistas_report3.htm⟩.

———. 2001b (2 Mar.). "Interview with Carlos Castano, Head of the United Self-Defense Forces of Colombia." *Washington Post Foreign Service*. 13 Mar. 2001 ⟨www.washingtonpost.com/ac2/wp-dyn/A47019-2001Mar9?language=printer⟩.

———. 2002a (16 Sept.). "Cocaine Trade Causes Rifts in Colombian War." *Washington Post*. 28 Sept. 2002 ⟨www.washingtonpost.com/ac2/wp-dyn/A22043-2002Sept15?language=printer⟩.

———. 2002b (18 Sept.). "24 Dead, but Alliance Endures." *Washington Post*. 28 Sept. 2002 ⟨wysiwyg://25/http://www.washingtonpost.com/ac2/wp-dyn/A31346-2002Sept17?language=printer⟩.

———. 2002c (29 Aug.). "Colombia Turns to Citizen Spies as Newest Weapon of War." *Washington Post*. 28 Sept. 2002 ⟨wysiwyg://28/http://www.washington post .com/wp-dyn/articles/A9071-2002Aug28.html⟩.

———. 2003 (6 July). "Commander of Lost Causes." *Washington Post*. 8 July 2003 ⟨www.washingtonpost.com/ac2/wp-dyn/A13583-2003Jul5?langu_⟩.

Wood, Elisabeth J. 2000. "Civil War and the Transformation of Elite Representation in El Salvador." In *Conservative Parties, the Right, and Democracy in Latin America*, ed. Kevin J. Middlebrook. Baltimore: John Hopkins University Press.

"World News in Brief: Colombia Militia Surrenders Arms." 2006 (8 Feb.). *Financial Times Information*. *LexisNexis Academic*. 27 Feb. 2006 ⟨http://web.lexis-nexis .com⟩.

Yin, Robert K. 1994. *Case Study Research: Design and Methods*. 2nd ed. London: Sage Publications.

Youngers, Coletta. 1998. "U.S. Entanglements in Colombia Continue." *NACLA Report on the Americas* 31, no. 5: 34–35.

Zald, Mayer N., and Bert Useem. 1987. "Movement and Countermovement Interaction: Mobilization, Tactics, and State Involvement." In *Social Movements in an Organizational Society*, ed. Mayer N. Zald and John D. McCarthy. New Brunswick, N.J.: Transaction Books.

Zartman, I. William. 1995. *Collapsed States: The Disintegration and Restoration of Legitimate Authority*. Boulder, Colo.: Lynne Rienner Publishers.

Zellner, Mike. 1999 (June). "Ending the War." *Latin Trade*. 1 Apr. 2006 ⟨http://www .findarticles.com/p/articles/mi_m0BEK/is_6_7/ai_54717578⟩.

Zin, Ilan. 1990. "A Question of Conscience: The Murder of the Jesuit Priests in El Salvador." First Run Features. Produced by Icarus/Tamouz Media.

Zuckerman, Mortimer B. 1983. "Battle Hymn of a Republic; Sojourn in Salvador." *New Republic* 189, no. 24 (12 Dec. 1983): 10–13.

# INDEX